THE BOOK *of*

LOVE LETTERS

ALSO BY THE EDITORS

The Book of Letters (2002)
The Book of War Letters (2003)

THE BOOK *of* LOVE LETTERS

Canadian Kinship,
Friendship, and Romance

COMPILED *and* EDITED *by*

PAUL *and* AUDREY GRESCOE

M&S

Library and Archives Canada Cataloguing in Publication

The book of love letters : Canadian kinship, friendship, and romance / compiled and edited by Paul Grescoe and Audrey Grescoe.

Includes bibliographical references.
ISBN 0-7710-3558-6

1. Love letters – Canada.   I. Grescoe, Paul, 1939-   II. Grescoe, Audrey

PS8351.L6B66 2005   C816'.00803543   C2004-906472-X

We acknowledge the financial support of the Government of Canada through the Book Publishing Industry Development Program and that of the Government of Ontario through the Ontario Media Development Corporation's Ontario Book Initiative. We further acknowledge the support of the Canada Council for the Arts and the Ontario Arts Council for our publishing program.

Typeset in Sabon by M&S, Toronto
Printed and bound in Canada

This book is printed on acid-free paper that is 100% recycled, ancient-forest friendly (100% post-consumer recycled).

McClelland & Stewart Ltd.
The Canadian Publishers
481 University Avenue
Toronto, Ontario
M5G 2E9
www.mcclelland.com

1 2 3 4 5   09 08 07 06 05

To all our Dears – kin, in-laws, and friends –
and to Taras, Lara, and Justin

❖

Contents

THE BOOK *of*
LOVE LETTERS

Introduction

"These are shocking things to put on paper"

In a land where the nights are long and the days cold, love illuminates the soul and warms the heart. Well before there was a country called Canada, newcomers to this land were writing loving letters to one another and sending them via sleigh and boat, cart and stagecoach. The earliest one in this book is dated 1786, written in ornate prose by William Smith, the chief justice of Quebec, to his wife stuck in the United States. In the generations since Confederation (in 1867), kinfolk, friends, old married couples, and especially young lovers have put their thoughts and feelings on paper to declare their caring, fondness, and passion. (And sometimes to announce the end of a relationship, as did a teacher who sent a dreaded "Dear John" letter to her soldier boyfriend overseas.) In the twenty-first century, love letters endure: the most recent one in this collection is a Valentine's Day paean that rock star Randy Bachman wrote on a laptop to his wife in 2004.

Thinking that such correspondence might help define a facet of the collective national character – and be highly entertaining – we pursued examples of the genre written over the past two centuries. We explored public archives across the country and appeared on radio and television programs and wrote magazine and newspaper articles to invite Canadians to send us submissions from their family archives. Sometimes we approached interesting personalities directly, collecting love letters from a Cambridge don, a prima ballerina, and a bank robber. What we discovered is that the Canadian soul, as revealed in loving correspondence, is not the dull, discreet thing that even many Canadians suspect it to be (expatriate actor Donald Sutherland once described his fellow citizens as being like children who press their noses against the window of life). In fact, it can be impassioned, theatrical, and sometimes downright sexy.

Of course, attitudes to sex have changed dramatically over the wide time span we cover. In the late eighteenth century, engaged men wrote about their dedication, zeal, devotion, and affection. A hundred years later the word *love* – and the promise of it – was common. Early in the twentieth century, artist David Milne wrote to his girlfriend about hugging and kissing her on the dimly lit platforms of railway stations when they were saying goodbye, and then advised her to burn or hide his letters, because "these are shocking things to put on paper . . ." During the early 1940s another artist, LeMoine FitzGerald, wrote more explicitly: ". . . you entwine me and draw me into you and absorb me and I enter you and absorb you and motion is one." Ed and Jean Brunanski – each consulting a different sex manual while he served overseas as an airman during the Second World War – wrote to discuss whether twice a week was the optimum number of times they should make love ("yes I think after awhile we can adhere to that rule if necessary," he remarked). Three decades later, while she was preparing to emigrate to Canada from Spain, Mercedes Roman told her beloved Pierre Trudeau (the chef, not the politician), "We shall have a naturel and satisfaction sexual life, with very profundo love. Our sexual life will be fantastic . . ." And perhaps signalling the liberated female, poet Susan Musgrave wrote in 1985, "I love it when you gather up my clothes into a bunch and pull me up to you. You can tear anything . . ." More recently, sex may be merely alluded to in correspondence – in phrases such as "my unexercised bed" – or recalled more directly, as when a young hostel operator ends a letter to his new love with: "P.S. My back and bum are still itchy from that romp in the grass."

In our three-year quest for love letters, we came up dry with only two groups: hockey players and gay couples. Through intermediaries, we approached all the players of the Toronto Maple Leafs and the Vancouver Canucks. No one on either National Hockey League team even responded, except the highly literate Ken Dryden, the former goaltender, Toronto Maple Leafs president, and current minister of social development, and his wife, Lynda. Yet even they had nothing to offer us. Fortunately we had delightful love letters from another goalie, perhaps the most prolific letter writer in hockey history, the late Jacques Plante. We faced a similar scenario with gay men. Through the kind assistance of Toronto lawyer Martha McCarthy, we circulated our request for correspondence to most of the couples across Canada involved in the fight for same-sex marriage. A vacuum – except for Joe Varnell and Kevin Bourassa, the authors of *Just Married*, who had no letters themselves but passed on our plea to a long-involved couple, a professor and a composer, who had corresponded often. Again, nothing. A gay friend suggested that perhaps because of the prejudice homosexuals faced in the past, they have never felt comfortable expressing their love on paper. Once more, fortunately, there was a backup: we did hear from others engaged in the same-sex legal challenge, lesbian couples who gave us a splendid sampling of their loving letters and e-mails.

(A digression: It's true that, because of convenient electronic communication – cheap long-distance telephone calls, cellphones, and the Internet – Canadians are writing fewer letters now than they once did. But the love missive remains one of the rare rationales for taking the time to think about, and then spell out, ideas and emotions at length. Sometimes this takes the form of a letter on paper; increasingly it's done as a protracted e-mail. A whole new way for lonely hearts to make contact and to court has emerged with a deluge of dating sites on the Web. We include an example of one couple who met and communicated on-line so zealously that they wound up married.)

Our initial fear that there would be too much of a sameness to letters of love was unfounded. One correspondent, a soldier, quoted Elizabeth Barrett Browning when writing to his wife: "How do I love thee?" The ways that Canadians expound on that subject are many and various. Some use beautiful or original language. Others are plain-spoken yet powerful in their directness. Whatever the writers' choice of words, all of the letters tell a mini-story, which may be moving, dramatic, or funny. Early on, we decided to be as inclusive as possible in defining what a love letter is. It's certainly more than the glorious gush of prose and poetry that people compose while in the first heady thrall of an affair. Among the most touching letters in this book are those penned by couples either entwined in, or even about to end, long relationships. But friends and family members write lovingly to one another too, although their sentiments are usually more contained, their voices less effusive (among the exceptions are fearful parents writing to their adult children fighting with the Canadian Forces overseas).

The first of five chapters includes correspondence that meets the traditional definition of Love with a capital L. In "New Romance" we've collected letters that tell the stories and express the tumult of passionate love – the overwhelming impact of a life turned upside down because a person has become preoccupied with an ideal other. The lovers may be adolescent or old, or any age in between; what counted for us was the newness of their romance and their astonished and novel reactions to it. We read hundreds of letters filled with prosaic protestations of love, and while we never doubted the sincerity of those who penned them, we were looking for fresh, unconventional, whimsical, and imaginative expressions. It's likely, for instance, that no one other than composer Sir Ernest MacMillan has written to his beloved that the contemplation of their future together made him so happy he could sing a "Te Deum." Has anyone ever before piled on terms of endearment as artist James Nicholl did in just one letter, calling his love Dear Puzzled, Dear Jigsaw, Dear Tiddley Winks, dear little prairie flower, dear Edelweiss, dear Pearl of the Hareem, and my dear little gazelle?

Because our letter-writers were separated, often for years (otherwise they wouldn't have been writing letters), we were interested in the devices they used to erase the distances between them. Some writers imagine astral travel: university lecturer Carolyn Harris declared, "Thoughts are remorseless voyeurs," and sent hers across the Atlantic and into the bedroom of her future husband in the Czech Republic. Fred Albright started a night breeze in Calgary and lofted it to Toronto where it stirred his fiancée's bedroom curtains. Susan Musgrave teleported herself into the prison cell of her new love and listened to him breathe in his sleep.

As well as trying to annihilate the space separating them, lovers strengthened their bond by creating indelible images of themselves. While he was in the North-West Territories in the 1870s, Richard Barrington Nevitt told his Toronto fiancée he was building a private retreat in a small clump of trees and bushes where he could sit alone with her letters – an image that might have helped

Elizabeth Beaty tolerate his four-year absence. In the same decade, Oliver Edwards, away for a year in England and Scotland, wrote an entire paragraph about having a very young girl on his knee – "the little thing . . . talked and laughed so merrily that my enjoyment was perfectly exquisite" – incidentally revealing to his future wife how much he loved children. More than a century later, poet Sarah Haxby told the first love of her life about taking a sparkler to the middle of a frozen lake: "I lit it and wheeled around under the great almost full-term waxing moon spinning madly with this sparkler until I was quite dizzy and the stars kept spinning."

Falling in love is an almost universal experience, and the letters in this chapter remind us of what we've all felt at some time – the ecstasy of reciprocal romance and the despair of unrequited love. Young architectural student Dave Witty, who proposed to Margaret Mitchell on the ninth day of their liaison, demonstrates the brain-chemistry-inspired ability of the lover to know almost instantly that he has found the right and only one. The obsessive correspondence of "Bob" (who wanted to smother his beloved with "purple kisses") develops a portrayal of rejection, and the sad, misspelled letters of Margaret Thompson tell a story of a jilted woman caught in a lethal family feud and publicly humiliated.

Even those in the flush of new romance need friends outside the closed circle of their rapture. The chapter on "Friendship" is where we allow professional writers free rein. We wonder if writers, given the solitary nature of their occupation, feel the need for pen pals more keenly than most people. Whatever the reason, they certainly have the craft and experience to put down on paper, with great imagination, their musings and feelings – and wit. The feisty sixty-eight-year-old writer Morley Callaghan tells a friend, literary critic Edmund Wilson, about getting mugged with a blackjack in his own home. Novelist Jane Rule, on the other hand, waxes profoundly on the nature of emotional dependence in a letter to a friend, writer David Helwig. Non-professionals can be just as thoughtful *and* funny, as Bridget the servant-girl demonstrates in the nineteenth century ("there's a servant-boy . . . that's throwing a sheep's eye at me") and Ruth the mother-to-be in the early twentieth ("I don't expect any relief till the little brat is born").

As life's practicalities – such as the demands of children – intrude on a relationship, love's fervour may mellow into devotion. Some describe the result as companionate love, others call it attachment. In *The Luck of Ginger Coffey*, Irish-Canadian novelist Brian Moore (*see page 252*) writes, "Love – why, I'll tell you what love is: it's you at seventy-five and her at seventy-one, each of you listening for the other's step in the next room, each afraid that a sudden silence, a sudden cry, could mean a lifetime's talk is over." In the chapter titled "Mature Love," seventy-year-old widow Margaret Crawford reconnects with a man she knew a half-century earlier and realizes that she has been "empty of that special feeling that takes place between people of like mind. Emotion. Appreciation." The young yet self-aware literary scholar Northrop Frye maintains that "love itself is ridiculous and grotesque, like the sex act itself. I could hardly be a lover without being a clown first." And a devoted husband beset with failing health and hopelessness writes an affecting love letter to his wife in the form of a suicide note. With maturity, youthful sweethearts may ripen into supportive soulmates.

In the "Family" chapter that follows, we haven't explored every familial relationship, but we have found examples of most: parent to child and the reverse; sibling to sibling; grandparent to grandchild; aunt to niece; and in-law to in-law. In these letters, relatives express their prescribed roles: fathers and mothers give advice or praise; grown daughters thank their parents for all they have done for them; older brothers try to control their younger siblings; a younger sister adores her big brother; a grandfather amuses his grandkids; and in-laws strive to establish and maintain the connection with their spouses' families.

Sometimes you have to smile as you recognize familiar family patterns. Egerton Ryerson, a doting Victorian father with high moral standards, follows his wife's wishes in sending his married daughter a cheque to buy a diamond ring, while lecturing her about the frivolity of personal ornaments, making it almost impossible for her to accept his money. Father Constantine Scollen, in nineteenth-century Saskatchewan, consoles his siblings in Ireland when their father dies, and then assumes a parental role, laying out his plans for the lives of younger brothers he hasn't seen in twenty years. Playing the role of the matriarch who sacrifices individuals for the family's social position, Mary Baker McQuesten tells her son how she squashed her daughters' unsuitable romances. A more contemporary French-Canadian father strives to put a good face on his remoteness from his son and his absences during the boy's childhood, but reaches out to build a relationship with the admirable young man the boy has become. Even when it's a tad self-serving, love drives all these letters: love that hovers over and releases, that accepts the inexplicable choices of children and rejoices in their accomplishments, that recognizes the debt owed to parents, that gives and seeks comfort in grief, that reaches out across generations and is the strength of families.

All the elements – new romance and ripe old love, the tight bonds of friendship and the blood ties of family – come together in the final chapter, "Love and War." War brings out the best as well as the worst in the people caught in its web, as illustrated by letter-writers corresponding from the battle and home fronts of four wars and a peacekeeping mission. Their letters often deal with the basic facts of life while the silent figure of Death lurks in the background. The distance, the danger, the heightened senses of family members and lovers living in the moment combine to inspire passionate communications. In particular, those in harm's way display their humanity as they write to their folks, children, siblings, in-laws, pals, and lovers. Wars kill and wound, but they also create relationships and nourish existing ones. And letters are often the only way loved ones can communicate with one another in such times. The intangible power of the written word and even the tangible qualities of the letter itself – the handwriting, the paper, the lingering presence of the writer – can be overwhelming. Receiving a love letter from his wife in 1994, peacekeeper Kurt Grant wrote from the Balkans killing fields, ". . . I knew that this one was special. At first I did not know why, but then it came to me; as I raised the letter to my nose and inhaled the delicate scent which emanated from its folded pages, I was struck by an overwhelming image of you. Not a picture you understand, but the essence of you."

Letters like these live on. Decades later, children reading them discover the youthful ardour of their parents, lovers recall their madcap days, a grieving survivor finds comfort in the familiar handwriting and the almost-memorized words. Outsiders read love letters from a different perspective, perhaps enjoying a reminder of their own romances, perhaps entranced by an imaginatively and exuberantly expressed passion. We find that these real Canadian love stories attract us because most of them were written in hope and optimism by people who, at least for a time, were seeing life through loving eyes.

Editors' Note

For practical reasons, we have not tried to reproduce actual letters. Often we had to work with unclear photocopies of original correspondence. In some cases the letter-writers' handwriting was nearly illegible. Occasionally we failed to figure out a word; in that case, we either take an educated guess, enclosing the likely word in [brackets], or indicate a missing word with a question mark in brackets [?]. To maintain each letter's integrity, we have not corrected the writer's spelling and grammatical errors unless we thought these might confuse the reader. In those cases, we have made corrections or provided short explanatory notes [in brackets]. We've preserved personal eccentricities as well as peculiarities of punctuation – for example, the habits of avoiding commas, using dashes rather than full stops, or starting a sentence with a lower-case letter. We sometimes omit sentences, or paragraphs, that seem less relevant or less interesting than the rest of the letter. We signal such omissions with ellipses (. . .).

We've done our best to obtain permission to reproduce all the letters in this book. Errors or omissions brought to our attention will be corrected in future printings.

This is the third and final volume of a trilogy that began with *The Book of Letters: 150 Years of Private Canadian Correspondence*. The second was *The Book of War Letters: 100 Years of Private Canadian Correspondence*. While continuing to read letters written by others with interest (and not a little voyeurism), we are no longer inviting contributions to this collection of private correspondence. We do, however, urge Canadians to save copies of their most interesting letters, unearth the little treasures in their families' archives, and share them with one another and even with the wider world. This country has major repositories for such documents, including the National Archives of Canada and the Canadian War Museum in Ottawa; provincial and municipal archives; and local museums and libraries with special collections that often include historical letters. Correspondence among

Canadians has helped historians and social commentators create human-scale portraits of the nation's past. Our readers' personal letters can contribute to this precious legacy.

Audrey and Paul Grescoe
Bowen Island, British Columbia

New Romance

❦

"All my body is electrify"

WITH ZEAL AND DEDICATION

*An important figure in nineteenth-century Canada, **Jonathan Sewell Jr.** was born in the United States in 1766 but fled the country with his parents and brother after watching a revolutionary mob burn down their home in Cambridge, Massachusetts, in 1774. As a young man visiting England, Jonathan wrote to his father in Nova Scotia, describing in one letter an early balloon ascent by Count Francesco Zambeccari in London in 1785 and a stormy sea voyage, during which he was "horribly sick but unable to puke." By 1789 young Sewell had settled in Quebec and embarked upon a career in politics and law. He became engaged to Henrietta, daughter of William Smith, an American who remained loyal to the British during the revolution and was later appointed chief justice of Quebec. About six weeks before his marriage, Jonathan wrote to his fiancée.*

Quebec, Aug. 8, 1796

My D. Harriet

The various emotions excited in my mind by your conversations last evening deprived me not only of the use of speech but of the power of thinking. To appearances I must have been remiss and not sufficiently sensible of your generous conduct. Believe me however it was to appearance only for I then felt and feel at this moment more than I can express or describe.

Your superior understanding and facility passed what I experience to remark only that I [am] without [doubt the] happiest of mankind – and for the happiness I enjoy I am totally indebted to you.

You have known me long and cannot think me ungrateful. You have proved me and know that my affectionate attachment to you is sincere and unbounded. These are only actions and convincing pledges of my future conduct – proofs of the zeal with which I dedicate myself to make you every return in my power for your candid and liberal behavior towards me – and provide assurance of our mutual happiness

To you my dear Harriet with every sentiment of love and gratitude is sincerely dedicated the life [of]

Your truly affectionate
Faithful and Sincere
Sewell

The pair were married on September 24, 1796. Their first child, a daughter, died in infancy. Their first son is mentioned in this letter from Jonathan to his wife.

Montreal, 14th February 1799

Mrs. Sewell
Palace Street
Quebec
My dearest Wife
I wrote you a few lines this morning at eleven and delivered them to Mr. Ferguson who was just getting off for Quebec – I have not there said one millionth part of what I feel and I have not at this

Jonathan Sewell, Jr.,
chief justice of Lower Canada
(Courtesy Janet Beale)

Henrietta Smith Sewell
(Courtesy Janet Beale)

moment time to say anything except to repeat my fondest affection and attachment and would to God I had words capable of Delineating their warmth sincerity and extent. It is however vain to wish, for no known language of the Tongue can do it – I refer you therefore to the language of the Heart that copious language which without a word, will convey to your Intelligent and equally affectionate Soul all that I feel – I say equally affectionate, I am sure of it, and I am rich beyond expression in the conviction that you love me with an affection equal to [my] own.

I am, thank God, as well as ever I was in my life and by no means fatigued . . .

I would at this moment give all the profits of my Journey for one half hour conversation with you and my dear William – Kiss him for me, and give him for me the fond blessing of his fond father.

I found my Mother and brother very well and happy also – My mother quite young with a Turban on her head or a Hankerchief rather put on turban fashion. If she likes it, I have no objection, but a Turban I think is too young for her . . .

 I need not bid you to keep in mind

Your fondest and most affectionate husband
J. Sewell

After many years of loving marriage and the birth of sixteen children (twelve survived infancy), Jonathan was still writing poems "For Mrs. Sewell, My Own Dear Jewell." His portrait hangs in the Canadian Senate, recognizing the many public offices he held (including chief justice of Lower Canada) and his preliminary role in Canadian Confederation in presenting a proposal to the British government for a federal union of the provinces. Maria May Livingstone Sewell, the recipient of the following letter, was Jonathan's daughter.

TELL TALE? NOT ME

William Henry Temple, born in Ireland in 1788, served in Canada in the 15th Regiment of Foot, the East Yorkshires. In May 1832 Captain Temple was in command of a detachment facing rioters at a polling station in Montreal. He gave the order to fire and three French Canadians were killed. Although he and his commanding officer were arrested, both were absolved – but that outcome was uncertain when he wrote this letter. In his late forties, Henry became engaged to twenty-eight-year-old Maria Sewell, who was living with her parents, Jonathan and Henrietta, in Quebec City. Maria, for some reason, wanted to keep the engagement secret.

Montreal, Sunday
[1832?]

My dearest Maria:

I hope and trust your violent rage & bad humour had subsided in very short time after you had dispatched your letter to the post office, & that your anger is by this time converted to your sweet pleasing smile, & still more amiable temper; for of course, Cornell [?] must have made his appearance either on Thursday evening or Friday morning, & by him I enclosed a letter to your brother Henry for you, & also a hurried one to him. My room was full of visitors as is common about half an hour before dinner to chat over the day & lounge on my most comfortable arm chair & sofa that I scarcely know what I said to him, with the tongues that were exercising themselves at such a rate, but I request you will make him Groom's Man when the ceremony takes place, and I also expressed a wish that every member of the family should form the Bridal Party.

So you tell me the secret has got wind & talked of all around. The person that asked your Father must have been on the most intimate terms to have dared to put such a question, & even then it was a great liberty, without first coming from the family. You appear to insinuate that I am the Tell Tale. Most solemnly do I declare that neither directly or indirectly did I ever give the Edens the slightest cause to suppose that such was to take place, nor has it yet escaped from my lips to a soul breathing on this side of the Atlantic, nor shall I ever mention it to your cousins although you say I may. Take your own opportunity of acquainting them & when they ask me, I shall reply yes, I am to be so blessed to have your dear cousin as my partner for life . . .

A palpitation came over me when reading that part of your letter that, should I mention the circumstance to your cousins, to bind them to secrecy for "fear any unforeseen accident should prevent it taking place". Oh for God sake do not distress my feelings with a doubt on the occasion, for really & truly if such were to occur it would break my heart & destroy the most anxious hopes of all my friends. I cannot nor will I for a moment, conceive that there can exist a doubt but that my happiness will be soon realized, & with a sincere hope there will be no occasion for the flight you have in contemplation. Suspense is hovering over me, even that refractory house of assembly keeps me in a state of despondency. I fancy it is pretty certain we military and Magistrates are to appear before it; and suppose I do, what have I to apprehend? Nothing. I have given up in a degree visiting, in short there is but one individual in this world in whose society I can be happy, nor can all the balls, parties & dinners make any impression to amuse me. There is no post today & I am fearful your patience will be again most severely put to the test with a thousand fancies of my apparent neglect, but rest assured you shall never have such a cause of complaint ever to make of me. It gives me a great consolation to find your cold is better. Pray take good care of yourself & do not catch another. We have had a good fall of snow both yesterday and today.

Kind remembrance to all,
and believe me ever affectionately attached
H. Temple

The couple were married in Quebec on January 9, 1833. In May, Henry was stationed at his regiment's headquarters in Kingston, and Maria was in Quebec. She seems to have had a miscarriage and to have heard rumours about her husband.

Kingston, Friday 10th May [1833]

My Ever Dearest Maria:

I know full well your anxiety to hear of my safe arrival at my present, indeed I may well say gloomy, destination, for without your society the most lively place must appear to me dull & gloomy in the extreme; but my dearest Maria, I must content myself with the hope that it will not be of a very long duration before I shall have the happiness of being with you & the rest of my kind relatives . . .

I should have written to you the day after my arrival, but really I had not a moment to myself . . . & then I was anxiously expecting a letter from your dear self which I was gratified by receiving this morning, & as you have expressed so tenderly if I loved you to write, depend upon it my own dearest Maria, to the hour of my death will I dote on you & trust you will have never cause to say otherwise; so with the greatest pleasure I now sit down to thank you for your affectionate letter & I feel happy to find your poor throat is quite well; but I am really much concerned for what has now occurred although you think I shall be glad, indeed I am not, for God sake take the greatest care of yourself & pray do not keep anything from me concerning yourself, for if you do I shall be truly wretched. Has your waist come to its original size? I do most solemnly declare that I did not gallivant with any lady in Montreal, although a female friend of mine once requested of me to take up my abode with her during my stay, which of course I civilly declined. I must say she is a kind-hearted, unhappy woman . . .

[signature missing]

The Temples had six children.

THE POET ENGROSSED

William Bruce was four years old in 1837 when his family left Scotland and emigrated to Canada, settling in Hamilton, where William attended school. As a young adult, he studied classics, the violin, and shorthand in the United States and worked in Canada West at a variety of jobs – bookkeeper, writing master at Hamilton's Central School, and bookstore manager. In 1864 he founded an evening academy, where he taught young men commercial and ornamental penmanship, and in 1867 he opened a patent office, where the first patent he registered was his own invention, a machine to train the hand to write. Keen on astronomy, William built an observatory on his property on Hamilton Mountain and was president of the Hamilton Branch of the Royal Astronomical Society. He also practised engrossing, an ornate form of writing and illuminating, and was hired to pen official documents presented to Queen Victoria and Kaiser Wilhelm. On top of this, he wrote poems in his beautiful penmanship for Janet Blair of Glandford Township, whom he called Jennet and married in 1853 or 1854.

March 9th 1853

To Jennet
They say that thou are poor, Jennet,
And so I know thou art;
But what's wealth to the noble mind
Or riches to the heart?
With all the wealth of India's mines
Can one great deed be bought?
Or can a kingdom's ransom bring

One pure and holy thought?
No! Vain your boasted treasure
Though earth to gold is given,
Gold cannot stretch to measure
The Love bestowed by Heaven!

⁓

They say that thou art poor, Jennet;
And so I know thou art;
But why should lack of sordid pelf
Thrust thee and me apart?
The pearls that sparkle on the lawn
Our jewels bright shall be;
As never met the fevered lips
Of fortune's gilded slave.
Could Lybian Croesus, dearest,
As wide a kingdom see
As the fair realm thou hearest
Belongs to thee and me?

⁓

I know that thou art poor, Jennet;
And so indeed am I;
But not the hoards of ocean's caves
Our poverty could buy;
For wealth beyond the miser's thought
We both alike control –
The treasures of a priceless love,
The riches of the soul!
Then at this hour divine, love,

To holy echoes given;
Let <u>thy</u> true vows and mine, love,
Be registered in Heaven!
W.B.

After their marriage, William continued to express his love in rhyme: "When on <u>thy</u> bosom I recline,/Enraptured still to call thee mine,/To call thee mine for life,/I glory in the sacred ties,/Which modern wits and fools despise,/Of husband and of wife." William and Janet had three children, one of whom was Canada's first impressionist painter, William Blair Bruce, whose art was shown in the Paris Salons of the 1880s. After the deaths of his wife in 1904 and his artist son in 1906, William Bruce was one of the founders of the Art Gallery of Hamilton, which has many of his son's paintings in its collection. He died in 1927.

LADY'S CHOICE

An act of the Scottish parliament in 1288 allowed women to propose in a leap year, and to claim a forfeit if refused. In 1864, **Ann Eliza Cairns***, of Hemmingford, Quebec, took advantage of the custom and made a valentine that she mailed from nearby Barrington to Donald McNaughton, who lived in Hemmingford. Ann's card, containing the following rhyme, was decorated with a painting of flowers – pansies, a red rose, and forget-me-nots – the meaning of which she pointed out by encircling the illustration with this message: "Within this bouquet read all I would say Love, truth and constancy. Leap Year."*

Ann Eliza Cairns in 1853 at the age of sixteen (Courtesy Ann Harris)

Donald McNaughton in the uniform of the 51st Hemmingford, Quebec, Rangers (Courtesy Ann Harris)

I've often wished to have a friend
With whom my choicest hours to spend
To whom I softly might impart
Each wish and weakness of my heart
Who might me in my sorrow cheer
Or mingle in my grief a tear
And to secure my happiness till life doth end
I wish that friend to be my Husband.
Will you be that friend?

Ann and Donald married the following February, when she was twenty-eight and he thirty-nine. They had six children before Donald died in 1885. Ann survived him by three years.

Love only me

*In 1861, thirty-five years before he was elected prime minister of Canada, twenty-year-old **Wilfrid Laurier** met Zoé Lafontaine, a piano teacher, who boarded in the same Montreal house he did. Six years later, when Wilfrid was practising law in Arthabaska (now L'Avenir), he wrote love letters in French to Zoé, but hesitated to propose marriage because he was poor and believed he had tuberculosis, a disease that had killed his mother: "Unfortunately, I fear that I am carrying in my lungs a germ of death that no power in the world can dislodge." By December 1867, however, he was convinced his condition was chronic bronchitis. Two months later, Wilfrid sensed he was in greater danger of losing Zoé than of dying.*

Arthabaskaville [February 1868]

My very dear good Zoé,

Yesterday and the day before were two long and anxious ones for me; your letter, which I'm used to receiving on Tuesday morning, arrived only today. Tuesday I still wasn't entirely upset; I believed that it was basically nothing more than a delay in the mail, and I counted on the following day, but the following day, there was still nothing. Alas, the tone of our correspondence over the past three weeks has caused me mounting uneasiness. In any other circumstance, this delay wouldn't have alarmed me much, but your earlier letters have filled my head with somber ideas; I feared everything without daring however to acknowledge my fears. Dear Zoé, I felt it more deeply than ever, because I have feared it, how hard it would be for me if I were to lose you. My friend, I could never love anyone other than you, and if I were to lose you I would never be consoled.

Sir Wilfrid Laurier, a young lawyer in the 1860s (Bibliothèque nationale du Québec #3223-44)

Zoé Lafontaine, a piano teacher before her marriage to Wilfrid Laurier (Sir Wilfrid Laurier collection, National Archives of Canada C-015558)

If there is really nothing but my health that worries you, dear, you can be perfectly at ease; not only am I better, I am perfectly [?]. I have at last found that cure that I have waited for for such a long time. At first you may not believe me when you read this, however, my friend, I am speaking only the truth.

The sitting [of court] finished on Tuesday. I am tired but nevertheless I am not [?] at all. Moreover you can soon judge the matter for yourself, because I am going to Montreal before long. Dr. Poisson to whom I mentioned that you said people think I'm consumptive says it is humbug and who would know better. Yes, my dear, if there is really nothing but my poor health that is the cause of your uneasiness, don't be upset, for once again, I am entirely well.

In your last letter, you wrote me things that would certainly have awakened my jealousy if I did not have absolute confidence in you: people say that men are fighting over you. I know very well that M. Valois loves you and it wouldn't surprise me in the least if your cousin also loves you. You can't prevent men from falling in love with you, but love only me and I will be content . . .

Farewell, my good Zoé, love me always; as for me, I love you very much.

Your friend
Wilfrid

Zoé had been waiting for Wilfrid to make an offer of marriage and when he did not, she agreed to wed Dr. Pierre Valois. About ten days before the proposed wedding, Dr. Séraphin Gauthier, in whose boarding house Zoé still lived, telegraphed Wilfrid to come to Montreal "on a matter of urgent importance." When Wilfrid arrived early the next morning, Gauthier told him that Zoé had confessed she did not want to marry Valois. Brought together in the library of the Gauthier house, Wilfrid and Zoé embraced and decided to be married that very night, May 13, 1868. Although childless and despite Wilfrid's romantic liaison with his partner's wife, the Laurier marriage endured for half a century.

DREAMING OF HETTIE

Oliver Cromwell Edwards *was born in Clarence, Ontario, in 1850 and became a medical doctor. Henrietta Louise Muir, born in Montreal in 1849, was an early Canadian activist for women's rights. She was the oldest of the "Famous Five" litigants from Alberta whose Persons Case, on appeal to the British Privy Council*

Henrietta Muir Edwards,
circa 1870 to 1875 (Glenbow
Museum NA-2607-6)

Oliver Cromwell Edwards in 1900
(Glenbow Museum NA-4035-140)

in 1929, established that the word persons *in the British North America Act included members of both sexes, thus allowing women to be appointed to the Senate. They were married in 1876.*

Portobello, Scotland
July 21st, 1873

My dear Hettie:

At last I am going to try and write quietly with nothing to hurry me. Many of my letters and in fact most nearly all have been written in the greatest hurry and then you know dear I have had some unfortunate accidents about some of your letters in regard to mailing them. I felt very very sorry at the time and many a time since that you should have gone that week without my letters – and nothing except sickness will ever permit it to occur again.

A week ago today I made my entrance into Scotland by the coast west & South of Edinborough & though the country was barren looking still it improved as I neared the city, and I found it much better East of Edinburgh in fact one farm I passed I was told was the finest in the Lothian district. Regarding Edinburgh itself – I am greatly pleased with it and have been the recipient of a great deal of kindness since I arrived . . .

I go from here to Glasgow & then up Loch Lomond & through the Trossacs & back to Glasgow by Sterling . . . Now will begin the glorious scenery & I am all enthusiastic anxiety to see it – but oh how very much I wish you were here tonight and would accompany me in the morning. It would be doubly delightful if you were beside me. A year ago tomorrow I left Montreal for my summer holidays. I have often wished since over here that I could dream of you and last night I had my wish gratified – for you came to me & I thought I was sitting & you came in behind me and bent over me & kissed me and I felt your soft arms around my neck – and oh it was so delightful & when I awoke and found it only a dream & I thousands of miles away ah me – but still the dream was so vivid & your face appeared so natural & so full of tenderness when you bent over me that when I woke I felt very thankful that I had had it – & dressed happily. Now darling good night – I scarcely know when my next may be dated from

With love believe me your

Oliver

Portobello Scotland

Aug 7th 1873

My darling Hettie:

How shall I begin to answer all your letters. On Saturday last I returned from my northern trip and found <u>eight</u> letters waiting

me and four of them from you. This morning the postman
brought me <u>six</u> and two of them from you – so I have six letters
to answer in this one. Did you ever experience in your travels the
getting of eight letters in a bunch – if not then let me tell you that
it is almost overpowering. For two weeks I had been north and
all the time contented myself & reassured myself & congratu-
lated myself that I would find letters waiting me at Portobello and
I was not disappointed. When I arrived here I was thoroughly
tired out and for the first time since I have been in Scotland really
hungry – having had tea I began the attack on the pile of letters
but succumbed before I finished for my poor body was so loud
in its calls for sleep that I could not enjoy the letters as I wished
to & so put two under my pillow & in a few moments all
thought of Canada & you were drowned. I woke on Sunday
feeling so much refreshed & then out came your letters & I was
again all attention. Oh! how I do enjoy your letters – they are so
very very sweet . . .

And now I must again come to a close. How very much I should
like to be with you in the drawing room on that sofa or outside
under the shade of the trees & talk to you about all I have seen –
this writing is so slow & So unsatisfactory. Oh I met a pretty little
dark-eyed girl a day or two ago at one of the friends houses in
Edinburgh & it was such a treat to have a child on my knees again
– I had not had one near me since I left Clarence & the little thing
made friends with me & talked and laughed so merrily that my
enjoyment was perfectly exquisite. She put her arms round my
neck & kissed me – & I patted her soft cheeks & while the friends
laughed at little Nellie making up so with a stranger they little
knew what was running through my mind & what the patting of
the cheeks & fondling brought back so very vividly to my mind.
The child clung to me the whole evening & chatted away so

happily I declare I have had nothing give me such pleasure since I have been away.

But goodbye darling goodbye . . . believe me with love
Ever your only
Oliver

In 1916, a year after Oliver's death, on the evening of what would have been her golden wedding anniversary, Henrietta wrote to her daughter, "My husband and I walked together in perfect accord for 39 years."

BLACKHEART

William Donnelly – known as Clubfoot Will – was one of the seven sons of James and Johannah Donnelly, who emigrated from Ireland in 1844 and settled in the Ontario township of Biddulph, in a community that festered with factional hatreds born in County Tipperary. In this dangerous place, grudges were settled with violence, arson, even assassination, and the Donnellys became known as the Black Donnellys, possibly because they opposed a secret society known as the Whiteboys and possibly because their enemies described them as "black inside and out." William, the second Donnelly son, courted **Margaret Thompson.** *Early in April 1873, Margaret sent William a picture of herself "in hopes you think as much of me as I do of you . . . I desire to bear testimony to the faithfulness with which you have laboured for my benefit and the kindness which you have ever shown towards me . . ." In two subsequent letters, Margaret mentioned a marriage proposal and the tempest that blew up when her family became aware of the romance.*

April the 30th 1873

William Donnelly

Dear friend

. . . I now wish to inform you that I have made up my mind to accept your kind offer as their is no person in this world I sencerly love but you . . . you can acquaint my parents about it any time you wish after the first of November . . .

Margaret Thompson

December 24th 1873

William Donnelly

Dear friend

I adress you with those few lines to let you know I am well and hopes you are enjoying the same blessing I wish to let you know a little about the performance I had to go through sence I came up here. My friends herd all about me writing letters to you which caused an awfull storm so that I could not attempt to ask to go any where and on that account you will please excuse me for not writing to you. Dear William I would rather be in the grave than home at present for the way my people abused me on your account hinders me of ever forgiving them. I will never have anything like a chance of fullfilling my promise of marriage with you except you come and take me away by force and if you think as much of me now as you did always I trust you will relieve me before long and if you will please send me my Letters to [?] and I will try to put up with all. I burnt your Letters when they commenced to abuse me about you for they would shurly get them if I did not do something with them. Excuse my bad writing for I am in an awfull hury as it is in the office I am writing it. No more at present from your loving friend

Margaret Thompson

In January, a person who signed himself P.Mc. wrote to Margaret's
father following "the excitement that took place at your house of
friday night last," warning Thompson that "the Donnely's are a
bad crowd to quarrel with not only them but the crowd that will
almost die for them . . ." And then **William Donnelly** *wrote to*
Margaret's father.

Lucan Jan 12th/74

Mr. W. Thompson

Dear Sir

. . . I was in the crowd myself and my sole business was to have
satisfaction for some of yr mean low talk to yr daughter that never
deserved it – at least she never deserved it on my account . . . in
the first place I will show you how you were wrong in saying that
their was letters passing from yr daughter to me as I defy her to
say that anything of the kind ever happened and secondly you
were wrong in saying that I was a son of a Bitch . . . for the long
length of time yr daughter was in Biddulph I defy her or any one
else to say there was one word of marriage passed between us and
for that reason would like to know what you abused her for and
talked to me in the manner you have done . . . I want you to understand that I will have my revenge if it cost the lives of both familys
which I am shure it will not for I can get crowd enough in allmost
any town to cary out my design . . . if the business must be done
on the way to church I can get any amount of men to do it . . .

Give respect to your daughter. Answer me if you like.

[William Donnelly]

James Reaney, author of a trilogy of plays about the Donnellys,
writes that William twice attempted to abduct Margaret in 1874.

In 1876 he married Hanora Kennedy against her family's wishes. Four years later, a vigilante crowd murdered the elder Donnellys, one of the brothers, and a cousin, and then walked the three miles to William Donnelly's house, intending to kill him, but shot instead his brother John. William died of natural causes in 1897.

Tied for Eternity

*Born in Savannah, Georgia, in 1850, **Richard Barrington Nevitt** fled to Canada during the American Civil War. In 1874 he received a bachelor of medicine degree from the University of Toronto, but, not being qualified to practise, and with not enough money to continue his studies, he joined the North West Mounted Police at a salary of $1,000 a year and travelled west with Colonel James F. Macleod, arriving in October at the site selected for Fort Macleod, the first permanent outpost in the North-West Territories. From there, Barrie wrote to his fiancée, Elizabeth, the daughter of Robert Beaty, a prominent Toronto banker, broker, and real-estate dealer.*

Fort Macleod April 23, 1875

This afternoon I took a walk down to the River and watched the rapid waters and to my delight found some willows really beginning to put out their leaves, the first that I have seen. I found a cosy little space just over the river in a small clump of trees & bushes that I am going to turn into a private retreat and in the summer will have a nice quiet little place to take your dear letters and read them. I will make a seat there – just under a bush & imagine you are in the bush. I will not make a second seat for you

for someone else might come and sit in it and I don't want them
to do that . . .

> With much love believe me
> Yours forever
> Barrie

Fort McLeod June 4th 1875

My dear Lizzie

A mail is to go out from here tomorrow. How I would like to go
with it. I am afraid that I would outstrip the mail. Dear me, I am
afraid that I am very blue tonight. I think I always get blue when
a mail is about leaving, but I must not think of the blues just now,
for you, by the time this reaches Toronto, may be thinking of
Miss Annie Taylors wedding. Dear Liz, I wish it were you and I
that were about to be tied together for life – for more than life,
for Eternity. Do you ever think of it? I do often and often I consider that in very truth you and I are
now so nearly and so closely united
in heart and mind and soul, that tho'
our bodies should never be united
still our soul-binding would last thro'
time and Eternity. Even now separated as we are by vast tracts of wild
desolate country, we are yet one and
should one of us be called away, the
other would remain faithful and true
until such time as Our Father saw fit
to place us together again. But my
own darling I am getting gloomy
again. Forgive me and let us talk of
something else. Say anything you

*Richard Barrington Nevitt, a
university graduate in the
early 1870s* (Glenbow
Museum NA-2859-1)

would like me to say to Annie Taylor on the 20th and I will become responsible for it. Why did she not choose the 21st of June, she would have had a longer day? . . .

And now my darling I must say good night – and for the present goodbye – I am quite well & have been. The only change is my smooth chin and fierce (?) moustache. Keep your spirits up old girl – our 20th of June will come round in good time and then – [?] –

With unalterable love I am

ever your own

Barrie

I inclose you a little flower I found in a most lonely desolate spot all by itself – no other green thing within some distance of it. It was bright and doing well & apparently happy tho' all alone – like

Your

Barrie

Barrie spent four years in the N.W.T. He sketched and painted Blackfoot and buffalo, performed what he thought was the first post-mortem examination in the area, and witnessed the meeting in 1876 at Fort Walsh between A.G. Irvine, the assistant commissioner of the North West Mounted Police, and Sitting Bull just after the Sioux chief had defeated General George Custer at Little Big Horn River in Montana. Barrie returned to Toronto, married Lizzie in 1878 (ironically, on June 22), and had a distinguished career in medicine.

CROSS GHOSTS

Helen (Nell) Macleod, the first white child born in southern Alberta, was the daughter of North West Mounted Police commissioner James F. Macleod. She attended Bishop Strachan School in Toronto but at the age of sixteen went to work as a cashier at Hudson's Bay Company in Calgary to help support her impoverished mother following her father's death in 1894. A.E. (Ernest) Cross was born into a wealthy Montreal family, attended a boys' school in England, a business college in Montreal, the Ontario School of Agriculture in Guelph, the Montreal Veterinary College, and the Montreal Brewing Academy before coming to Alberta, where he started the famous a7 Ranche at High River in 1886 and the Calgary Brewing & Malting Company, the first brewery in the North-West Territories, in 1892. When he was thirty-seven, with three failed engagements behind him, Ernest fell in love with nineteen-year-old Nell Macleod following a horse race in which Nell demonstrated that she could ride as well as a man. The pair became engaged in 1898, the same year Ernest won a seat in the North-West Territories legislative assembly in Regina with the party led by Sir Frederick Haultain. Helen wrote to him from Calgary.

Sunday [April 9, 1899]

My dearest Ernest

Imagine me sitting at my desk in the sitting room with your photograph & the roses which came yesterday in front of me. Mother, Norman & Jean are at the Pinkham's & I am all by myself & it is raining out of doors & I am very lonely & wish you my dearest love were here. I was very disappointed not hearing from you this morning but I must not say too much as I took such a time to write my first letter to you. But if I don't hear soon, I shall begin to be alarmed. Now do write soon dearest & tell me all about your dear self what you are doing & all that kind of thing. I left work last night at 7.30 & after tea washed the dishes. It did seem a shame to put my ring in dish water & Mother objected at first but I must help in the house & it wont hurt the stones & when you come back you will take the ring off & we shall clean it. I dreamt last night that you were helping me with the dishes or rather that you were talking with me while I did them . . . I wonder if you have been to church today & I

Helen Macleod Cross on her wedding day in 1899 (Glenbow Museum NA-2536-4)

must get ready for evening service now so Good-bye for the present. Well I had a struggle to keep awake during the service but did manage it. We prayed for the Lt. Governor & Legislative Assembly & I thought of you most particularily dear, & of Haultain's supporters in general . . . Have you any idea of when you will come up? Good night dear & may God watch over you & bless you. With very very much love & hoping to see or hear from you soon.

Your very very loving
Nell

Regina, Apr. 11. 1899

My dearest Nell
Your sweet letter written on Sunday arrived this morning . . .

I cannot stand your being lonely and there is a beautiful political excuse so I shall take a trip west and arrive in Calgary next Saturday morning when my spirits will reach the heavens. Your

sweet influence seems to have absorbed all my heart and soul
Nell, and I am afraid politics are a very secondary matter . . .
Very many thanks for the pretty flower which I prize more than
the finest gem. It is almost impossible to write as the M.L.A.s all
round are talking rubbish so I shall say goodbye dearest, from
your ever loving

Ernest

*The year he was married, Ernest bought a house on 8th Avenue
in what is now the Inglewood district of Calgary. He installed
Nell there, leaving her frequently in the next fifteen years as he
travelled on business, but writing almost every day while he
was away. In March 1902 he was in Milwaukee studying beer-
brewing methods.*

Mar 31, 1902

My dearest Wife
I have been working hard since early
this morning trying to get all the
information possible and have succeeded in getting a good deal, but
will have to remain over tomorrow
as there is more than I can get
through. I shall send little Helen a
birthday card to show I remember
our dear little ones welcome coming
into the world . . .

In one way I hope my love is not
getting too lonely, it is hard to feel
that way, while in another it would
please me beyond description to

*Alfred Ernest Cross, member
of the Legislative Assembly in
1899 (Glenbow Museum
NA-165-4)*

think I was very much missed by one who is dearer by far than one's life. And our dearest little ones. I keep wondering how they are and how much they are growing each day. Selkirk must be nearly walking . . . God bless and protect you all is my fervant prayer; kiss the little ones from me. Goodbye my own darling wife, as I must be on the go once more.

Ever your loving husband
Ernest

Two years later, little Helen and Selkirk died of diphtheria within twenty minutes of each other. Their baby brother, James, was seriously ill but survived. Ernest and Nell continued to live in their house on 8th Avenue, raising six children to adulthood. Given historic designation in 1977, the Cross House – now the location of a restaurant – is said to be haunted by a couple whose ghostly image was once caught in wedding photographs, dancing among the living guests.

Don't get sunburned

David Milne, who has been called one of the three most important North American artists of his time, was born in Paisley, Ontario, but spent almost half his working life in the United States. In 1903 when he was twenty-one, David went to New York to become an illustrator and to study at the Art Students' League. Three years later he met May (Patsy) Hegarty, a sixteen-year-old cashier and assistant bookkeeper at the drugstore for which Milne dressed windows and made showcards. That summer while May was vacationing out of the city, David wrote to her and tried to find the time to visit her.

[August 1906]

Can't decide what to call you, Patsy, so I'll just start without calling you anything. I've been studying the dictionary all day and I can't find a name half sweet enough.

Anyway why should my letters to you begin the same as other people's letters to other people begin? Our letters are going to be different from all others aren't they? – different from any that were ever written from the time Adam and Eve scribbled theirs on a fig leaf till now. They are going to be just our thoughts, our very inmost thoughts at that.

Patsy, I'm never going to let you go again the way you did Sunday night. Even if I have to wade back I'm not going to let you go away by yourself in the dark to a strange place. Of course I know you're safe but – well I don't know what it is, but I think I'd like to have you spend your future vacations somewhere round the end of my finger tips. Why didn't you look back, sweetheart? I stayed there until you were out of sight and then turned round to walk away, and butted into the wrong place about half a dozen times before I woke up . . .

Patsy, how much do you think I'd give to have a certain little color scheme of red-gold and navy blue snuggling up against my shoulder and two arms that I know stealing round the place where my collar ought to be (it isn't) and two lips that I also know just touch mine like a butterfly. You needn't guess, you couldn't guess enough . . .

How's the water, Patsy? . . . If you don't wear a bathing cap – a bigger one – there's trouble waiting you. And get as much sunburned as you like but don't do it all at once; if you do you will be so sore that no one can touch you and you know, someone might want to   well, I want to shake hands with you

I looked up those trains to-day, and I find that there are no

David Milne, circa 1903, before he met May (David Brown Milne collection, Library and Archives Canada C-057170)

May Hegarty Milne before she and David married in 1912 (David Brown Milne collection, Library and Archives Canada C-057191)

very early ones on Sunday, but I shall go down on the first one, and come back on the last, and, though that doesn't give us much time, it's about the best we can do, little girl. I hope the Asbury Park station is something like the Long Branch – not too brilliantly lighted – you know how lighting uses the eyes – and the people seem a little shortsighted. I don't think they'd look – Patsy, turn your face this way – good-bye. You darling, I'd just squeeze you to pieces if you were here.

These are shocking things to put on paper, Patsy, but you understand, and I'm not writing to anyone else. Still Patsy other people wouldn't understand, even if they knew that I love you and that you love me – you do, don't you, "Little friend of all the world". So it would be very much better to burn these letters or bring them some place where they'll tell no tales to any one but you and me. I don't care though. It's you who takes the risks. Wouldn't I like to be there the day your aunt decides to help you fix your room, and a certain pile of letters tumbles open at the very worst page of course. Has your aunt a very strong constitution?

Why, May, it's half-past ten – just time to get you home. Shall we say good-bye – in the usual way?

Next time you write you must tell me every little thing about yourself, that is every little thing that concerns me, and to-morrow I shall look for a letter, one all your own. Good-bye Patsy, darling. I can almost imagine I have you in my arms, and this time I'll not let go. I don't need to, do I?

Dave

Three years later, when they still couldn't afford to be married, David wrote, "I have never wanted anything Patsy as much as I want to have you all to myself in a little house, and I think when people want a thing as much as we do, and work as hard as they can for it, they are pretty apt to get it." Heading to the Milne family home in Paisley for a vacation in August 1912, David and May made an impromptu decision to marry, using bogus local addresses to get the necessary licence in New Rochelle, New York. In the next few years, Patsy was often the painter's model for domestic scenes in their apartment in New York. The couple came to live in Canada in 1929, but separated, childless, in 1933.

WILL YOU GOSSIP?

Maude E. Parkin was born in 1880 in Fredericton, New Brunswick, and educated in Switzerland and at Bishop Strachan School in

Toronto. In 1902 she obtained an arts degree from McGill University and became warden of Ashburne Hall, then a women's residence at the University of Manchester. Born in 1872 in Halifax, Nova Scotia, William Lawson Grant attended Queen's University (where his father was the legendary energetic principal George Monro Grant) and Balliol College at Oxford. William taught history at Oxford and at Queen's before becoming headmaster of Upper Canada College in 1917. Maude and William became engaged in 1910 when she was thirty and he was thirty-eight.

[1910]
The Oaks
Fallowfield, Manchester

Dear Will,

I have had two letters from you today – one little one (a gem) and one big, splendid, long one which has made me gloriously happy. You are a dear to write me such good letters and I think you would feel rewarded if you knew how glad they make me. And I am just dreadfully proud of you – really uplifted. The account of the [oral exam] thrills me. Oh, my dear, I do love it that you did it well. I am going to keep the account you sent me in your letters for myself . . . I wish I had been there. It must have been a rather wonderful moment for you to find yourself standing in your Father's Hall – doing something and fulfilling a purpose that would have made him glad & proud. Dearest, among the many things that make me rejoice, I rejoice that you are his son. But most of all I love you for being you and for being all you are to me. Yes we'll both have to put up with each other because for one thing we can't help it now – it is stronger than any prejudices & impatiences, isn't it? And I am so glad it is!

I just <u>love</u> your expression "wild flurries of trying to be strong" – it is so dear & funny & like you to make fun of yourself. There – I just kissed you to show you I have a special kind of love for you when you are funny . . .

When you talk about me as you do, it makes me a little afraid. Beloved, after all I am very commonplace & earthy [?]. Only I have this to the good, that I love you and want to make you happy, splendidly happy.

Always yours,
Maude

Sunday, Oct. 30, 1910

Willie, dear,

. . . I . . . feel like writing to you – just to tell you before I go to sleep that I really like you most awfully much – and that I am glad that any one in the world who wants to know that fact can after tomorrow . . .

Tomorrow late: Such a day! With not a moment in it to write to you. And now it is no more a secret. I have told the children here – tonight, and I feel really launched on the sea of the future. You know what I mean, don't you? The future began on August 3rd really, but that was especially yours and mine – and now that everyone will know it is different. I am awfully glad for I have been longing to tell the world – and so have you, I know. Dearest, dearest, I am just a little afraid – for it has always been easy to me to be a great deal to a great many people – but can I be everything to one person? Our lives, by the very reason of what they have been so far, are sure to be filled with many friends, and interests & duties, but we won't let that fill up all the space, will we?

To tell the girls, I had a tea party – a very superior one in my

room at 10 o'clock – for seniors only – the ones I had known
before this year. They were so dear & nice & glad & sorry . . .

Good-night, beloved,

Maude

Au lit

Thursday, Nov 10th 1910

12:30 a.m. or Friday

Beloved,
As you have not yet expressed your strong disapproval of my
writing letters in bed, I think I won't stop the bad practice –
anyway not tonight, for I awfully want to talk to you a bit . . .

. . . after being tired & depressed all day – almost all, I got
into an exultant frame of mind – largely because I was thinking of
you & how nice you are & will be! I wish I could describe it. It
was really exciting, thrilling & I love you for being the cause of it
and for everything else you are to me.

I sometimes wonder what it will be like to change from living
with 65 women most of whom I rather love – at least in theory
and on the whole in very actual practice too – to living with one
man whom I also rather love – anyway most certainly in practice
and I suppose in theory too! I think it will be very nice – if only
you'll be gossipy & awfully friendly and like a woman friend to
me. Sometimes I ask a very great deal of you, don't I? . . .

Till tomorrow

M.E.P.

*Maude and William married the following year. Their four chil-
dren, one of whom was philosopher George Grant, and their thirteen grandchildren (among them writer and historian Michael*

Ignatieff) have had prominent careers as academics, writers, painters, teachers, administrators, social-justice advocates, and human-rights activists.

A SONG OF JOY

*Internationally known conductor, pianist, and organist **Sir Ernest MacMillan** and his wife, Elsie, always referred to June 25, 1913, as their "day of revelation." On that day, Ernest, who was only nineteen, was leaving to work for the summer as an organist at a resort on the Saguenay River in Quebec. Before boarding a steamer that would take him through Lake Ontario and up the St. Lawrence River, he went to say goodbye to **Elsie Keith**, a modern-languages student at the University of Toronto, who was his German tutor. In that moment of parting, the pair confessed their love for one another and agreed to announce their engagement when he returned.*

Kingston [a steamer]
June 25th 1913

Meine Geliebte [my beloved]: –
This is my first attempt at a love-letter, so if you find any faults in it, they may be set down to inexperience and – may I hope it? – be pardoned. Dearest, I am still a little dazed by the events of today (and it will always be a red-letter day in my life) but the one fact that stands out dear & glorious is, that you return the love which I have so long felt for you. And I cannot begin to say how great that love is. If you only knew how constantly you have been in my thoughts, particularly during the past winter, and if you realized what you have meant in my life ever since I first met

you, you might begin to form an idea of what my love is. And I know, darling, that your love for me, though new-born, is no less than mine for you. Oh, Elsie, can there be anything more glorious in God's earth than a strong & steadfast mutual love? I thank God for your love & for you & I only pray that I may prove worthy of it.

Mr. Gibson is an interesting companion, but I did not want to talk to anyone for any length of time, so I excused myself, & retired to my stateroom, where behold me being in a rather unromantic but comfortable position on my stomach in the upper berth with no thoughts save of you. And now, although I have so much to say I can think of nothing but to repeat – I love you, I adore you. Don't forget to tell me the same when you write, because I cannot hear it too often.

Absence may make the heart grow fonder, but under the circumstances don't you think, Elsie mine, that separation for us is a great shame? It reminds me of the little poem – "Platonic" – where the two "friends" found out that they loved one another just as they had to part. I shall always love that poem, & hope to hear you recite it soon.

You know, sweetheart, you seem so different since I told you of my love, & yet you are the same dear little woman I have so long adored. You are not perfect thank Heaven, but there is not a feature of you that I should wish to see changed. I love everything about you, but nothing more than your complete sincerity and openness. I could imagine you doing anything rather than deceiving any one. And this augurs well for our future, dear, because only the most complete frankness between us will prove to be in the interests of our happiness.

I told you, Elsie mine, that I was frightened of you, & it is true in a sense. I never realized until today all that love means to a woman, and I tremble lest I should prove unworthy of your affections. I suppose that together with complete sincerity, great tact must be used between lovers, and I should hate to think that I might inadvertently hurt you by some thoughtless remark or action. Now, dearest, I want you never to fail in telling me if I ever do anything which you do not like. What I want is always to please you in every way I can.

I am sure you must feel as I do the responsibility we have taken upon ourselves, but a love like ours will bear any load, & our happiness will certainly be assured . . .

. . . more love than you can imagine goes with this letter; love for your mother & father & all the rest; love even for Prince & the cat (love me, love my dog!) and — I can never begin to say how much love for your own dear self.

Thine always
Ernest

Kingston June 25, 1913

Dearest: –

. . . I told you today that you always seemed part of my music, & my music seemed part of you. You have encouraged me more than I could begin to tell you in the study of my beloved art. No greater happiness was mine than to play the things I loved to the little woman I loved best. Quite apart from the fact that I loved you (if such a fact can be separated), there was no one I loved better to have with me at concerts, for you were so appreciative of all that was good and beautiful, that your dear companionship gave me inexpressible delight . . . oh my dear dear friend and love! To know that you are willing to be my life-companion is surely enough to make me sing Te Deum.

And what you have been to me in the past, I know you will be in a fuller & richer sense in the future. But at the same time I want to undertake the duty and the pleasure of interesting myself in some of the things which interest you. If I can help you in any way, it would be the greatest joy of my life to do so. We can work together, live together, & love, so that our love will grow ever greater and wider as life goes on . . .

Now it is getting late, so perhaps I had better say good-night. I feel sure I shall dream of you tonight, as I often, often have done. Do you ever dream of me, sweetheart? And was I less aggravating in the dream than in real life?

So – "Sleep rock thy brain,
And never come mischance between us twain."
> Good-night, beloved,
> Ernest

> 416 Markham St.
> June 27/13

You dear, dear man

I haven't a single excuse for writing as I sent you a foolish little note this morning and I haven't a thing to say – except that I love you twelve hours better than this morning. I think it will go on like that always – Goodness me, you'll have to die young or I'll never know where to put all the love and love and love that is yours. There, am I not getting fearfully bold? I could not have written that yesterday without, well, almost blushing. I know it's silly, but it is all so new to me. I have always counted those things so sacred that I cannot yet be quite free & familiar in speaking of the utterness of my love. I got your ship letters just a moment ago (I have read them all 3 times) so maybe that is what has made me feel so much braver. O darling, you make me feel so ashamed and so proud and so happy all at once that I don't know which is the greatest. Ashamed, miserably ashamed, of all my littleness and the million ugly horrid faults I know I have. But at least your praise makes me want to merit it, and to wipe the faults away so that you will not have to see them – for I could not bear that, and yet it would be worse to hide anything from you. And then I am proud, proud – just "busting" proud to think that, however unconsciously, I have won your love. I have always looked up to you so, dear, (even if you were a sophomore) and have always so admired your manliness and chivalry & idealism that I feel as though a great beautiful gift had been given me in your love – and that I should be chosen as the object of such a Godsent gift however undeserving, it makes me proud, proud . . .

You are so wise and right, dear, in what you say about there being perfect frankness between us. It is the only way to have com-radeship – & we will be comrades as well as lovers, won't we? I want to hear everything about you that you want to tell – and everything about me is open to you . . .

Goodnight now dearest.

Yours for always
Elsie

Ernest was in Bayreuth attending the Wagner festival when the First World War began. Interned as an enemy alien, he did not return to Canada until 1919, when he and Elsie were married. During their long marriage, Sir Ernest (knighted in 1935) held the major positions in Canadian music (conductor of the Toronto Symphony Orchestra and the Toronto Mendelssohn Choir, princi-pal of the Royal Conservatory of Music, dean of the Faculty of Music at the University of Toronto), and Elsie was, according to biographer Ezra Schabas, "his confidante, a sounding board, and a constant support."

THE STARS WHISPER

Fred Albright met Elnora Evelyn Kelly at Victoria College, University of Toronto. After he'd received his B.A. in political science, Fred came to Calgary in 1910 to learn law and began to write to Evelyn, who was still studying English and history. As the correspondence developed, he told her about events such as the first Calgary Stampede in 1912 and the opening of a Hudson's Bay store in 1913, and they exchanged views on topics such as feminism, women's suffrage, temperance, eugenics, politics, and popular entertainers. They were engaged in 1913.

Sept. 14/13

My dear little "True Heart,"
I wonder if you are lonely for me tonight as I am for you. Perhaps at this hour you are fast asleep, but I have a fond fancy that even

Fred Albright (Frederick and Evelyn Albright fonds, University of Western Ontario Archives)

Evelyn Kelly Albright some years after Fred's death in 1917 (Frederick and Evelyn Albright fonds, University of Western Ontario Archives)

in slumber you are thinking of me. It must be so. If there is any compelling force in love my heart must hear an answering echo to its beat in your heart tonight. Oh, my dear, dear girlie, I think I never knew the meaning of homesickness until today. The preacher in the pulpit this morning, the flowers and trees this afternoon, the flickering light of the grate fire, the friends with whom I have been talking, the moon and the stars and all the wonderful stillness of a Western night have been insistently and lovingly talking of You.

I went out at Fritz's for supper tonight thinking I might there forget the dull ache at my heart, but seeing them in their happiness, I couldn't refrain from speaking of you, and though it was good just to have someone to whom I could talk about you, and who would understand, the homesickness became worse. I felt I couldn't stand to sit quiet in church so I stayed for a time at Fritz's then came out into the wonderful starlight and moonlight with the clear bracing air of a September evening. The stars whispered 'Elnora' and it seemed as if the breezes must waft that gentle name across the leagues and leagues of land that separated us and gently stir the curtains of your room, reminding you that far away across the vast spaces, but conquering even space in its spiritual flight, my heart is beating with yours. Oh, the unutterable longing for your presence tonight! That I might clasp you in my arms and hear the sweet words from your lips, and see the glad wonderful light in your eyes that tells me you are mine, mine to protect, and love and keep, my inspiration, my anchor, my wife, my joy – my wife.

I had a thousand things I wanted to say to you but the dull indefinable longing and ache for a sight of your face tonight makes it hard to talk about other things. Oh, my dearie you are beginning to understand me, aren't you? I can't find words to tell you how much you are to me, but your own heart tells you what I cannot express doesn't it? I haven't got over my schooled reserve of so many years, and I can't say what I would say, but perhaps on account of that very reserve and self repression the surge of my pent up feelings tonight is so hard to bear. I want you, oh I want you my Love – my Life.

What can I give you in return for what you are to me? The exchange is all one sided, you, one of God's women, with your wonderful truth and faith and steadfastness, with your marvellous power to see and know and understand beauty, with your fresh unspoiled outlook on life, you to give yourself to me, an ordinary grub in the world's professional back yard. The thought often comes and fairly overwhelms me. What if in the future days my little girl should be disappointed? How will she look upon me when she is disillusioned, when she finds that she has over-estimated me? Will she cease to love me? Oh, my love, I would a thousand times rather you thought less of me now, yes even did not quite love me than that in after years your love should wane. Please, please don't expect too much. If you were anyone else but yourself, I think I couldn't bear these thoughts. But in spite of all such doubts, I feel you will never love me less will you? Your eyes are too deep and true and your soul is too steadfast . . .

Yesterday afternoon I had a glorious ride. The air was just perfect – cool enough – and yet not too cool. How I wished you were with me. As it was I had the company of Miss Bailey, a fine girl, Mr Oaten's chief assistant. She knows I'm engaged. Say, do you object to my going out riding with any other girl? Unless you object I expect to occasionally, but if you think I shouldn't please don't hesitate to say so. Above all things let us be perfectly frank

Fred Albright and Evelyn Kelly Albright at their wedding in June 1914
(Frederick and Evelyn Albright fonds, University of Western Ontario Archives)

with each other. There is so much more I want to say but I must close. Good night my dearest. Never so dear to me as tonight. May Heaven's guardian angels watch over and keep you this night.

Your own true love.

Fred

While Evelyn's letters were equally loving, she had reservations about the institution of marriage, which she expressed just two months before their June 1914 wedding.

Thorold, Ont.,
Apr. 6, 1914

My Dear Fred, –
One thing I don't like about getting married, is that I'll have to take your name, and I like my own better. I don't want to be a "Mrs." either but I suppose I "gotta" do both. Then sometimes I wonder if I really want to be married to live in a place I certainly should not choose for myself, to make another person's friends my friends. It seems so, so lamblike a course that it makes me mad. But that's the result of happening to care more for one particular man than for all the rest of them put together, . . .

[Evelyn]

After they were married, the Albrights lived in Calgary until Fred enlisted in 1916. His last letter to Evelyn was written just before he was killed on October 26, 1917, at Passchendaele. Afterwards, Evelyn studied law, becoming the second woman lawyer in Alberta. Instead of practising law, she taught in the department of English at the University of Western Ontario until she retired in 1951. She died in 1979, having never remarried. In their periods of separation, Fred and Evelyn wrote 550 letters, now held by the D.B. Weldon Library at the University of Western Ontario and available on the Internet.

WILL SHE? WON'T SHE?

Hilda May Willison *was twenty-eight years old when she drafted these letters to Art Stromberg, to whom she was engaged for a time. Hilda was the fourth of six daughters born to a Swedish couple who lived in Muskoka, Ontario, before moving to Calgary in 1900. In 1926, when she was trying to decide whether to marry Art, she was working as a teacher for the Calgary Board of Education.*

326-2 Ave. N.E.
Calgary, Alberta,
August 30, 1926

Art dear,

What on earth do you suppose possessed us to decide to get married? That is the question that has been puzzling me off and on ever since we decided to do it. There is absolutely nothing in marriage that I cannot get without it, unless it is perhaps your love which I could still have if you only <u>would</u>, and I would be losing so many things I now value – money, family, friends, name, freedom. Now about your side of it! What would you gain by marriage that you haven't now, or could have if you wished? Nothing, Art, if you could only see it that way. You could have a <u>home</u> if you are tired of boarding – rent a suite with some other boy, and have some woman come in to do the work for you (for I take it

for granted you wouldn't care to batch). You would then have
better meals, too, than you would get if I tried doing them. You
like girls – you could then have as many girl friends as you like,
not just one, which by the way, you would soon find very monot-
onous. You could take out any girl you wished, any time you
wished, pet to your soul's satisfaction and no one to forbid it, even
your conscience, having already been trained along the correct
lines! You can take a <u>drink</u> when you wish, without some fool
woman at home breaking her heart merely because you are a
"good fellow" with the rest of the boys! You have money, more
than enough to have a good time on. You can save enough in the
next few years to take, say, six months off and just travel or do
anything else you might wish to.

Now suppose we get married next summer. It will mean a great
deal of trouble arranging about the purchase of lots and getting
the house built, and, what's more, paying for them; worry about
money ad infinitum; tied down to your job even though you'd like
to drop it on the chance of getting something better, because you
have a wife and a million (more or less) youngsters dependent on
your salary; you could no longer take chances on horses, oil,
wheat, etc., etc., – you wouldn't have the money to spare; you'd
always get punk meals and not half enough even of poor food;
couldn't casually invite any girl to a show without inviting your
wife, and oh, how tired you will be of her continually tagging
along! But goodness, Boy, what's the use of going into all those
details? You know them only too well without having them rubbed
in! <u>Then why get married</u>!!!!

I know what you are saying – so you can have each other
always. The romance in that is appealing, isn't it? And we are not
the first to whom romance has appealed more strongly.

326-2 Ave. N.E.

Calgary, Alberta

Sept. 7, 1926

Dearest Boy Mine,

The postman didn't come around until five-thirty tonight, and here I had to wait all day for your letter. 'Fraid I wasn't very patient either. You should have heard all the direful things I threatened to do to that postie if he didn't come soon! The poor chap couldn't help being late though, for he had three days' mail to deliver.

I am so very sorry Boy dear, that my letters made you feel bad. I'm a horrid, selfish pig, Art, and I don't deserve your love a bit. I was afraid you would be disappointed in me when you knew me better. Are you, Boy? I don't think I could stand that. I have always been the cause of more worry than happiness to you, Art, and I don't want to be that.

I don't know why I remarked that I loved you that night – unless it was because I <u>did</u> love you. Of course I love you all the time, silly boy; I suppose it was just because I loved you more than usual that night that I said it.

No Art, I don't think I have been sorry that I said "Yes". But since you ask me to be entirely truthful about it I'll have to admit, Art, that several times I have been filled with a most sickening fear of the future. I know I shouldn't be afraid, dear, and I'll try to not be. Most of the time I have been <u>glad</u> that I said it, for a girl needs love – a man's love. Please try to understand now, won't you Boy? Remember you asked me to be perfectly truthful. Marriage appeals to me no more now than it ever has. I want your love & marrying you is the only way you will let me have it.

*In the midst of her dilemma, Hilda turned to her friend and fellow
teacher **Carrie Northover Kosling**. Six years before, Carrie had
gone through her own struggle over Fred Kosling. She'd written
to Hilda: "I want a Star – he offers me a Man. I can't get over his
nationality, his rather rough ways, his fair hair! Otherwise he very
nearly measures up to the Standard."*

Kew Post Office, Alberta
October 24/26

My dear Hilda:

. . . I rode down to Kew (about 7 miles) after the mail on Friday
after school. I quite enjoyed the ride, especially as I met several
old acquaintances, who all seemed glad to see me. How vain we
are, after all! But it seems as though that is what makes up our
happiness in life – the fact that we are liked by, and like, others.
Which brings me, naturally, to the topic of the day – your Love-
affair (if I may call it so.) I am so glad, Hilda, that you have had
this come into your life (even supposing it should not turn out to
be The one.) Surely life would be empty without Love. But it
seems so hard to have to give one's whole self up to it. It does
seem to ask too much of one. I remember at one time I felt this
very strongly. I accept it now, as a matter of course. I often wonder
how I ever came to offer myself up (it amounts to that) on the
altar of love. I was so selfish (and still am), that it must have indeed
been an overmastering, irresistible force to make me give up my
precious dreams, my wonderful ambitions. I will not say that I
have never regretted it, never longed for the flesh-pots of Egypt.
Who could help but do so? I think every married woman who has
had the chance of a future must inevitably at times feel the same
. . . Strangely enough, there seems to be no bitterness as to what

"might have been" in my thoughts (except perhaps, to be strictly honest, after a spat with Friend Hubby), but rather a sweet regret, as one feels over any precious past memory, which can never return.

But to come back to your case. I do indeed, Hilda, understand very, very completely, I think, just how you feel at this particular time for if ever mortal soul passed through the tortures of doubt, fear, and great uncertainty as to the genuineness of love, I am sure I did . . .

It is the farthest thing from my thoughts, O beloved, to attempt to persuade you that you have found your Knight. You, and you, alone, can know that. I know only too well that married life, even with one whom you truly love, is not easy, at times indeed, just bearable, and no more. And God alone knows the agonies of poor humans when Love turns to hate. I know you realize this, and no doubt it forms part of your doubts. But I do want to tell you that I quite understand your feelings, and I do not think that simply because you are in doubt, you shouldn't do it. If you take time, I'm sure it will come to you whether this is the Real Thing or not. In the meantime, why not be just as happy as you know how to be? Moreover, one can hardly expect a man to wait on "the door-mat of a woman's indecision" (from "The Rosary") for long, can one? and sooner or later, one has to decide one way or the other . . . I have not been writing steadily all afternoon. About halfway through Friend Hubby came home, bringing with him a neighbor & his two kids, for all of whom, I had to provide food . . . I have since washed the dishes, rescued Joan from falling into the pig pen, fed the cats, brought in a pail of water, etc. etc. Beware of married life!

. . . I think it is much nicer for you and your Beloved to be separated at least part of the time. It seems so hard to act always the way one resolves to when the dear creatures are so lovable and so determined, and yet withal so pure that you are so safe when under their wing (as indeed one is with the <u>good</u> sort) . . .

With much love to My Own Big 'Un (who from now on will not have quite so much love to spare, I am afraid, for)

Her Little 'Un

Hilda did not marry. For most of her life, she lived in the family home with her sister Mary. She retired from teaching in 1959.

FATHOMLESS TEARS

In 1928, the year John Barrymore was at Lake Louise in Alberta filming Ernst Lubitsch's Eternal Love, *Ethel Thompson of Calgary, who worked in the accountant's office at Chateau Lake Louise, was wooed by the lachrymose and persistent* **Bob,** *who was also working at the resort hotel in the Rockies.*

[July 3, 1928]

My Flower of Moonlight

Love – Pity the hearts that know – or know not – Love!
Fancy! what words come to my mind when I am thinking of such a sweet little girl as you are Ethel. Tonight when you came down I was dazzled at first by the most exquisite array of colors. I felt like crumbling you in my arms and smothering you with purple kisses. Ah! My Angel, you are so pretty and frail. I would not hurt you in the least. In my loneliness last evening I scribbled down the words of a song. Guess the title. One of the most famous of song writers on the American Continent wrote "Why are There Tears in Your

Eyes" My title was "There are tears in my eyes." Underneath in fine words I penned some little phrase regarding the above.

I am transcribing the song tonight if we balance early and forwarding same to my Publishers in New York. Please do not say anything to anyone, Ethel. It is for a certain reason which I am afraid to mention to you. I trust you.

Ah! last night. My eyes filled with tears of silent pain.

I am sorry Ethel. I was so lonely. I thank you a million times for calling down tonight. I feel better now. It's a wonder my passionate lips did not caress your lovely eyes and hair tonight.

I wish you a joyous sleep. Night-night. A kiss to your eyes,

Votre ami sincere,

Bob

July 10th/28

'Little Darling',

My you sure are like a little bird fluttering around the Dance floor. I admire your graceful swing on the dance. I long for you more because I know there are others that would very much like to take you out. I heard a few nice words about you last night, but if you were mine I would be far gladder, although it is a credit to you anyhow . . .

A beautiful day today, it would be nice if you would come for a hike this morning to the 'Tea House' but as you will be working hard I am afraid my hopes will be shattered. What is your best magazine?, and I will send away for it tonight and you will receive same by return mail Ethel . . . I do admire you Ethel, I cannot get away from it at all. Your nice ways and you talk so kindly that anyone must take a liking to you. That is why I have to be careful as you will be rushing out with all your other nice admirers, far nicer than poor Bob. Your beautiful figure and pretty little head set you off to a tee. You dance like as light as the swallow on the wing. I sure will write you some letters before I am through. I do not mean that I will give you up as nothing on earth will alter my liking for you. Now just try and come out with me tonight, after your swim if you care. It is so nice being out at nights especially when the weather is fine . . . Oh Dearest Ethel why do tears come to my eyes. I cannot explain to you. It is something that I am unable to fathom. Why are you here 'Little One'. Would I like to leave you now, there would be no joy left in me. Come to me tonight under all costs and let us go for a walk, I want to see you and treat you at the store.

Darling Ethel, it is torture for me when I do not see you. No one can understand, I could not write in words my sorrow. Do not forget tonight 'Dear Heart'. Fare-well 'My Love'. Do not do any work today but just take things easy.

Just,

Bob

July 26th/28

Dear Little Heart,

If I could write you the best letter in the World I would gladly do so or even give you the best gift you have ever received but I am afraid we are not made for each other. We never seem to get on well together, the little bit I have seen of you Ethel all these months. I am at a loss to puzzle it all out but there is some reason which I cannot fathom. Others have nice times together but we do not enjoy ourselves a bit at all . . . I feel like killing myself these days because I have studied you from all angles and I sure think the World of you 'Dear Heart', but I am losing nerve to ask you

to come out time and time again. I shed tears for you all day in
bed but what's the use . . .

Yours as ever,

Bob

P.S. How about tonight?

Ethel did not marry Bob.

THIS HEAVENLY LOVE

*Following the First World War and the Russian Revolution,
Mennonites in Russia began to emigrate to North America. In the
village of Alexandertal, Molotschna,* **Helen Toews** *and* **David
Pauls** *celebrated their engagement on September 1, 1926, three
days before Helen and her brother set out for Canada. When they
were examined by Canadian medical officers in Holland, the siblings were found to have a chronic eye infection and were not
allowed to continue their journey. Meanwhile, David was permitted to leave Russia. That November he sailed from England to
join members of his family who had already settled in Arnaud,
Manitoba. Helen's parents and other siblings joined her in Holland
before they were all transferred to Atlantic Park in Southampton,
England. In 1928 most of the Toews family was allowed to travel
to Coaldale, Alberta, but Helen was detained until August 1929.*

Arnaud, April 6, 1928

Helen my love!
It's 4 p.m. All is quiet in the house . . .
There's a reason why I'm writing this note today. I'm moti-
vated by a deep longing and an intense and sincere love for you.

Words cannot describe the deep inner feeling that I have for you. Love is such a great thing. <u>Love</u>. This short and yet so unfathomable a word! It became so precious to me yesterday as I unpacked the sack. It was more than a powerful sermon for me. Because of love you are prepared to leave your mother, your father and your siblings. Now I am to envelop you with the love with which they have loved you. When I think about it, I'm filled with fear and trepidation.

I have considered the marriage relationship for some time now, here, as well as in Russia. It seems to me to be such an awesome responsibility. The man must be so careful to take care of the treasure that has been entrusted to him by God. So many things happen in a marriage. The good thing about it is that the positive things overshadow the negative things. However, if the marriage is sanctified by divine love, there is no problem. How beautiful that both of us can sun ourselves in this heavenly love. We are so privileged! That we feel more and more committed to each other in spite of the prolonged separation, is evidence of the fact that our love for each other is genuine. I am so deeply moved when I think how fortunate I am. I only hope that you will sense that love in me. This one thing I know; if we will love each other the way we have 'til now, we'll be happy.

I wanted to touch upon these things yesterday already but sleep prevented me from doing so. Now I'm refreshed and happy. I have much more to tell you but will wait and do it personally. In the meantime I will be praying for much comfort and grace for you.

With deepest love,
your David

Helen wrote to David after her family had travelled ahead of her to Canada.

Atlantic Park, April 22, 1928

My dearest!

Because I'm lonely, I'll write to you. It's Sunday evening and it seems so long ago that I wrote the last letter to you. Much has happened in the meantime. One of the things that has happened is a letter from you with the letters from John, Lydia and Dad enclosed. It arrived last Monday. I was so happy! Many a tear coursed down my cheeks. My loved ones are with my David, and I? – But, dear be thankful with me that I can say, "Lord, as you will." In response to your question as to whether I am still able to trust my God, I can say "yes". Yes, David, I am aware of the fact that I have a strong anchor. Otherwise I would be in a bad way indeed.

But, Duchen, I am so lonesome for you. Dad's comment, "Your future home is small and neat. I think you'll be happy here as long as this is your mission field," has made me unspeakably happy. You, my second 'I', I'm longing so much to be united with you. That you have lost so much weight, as Lydia indicates, makes me very sad. Things are certainly too difficult for you. Now I'm praying that the Lord will at least permit me to join you in time for the harvest so that I can help you then. I'd be so happy to be able to care for you. I just can't imagine what it will be like once we will be united forever – to read the Bible together, pray together and experience everything else together. I'm so glad that God has ordained for people to be meant for each other.

Monday, the 23rd. I'm glad I didn't mail this letter yesterday. Oh David, my David, I'm so happy today. I got up at seven already in order to wash the laundry the first time. But when I went out to wash myself Mr. Hildebrand came in with the mail. He had got up early as well because he had to go to the harbor at eight. He gave me two letters, one from Dad and the other one from my

David Pauls and Helen Toews Pauls,
reunited and married in August 1929
(Courtesy Michael and Sheila Pauls)

dear Ego. I forgot all about the laundry and everything else for joy. Like a thirsty person I drank and my thirst was quenched. David, I'm not worthy of you. I pressed the note written in pencil to my heart. It's so precious to me. I thanked God that he has given me a man who exhibits sacred love towards me. I'm glad that I could also show you some love in that I let my loved ones go to you. Yes, Duchen, for you I can do it. As regards marriage, the apprehensions that I had earlier are gone. I'll be happy with a man who considers his wife a gift entrusted to him. Every day I pray that God will prepare me for you so that we can be to each other what we need in order to be happy.

[Helen]

David and Helen were reunited in Winnipeg August 20, 1929, and married five days later. During the nearly three years of their separation, they exchanged 150 letters, which were found in a suitcase after Helen died in 1996, six years after David's death. Their letters have been translated from German.

Advice to the Perplexed

Artists **James Nicholl** *and* **Marion Mackay,** *both of whom were elected to the Royal Canadian Academy, met in 1933 at the Sketch Club in Calgary. Marion was a Calgarian who attended the Ontario College of Art and then studied at the Southern Alberta Institute of Technology & Art, where she became a teacher in 1933. Born in Fort Macleod, Jim grew up in British Columbia and trained as a civil engineer at the University of Alberta. Following his First World War service, he worked as an engineer, and in 1930 he began to paint. After retiring, he painted steadily for eight years. In his two letters here, Jim was responding to Marion's letters in which she pretended to be a lovelorn woman, Puzzled, seeking the advice of Heart-bomb.*

[Ottawa, Chateau Laurier]
July 9ᵗʰ [1934]

My Dear "Puzzled"

"Heart-bomb" is on a protracted vacation due to alc[o]holic poisoning, and if he never returns it will be soon enough, so I am endeavoring to console the wounded heart in his absence.

I have read your letter from beginning to end and vice-versa, and my heart bleeds for you, in fact I sob silently to myself the greater part of the time.

I notice that you are Twenty Five (25) years old and are you a bachelor girl or a spinister, as this has a great deal to do with your problem.

The triple underlining of the word innocently creates a certain doubt. Dear Puzzled, have you never heard of the lady who protested too much? Your writing leaves something to be desired as I am unable to discover whether this bird is hopelessly or helplessly

*Marion Mackay Nicholl and James Nicholl in Calgary in
the 1940s* (Glenbow Museum PA-24354)

infatuated with you. Sez you! The hinting of things (not indescreet) may be only feeble mindedness on his part. One of these days Dear Puzzled, he may wake up and make you a proposition. On the other hand his reticence Dear Jigsaw may be discretion, as if you weigh 240 pounds and he only weighs 95 obviously discretion is the better part of valor, but do not lose heart dear Tiddley Winks, as you may overtake him and can then rub his perishing little nose in the dirt.

Besides dear little prairie flower when you say you cannot care for him the way he wants you to, how exactly do you think he wants you to care? I have grave doubts regarding his intentions, which you may find are strictly dishonourable dear Edelweiss, so don't you care if you do blight the blighter's life.

Yes, or rather yeah dear [?] a young gurl should wait until her heart speaks. If you find that when the young man approaches, you have as it were an all overish feeling, and no desire for likker, 9 to 1 or at least 6 7/8 to 4, he is Mr. Right, but will probably do you wrong.

I hope that you are successful in holding him off, until you hear from me, and that you have not become hopelessly entangled or compromised. My advice dear Pearl of the Hareem, is to let your concience be your guide, but under no circumstances to lose your lure.

In hope faith and charity and with love and kisses

I remain yours

as ever was

Heart Throbs.

Funnily enough I have also received a letter addressed to "Heart Bomb" from a youth who signs himself "Skinny".

He says he has a dimple in his chin, and thinks he has S.A. [sex appeal] but seems to be unable to make an impression upon

the object of his affections or what have you, and I have told
him to be persistent and also that what most dames require is a
slap in the pan every now and then or a good sock in the jaw,
so will it not my dear little gazelle be a remarkable coincidence
if it should be your boy friend and he does take my advice. Oh
goody, goody.

I forgot to tell you that if he does hint, or ever come right out,
with indescreet remarks, your cue is to leap like a startled gazelle
and standing just out of the reach of his fist, gaze upon him soul-
fully, somewhat after the manner of a wounded fawn.

Let us all now join in singing "She was poor but she was
honest".

I am addressing this in care of Miss Marion McKay who I
understand goes out your way & will deliver it. I hope.

[Ottawa, Chateau Laurier]

Sept. 4th [1934]

Dear "Puzzled"

Your heart rendering letter arrived, and as I read each word apart
or by itself, I could hear the heart-strings in your aching boosom,
I think the C string is a little flat; or maybe the shoulder strap or
brassiere string has busted. My heart throbs in unicorn, excuse it,
I mean unison with yourn, but upon reading and re-reading your
letter, I am at a loss to know why you still sign "Puzzled". I think
you must now know everything, including the fact that there is no
Santa Claus.

So you married the brute and now have seven children. Wot a
man. Wot a woman. Did you say the name was Dionne. Prolific I
calls it. To think the brute beats you with your own children, and
that you are black and blue in spots I would never suspect. Oh I
dono I am a fair suspector. I am not sure that it would not have

been better to have remained as just friends instead of getting married, but I suppose the seven, or is it nine by now, children would have complicated matters . . .

I think you are wise to leave him dear Puzzled before there are any more children, and if you do not bring more than three I can put them in the clothes cupboard, but I am sure that every time I see their cleft chins and swivel eyes I will throw them in the canal and eventually we will be alone at last . . .

It is only fair to warn you unpuzzled, that I am a tough guy, and I have spat more holes in the pavements of Ottawa than all the senators together, and if, as, and, when, or and/or, as us legal people say, you arrive[,] you do not leap like a startled gazelle when I speak, while in fairness to myself I must say I am not a toothbreaker or hair puller, you will most doubtless be blacker and bluer in places that even you do not suspect.

However that is in the future. In the meantime, as I am just too full of advice, I suggest that you obtain a pick handle, or a wagon wheel spoke will do, or even a baseball bat, but be sure you select a straight grained one that will not break upon impact, and bend it over his dome, every time he looks sideways at you, and especially if he suggests more children, as eleven is quite a quiverfull, and it would seem God not only smiled on you but apparently went into hysterics . . .

Be sure to wire me a couple of days before you start with the kids, as it would be only fair to give me at least two days start on my get away. Hoping you are the same, and remember if you are good you may be happy but also damn lovelorn.

As ever & more so

Heart Throbs

In July 1937, Marion learned she was to study at the London Central School of Arts and Crafts in England. Jim was in Nordegg, Alberta, when she wrote this reassuring letter.

Friday July 30/37

My Darling: –

You are my pet goop & please don't crumble, or is it crumple? I love you and I'll always love you & what's more, mister, you're going to marry me when I come back. I mean right after I get back. All I'm doing is marking time until you're ready for me . . .

I've kept all your letters this time to read when I'm lonesome. I sniffle & my eyes look like boiled gooseberries, but I like it. Loving you is a swell business & its one of the nicest things about me – loving you I feel as tho' I'm showing such good taste. That's rot, isn't it? I don't know what's driving me. I'm as nervous as a lady school-teacher. I want to lie in your arms & go to sleep. You're silly to be afraid of London – after all I'm 28 & supposedly mature & I've loved you all my life – not many women are as fortunate. Of course I'll ruin as many lives as possible – in a perfectly nice way, of course – but it's you I want. It's you I'll always want – all my life . . .

My darling,

Your

Marion

The Nicholls married in 1940 and were fixtures in the Calgary arts community until their deaths – hers in 1985, and his a year later.

Solace in Milk

W.O. (Bill) Mitchell met Merna Hirtle in 1940 when he was selling the World Book Encyclopedia *in Edmonton. Bill had learned from a junior-high teacher that the Hirtles at the Baptist parsonage were a likely prospect for a sale, because young Spurgeon (Spud) Hirtle wasn't doing well in school. He convinced Mrs. Hirtle to buy a set. The next day, when he came to deliver the books, dark-haired, dark-eyed Merna answered the door. Bill found her intriguing but young; he was twenty-six and she was just twenty. In June, however, Bill, a skilled springboard diver, began hanging out at the pool where Merna was a swimming instructor. By August they were in love, and Merna's other suitors, Elgin Brisbin and Bob McDermaid, had backed off. That month, when Merna was in Banff at drama school, Bill, Elgin, and Bob wrote her a joint letter, partly in French.*

lundi

chez Elgin.

[August 1940]

Ma plus cherie Myrna:

Elgin et moi avons decidé d'ecrire une lettre en français et par cette moyen tuer deux oiseax avec une pierre. Maintentant nous buvons parceque il fait très chaud cette soir.

Nous avons fini déjà deux bouteilles et Robert est sorti de la maison pour achéter une autre, plus grosse.

Nous desirons te temoigner la grande nuage noire de malheureusement ou nous somme après tu a prendu congé de nous. C'est parceque cela que nous buvons maintenant si grands quantités du lait.

Comment ça va pour ton père et ta mère et surtout pour Spurgeon le seconde.

W.O. *Mitchell and Merna Hirtle Mitchell, wed in* 1942 (W.O. Mitchell
fonds, University of Calgary, Special Collections MsC 19.14.1)

Je te remercie mille fois pour les photogravures qui tu a manqué chez Elgin pour mois. J'en ai donné une à Elgin. La reste sont à ma chambre à côté des cesla de ma famille dans la mirroir de ma bureau.

Votre père et Spud ont ils eut difficulté en montant la tente à Jasper? Nous esperons que tu ne laisse pas votre mère travailler trop durement ou somme nous trop comme les chats quand nous dison des remarques comme ça?

Je ne souffre pas d'ennui parceque j'ai ma fille avec des cheveux de couleur de paille. Elles est très intéressante mais tu n'aimerais pas si tu peuve la voir.

Elgin passait la nuit avec Natalka le samedi passé après nous sommes allées chez tien. Il dit qu'il l'aime beaucoup coucher avec les filles étrangères. Je vais coucher moi-meme avec ma blonde cette soir; je n'expecte pas dormir de tout. Je pense que ceci est assez de francais pour cette soir.

Bob's come back with another bottle of milk and we're drinking ourselves to death. We started hitting the bottle soon after you left and haven't let up for a minute. All of us still have our colds down around the chest. It's unfortunate because it's been lovely weather for swimming.

Elgin has gone back upstairs to his French and I thought you might be interested in knowing that I still loved you. Mother has always told me not to put statements like that into writing but what the hell I don't care.

I've started missing you already and have been making burnt sacrifices daily to Jehova that he may send quantities of rain down in the vicinity of Jasper so that you'll have to come home.

I sent Mr. Twill on his way yesterday and have done a thousand words on Jake and Frobisher . . .

This is Elgin.

I have read Bill's portion of this epistle and you now have no secrets from me. All is not lost I shall preserve a discrete silence. I do not like French or anything about it but manage to study a half hour or so a day and may get there. We all miss you terribly, especially me, Bob just looks cynical and ignores everything. He is trying to kid himself he is a philosopher. No doubt. Farewell or mebbe aurevoir.

Good bye mug. I still insist that I love you and this isn't Elgin.

Bill

In their biography of their father, Barbara and Ormond Mitchell write, "Merna was the first person in whom Bill confided in any detail about his writing." In this letter he mentioned sending Mr. Twill, *a novella, to a publisher and working on one of the early "Jake and the Kid" stories. Merna and Bill were married in 1942. "It was," write their biographers, "a marriage that lasted a lifetime – and adoration and laughter were key to its longevity."*

PRINCIPAL AS LOVER

Irene Heywood was eighteen in 1931 when she began studying at the Winnipeg School of Art, where the principal and chief instructor was forty-one-year-old **Lionel LeMoine FitzGerald,** *a Winnipeg-born painter who exhibited with the Group of Seven before being admitted to the group in 1932. Irene wrote in a memoir that she and the principal, who was married, developed a student-mentor relationship during her second year and then fell in love. Later, in 1940, when she was on her way east to work in*

Toronto, she visited LeMoine: "I asked him to become my lover and he did." The pair corresponded and saw one another when Heywood visited Winnipeg. LeMoine's letters, whether typed or handwritten, are scroll-like, long, narrow, and unparagraphed, without a salutation and signed with an ornate monogram.

23-5-42 — The clock has stopped ticking for another season. Silence has returned to the ancient halls – the dust can settle undisturbed and any little mouse or spider can go its happy way without interference during the lazy summer days. But there is no letter from you. Perhaps you mailed it on the 22nd and it is now in the mail. I hope nothing has happened to you that you are or were unable to write. If you havent written, I am afraid that you will have to leave it until the fall . . . anyway here I am and feeling rather dilapidated after a more than usual hectic windup. A lot of extra things came up for finishing at the last moment and I got pretty frayed so I feel really quite tired and pretty well pumped dry. Am ready for a period of entire relaxation in the open where I cant even hear the phone or the voices of many people . . . I am very happy that you have made the change to your new place and have started back at the studying again. I am absolutely sure now that you will never be able to get any real happiness out of life without answering the urge for painting. If, after all this time and with the things that you have been through, you still feel as you do, then you can be very certain that you have the real thing. But dont despair of not being able to spend your whole time at it. Maybe the having of other work is an advantage in that whatever you do in art is free from the necessities of commercial art and you can express your real self as you decide. All that I hope is that you will have sufficient physical energy for the extra work. And you are certainly not old even though you may be thirty next July the 10th.

All the experience that you have had in the last twelve years is highly valuable even though it has not been directly in line with art. You have developed a confidence in yourself, you have seen many more phases of living and experimented with them much more fully. All this will enter your work. And I know somehow or other that no matter what you may say of your exterior, beneath is you. I know that the purity of YOU cannot and has never been touched by the acts and necessities of the moment. Forget the measuring by years, even the future, and only dwell on the advancing of your powers of expressing in material form, the beauty that is locked in the inner chamber. Accept every act and experience as contributory only to the revelation of all the loveliness of your spiritual being. You are beauty. Nothing can soil that. Nothing ever will. What your hand touches and what your eye sees will always be translated into beauty. There is nothing sordid or vile in life that can finally penetrate you. You are extremely human and love life and have a sensitive balancing force that knows what to throw away and what to treasure in your soul . . . To you I have always written freely, expressing ideas and thoughts just as they came to me, at many times never rereading them just as in a conversation. I have written of things of the flesh and of the spirit, with the conviction that they are inseparable and have their relative importance to the whole. I like to think of the joys of the contact of flesh to flesh and of the passionate stimulation to such contact and have written it to you knowing your joy in it. Your lovely nakedness is indelibley there in my mind through the eye and the touch that explored every last little particle of it and found it beautiful and treasured it. I have dwelt in some of the recesses of your mind and sensed the basic you, discovering its potentialities. You gave them to me as beauty and they dwell in my innermost as beauty – sacred treasures. I have written of aspirations that never materialized and of some that did in a measure . . . And so for this long time we have been revealing to one another some of our pleasures and pains and have enjoyed something of each others being. – as I write this note, the last for some time, I am hoping that you will be able to continue the new start you have made with painting again and that it will keep growing, and not be interrupted by anything this time. May peace and tranquillity enter your lovely being and dwell in the purity that is you. And may you have strength to dwell in the air of destruction and uncertainty that surrounds us at this time. I am a little sad that no word of you came today. I had hopes of hearing of many things that have taken place recently. Momentous things have been yours in this more than two years and I would have like to know the effect of your latest move. I am still uncertain of the summer excepting that I am going to work. I am so glad to be able to relax my mind for the moment that I dont bother thinking of a plan. But I have plenty to do and wherever it may be is not important. Goodbye now and the best of health to you.

30-1-43
The snaps were lovely – it was swell seeing you again – and you look so much the same only you look plumper – are you? . . . your letter was so beautiful, I still feel the effects of being with you and touching you and the smell of you came to my nostrils from the paper, very delicate but you and only you – I would like to reach out and touch you . . . I must away now – will write from day to day again and send along later – I enfold you – around you is a space with me enclosing you and entering you and saturating you with knowing – and with it peace – and you entwine me and draw me into you and absorb me and and I enter you and absorb you and motion is one and we dwell in a oneness

of ethereal light a silent calmness surrounds us and a radiation passes through our oneness of warmth and understanding and we dwell suspended in a passing into and out of each, of a living current, and time is not –

Irene Heywood married Wade Hemsworth, a Canadian folksinger and songwriter, and became an art reviewer for two Montreal newspapers. After his retirement from teaching, L.L. FitzGerald continued to paint until his death in Winnipeg in 1956.

THE LOVE THAT DARED

In 1957, when **Reva (Rita) Hutkin** *was twenty-two and married and* **L.G.** *was nineteen and single, the two women were completing their high-school education at night school in Montreal. Friends at first, they soon became aware of an attraction not easily explained.*

[1957]

Dear L.,

I am strongly fascinated by you. I am drawn as a moth to the flame and I cannot explain or stop this strange desire to bask in your company. I live in constant fear that you will wake up one morning, decide I am just like anyone else on earth and that my company is no longer desired by you.

In vain I have tried to analyse my feelings for you. The attraction definitely is not sexual because I have no thoughts of doing anything physical with you, other than sitting very close, shoulders touching, hearing your heart beat and your low laughter in my ear. I get deep pleasure in watching your face crinkle into that slow smile which so becomes your personality. Every tear you shed is doubly spent, for in my heart I cry with you. I am a person of varying moods, but you seem to pervade them all, penetrating to the core which is my own.

You once said to have two friends in one lifetime is a rare thing – our friendship is young – it has not gone through any experiences that have in any way tried it, as with E. and myself or you and A. I feel safe in my friendship with her because I know, come what may, she will always stand beside me. You are a person very much guided by mood. I have surrendered myself completely to you and I now consider you a friend as well, still new in its context, not really heavily taxed but a very dear friend. I only fear your moods will lead you away from me and that unwillingly our friendship will fall apart in reckless confusion.

The fact that I so desire to speak with you each day, to see you, to be near you, disturbs me. I am drawn to you and look upon our acquaintances as enemies, for they rob me of your company. I feel sorry for people like E. and A. because they were close to us before our friendship and somehow, inevitably, they are shut out of this great, complex relationship that has grown between us.

I still cannot bring myself to call this a clinging relationship – even though we are wrapped up in each other, there still exists a recognition of our separate lives. There are many ways to love and many different kinds of love. In all honesty, I can say I love you, in a very specific way, in a way that can only belong to you. I know you love me in a specific way, too, and it must be very similar to my own.

You are very engrossed with the subject of homosexuality right now. I wonder to myself if you think of me at all in this way. It wouldn't make any difference to me either way but I hope for your sake, you can divert your sexual energy towards the male, where it rightly belongs. To be homosexual is to be ill – society should not recognize it as a third sex but should accept its existence and extend the helping hand it so badly needs. Because I love you, I would like to see you whole and wholesome. Don't slide just because it is so easy.

Rita

Dear Rita

I sat down in class and opened your letter. As I read the first couple of words my heart began to beat very fast and I was compelled to put down the paper for I felt all the people in class would notice the sudden creeping of red that spread through my body. I became feverish and my senses were swirling. I could not think clearly but I was magically drawn to read, not once but several times, the letter of yours. It does not seem possible to me that I could feel the way I do. To honestly say I do not love you physically would be a lie. I am deeply in love with you, both physically and spiritually. Words seem inadequate to express the deep emotion I feel. When I am near you, I irresistably wish to touch you, yet I seem to be without hands, to kiss you – not to arouse any great passion for I do not know how to go about it – but to express the feeling I have locked deeply in my soul – yet I seem to be without lips.

I realized from the beginning how I felt, yet could not admit it to myself. The cravings I have are wrong, for in some indirect way I am destined to hurt you. The pain that is clutching my heart now is real for the last thing in the world I would want to do would be to hurt you. When I met you, I knew but suppressed these emotions for I was afraid of being repulsed. I am glad I am writing this for it sets my soul free.

I realize you do not feel this way, or as strongly towards me but I will be satisfied with the little crumbs of your friendship I can hope to acquire. They are stored in a secret room in my heart and will remain with me forever. When I think of it now, I know that I have never known love until I met you. It seems to have been a uniting of the souls, the key to life.

Your words have touched me deeply and I am moved. Since I met you, my outlook on life has changed. I walk alone yet you are always with me. I awake with your name on my lips, go to sleep with your image before me. When you smile, my heart is filled to overflowing for I feel radiant.

But it is wrong – I should go away and never see you again. If I do, I leave my heart with you. It would be harder to give up breathing. But I am a coward and will persist. I will hurt you deeply but it is beyond my control. When your eyes look into mine I am anointed. I can say I will never see you again but, I do not want it that way. I will continue our relationship as you wish. You are the Queen, and I your slave. Please do not let what I have said affect you too deeply for you are happy and I do not want to spoil this.

Love, L.

Dear L.

. . . When you say my feelings for you are akin to your own, you are right. I have a question uppermost in my mind – suppose I do love you in the same way you profess to love me – suppose I am not married – what kind of life do you envisage? What kind of love is there on which to build a future life? Is it not better to suppress such feelings, to channel them into new and more trying directions? If I were to give in to my impulses at this moment, I would probably leave G [her husband] and have you by my side, always. I also look into the future. Somehow I feel such a love cannot last a lifetime, under any given conditions, especially the ones we would presently be forced to accept.

I would like to think we love each other and from this love gather a kind of strength. We need not manifest our feelings to recognize their existence.

Please do not talk of leaving me because I could not bear it any more than you. My emotions are terribly tangled up in you, as much as yours are in me. Life is so short and real happiness is so rare – I am happy when I am with you – we need not live together to make this happiness complete.

Last night I wanted very much to put my arm around your shoulder, to cradle your head against my bosom but, I was frightened and paralyzed. I could only look dumbly upon you, mumbling incoherent sentences, telling you to do things against your nature.

We are two very complicated people, sensitive and unyielding to the will of others. This we cannot help. I am slowly learning to accept myself. I am sometimes puzzled by my thoughts, feelings and actions but, I don't question too closely. You must soon start on your campaign of accepting yourself. I can accept you because I love you but you must also love yourself. I do not ask you to integrate into society but if you want to be accepted by others, first start by accepting – recognize the fact that society exists and that some compromise is necessary, no matter how slight. Above all, do not lose your ability to smile so readily: That is when I love you best.

Love, Rita

Dear Rita,
. . . I feel extremely sorry for G. He had you and you slipped through his fingers. He is now left with a shattered world lying all about his feet . . .

I wish I could be with you right now, to lessen any heartache that might come your way but I cannot. I hope you find my spirit with you always, when things are bad or good; it should lighten your load for I carry it with me constantly.

There is a lot of misery in store for you and I hope we are both strong enough to see it through and come out on the winning side. I love you very much, Tiger, and all that matters is your happiness. Know your own mind and be proud of what you are. What you have done or might do is out of your hands but come what may I will see it through beside you.

You are a mysterious scented blossom and contained in your smile are rarest perfumes. You smile, the petals spread and there is released a spray of ecstacy blanketing troubles. As long as you can smile life is still worth living . . .

Through all these mad days, it is hysterically funny, I have been happy. I have never really known what it is to see the sun shine until I saw it through the eyes of love. I have decided within myself that this is right for me. Therefore, unable to do otherwise I shall persist until –

. . . I would like to move out of the house and in with you but first of all, right now, you have to be alone for awhile and secondly I have to think of my parents. They would never allow it and it would hurt them deeply, so all I can do is wait until I'm 21 and then do as I please without objections or hurt feelings

You have captured my heart and I am glad. I love you always.

L.

In the repressive 1950s, Reva and L.G. knew of no models for the relationship they wanted to have. Reva's parents took her on a long vacation, hoping she would forget L.G., but she could not ignore her overwhelming emotions and "could not be deterred from this trajectory." She obtained a divorce and lived with her lover. After the eight-year-long relationship ended, both women eventually found lesbian communities and other lesbian partners.

BLINDSIDED

It began as a blind date during the Winnipeg Pan-American Games of 1967. **David Witty** *figured he'd never see Margaret Mitchell again, and so, inspired by the tan he'd acquired working outdoors at Clear Lake for the National Parks Service, he introduced himself to her parents as a soccer player from Uruguay. Later, during the first week of August, Marg, on a break between her second and third years in a nursing program at St. Boniface Hospital, came to Clear Lake with a girlfriend, who was dating a friend of Dave's. "Somewhat unenthusiastically," Dave agreed to take Marg out again. They picnicked in secluded spots (his special "move") and travelled around in his TR3, visiting normally off-limits parts of Riding Mountain Park. On the fifth day, Dave was ready to marry Marg, but thinking he might be rushing things, he waited until the ninth day, when he proposed and she accepted. After only two weeks together, she returned to Winnipeg to complete her nursing studies and he went back to the University of Waterloo to finish his fourth year.*

Sept. 28/67

My Dearest Marg:
Never before have I felt so frustrated, confused and lonely. This past two weeks has been long and unending.

Your voice sounds so pretty, so near; yet it too is frustrating. When I hear you I'm lost for words then the call is over. I want to tell you so many things but the calls ends, I wander around empty, lost.

Marg what can I do or say to show you how much I need you. You're my whole life but so far away that I worry about you. You see I'm very jealous at times and now is one of those times. Not jealous in the normal sense of the word. Rather, I'm jealous of all Winnipeg, of the patients, of guys who pass you on the street; for they see you or talk to you. And I'm jealous; for I must be content with letters & your pretty voice (it's bubbly (sp?) & full of life).

Marg you are my whole being. My future. Never for once doubt that I love you.

I still can't figure out what I love about you the most. You are so wonderful, pretty, considerate and fun to be with . . .

I want you desperately for my wife. Marg, I wait only for that day when I kiss you with more meaning & love than either one of us could ever dream possible. I will hold you & love you with so much tenderness, so much love.

When I see people, especially on campus, walking hand in hand smiling at each other, I feel two things. First, I wonder if they feel as we do but that seems impossible and secondly I feel sad & lonely.

When I hear of broken marriages or marriage problems I get angry and bitter that we, so deeply & truly in love, must be separated by miles while those wishing they [were] miles apart act out the marriage game. Is life just? The only words I can say "I love you Marg more deeply & tenderly with each day. You are my answer to life. The key to my door together through which both of us will go until eternity.

I wish to touch your face, run my fingers along your nose, under your eyes; until I cover your cheeks with my hands and pull you to me feeling the touch of warm lips of love; of a body so loving, so tender . . .

And when I look down I long to look at pretty blue eyes, a pretty smile; but most of all I long to look at my wife.

Marg. Oh, to whisper in your ear that I love you, to lie awake watching & listening for you as you stir beside me, to feel your body warm & loving next to mine. To reach out and caress you and to bend down & kiss you while you sleep beside me. This my love is our future together . . .

But now this torture only grows. I must say goodnight. In less than one year I'll say goodnight holding, loving & kissing you. Whispering in your ear the love that I have for you. And as you fall tenderly into my arms and close your eyes I will then realize that no other human could have been so happy.

Goodnight my love

I am yours forever

Dave XXX

Marg and Dave saw one another only twice in the year they were separated. When Marg first came to visit him, Dave took her photo to the train station so that he'd be sure to recognize her. On August 10, 1968, a year to the day of their engagement, they were married. They live now in Winnipeg, where Dave has been dean of the faculty of architecture at the University of Manitoba since 2001. They are still crazy about each other.

Viva mercedes! viva pierre!

In 1971, while he was touring Europe on leave from his job as a cook at a catering company in Gillam, Manitoba, **Pierre Michel**

*Trudeau met **Mercedes Roman** at a dance in Madrid. After the dance, she gave him her home address in Bilbao, and a month later he came to see her. They spent fifty-three days getting to know one another ("no monkey besseness") and falling in love. Before Pierre returned to Canada, he promised they would be married in a year. With the determination of her Basque ancestors, Mercedes began to undo her life in Spain – telling her family she was going to marry and move to Canada, deciding what possessions she would give away or take with her, and, finally, quitting her interesting and secure job. During a 440-day separation, the pair continued their courtship in probing letters, written in English because neither could speak the other's native language well. They asked questions ("Can you drive?" "What song you like more?"), discussed philosophy and morality, and arranged the practicalities of their wedding.*

Gillam May 14 – 1972

Amor mio Mercedes.

I hope you are very well, I receive you letter of May 1 . . .

Mercedes don't be fear (miedo). I love you profondo, whit admiration, I think about you every day, I just think the day we be together for always.

I sufriendo [suffer] also, here not very, very interressing specialy for the moral[e], you know Mercedes I live here in Gillam just for you that very true, if I never see you or never rencontror you angel mio I think I live for september to try find a job any where, specialy in the big boat (barco) go every where in mondo.

But I am responsable of our love, I live just for that to be with you, amor, and it is necessary make sacrifice for me and also for you. I know it is difficult.

Mercedes, I want married you, I love you profondo, I never love before. I think not to many angel like Mercedes in the mondo,

I know. But, you pensor serious the difficulty, the sacrifice for you here in America, specialy in Canada that not a dream, that reality . . . I want you whit me to be happy not be sadness, the married that for always . . .

If I have $5000 today, I going to married you tomorrow. You understand not just a question of time (day), question also of money security . . . I tell you the situation here, now, all goes well . . . I can put in banco, 25,000 peseta by month. That very good money . . . Confianza in Pierre . . .

That all for now. Hasta pronto angel mio. I love you profondo whit all my alma [soul], my hearth, my mind.

Bye! Bye!

Pierre xxx

Bilbao España
June 25, 1972

Querido [beloved] and amado Pierre:

Hello, amor mio, how are you? Today I have received your letter 16 June and pretty card and Kettle Project Manitoba Hydro and photo of parkas . . .

Pierre, amor mio, I'm very very happy because I have given to you sorpresa [surprise] with my big photo, but now I have sorpresa because you tell me I'm pretty and beautiful. You never tell me that before.

Always everywhere the people tell me I'm very pretty <u>less you</u>. I was a little timid with you because you don't see pretty at Mercedes.

Amor mio, why do you give so much (tanta) importance into physical? I think is more import the quality and to be virtuous.

You tell me I have great personality. Is true. Everywhere the people tell me too. I think perhaps I have excess the personality . . .

Pierre, vida mia, I want what your moral[e] to be good. If some time you are triste (sad) or your moral is low (baja), you look at me in the photo and you think what my eyes it's to emit (dar) ray of amor at Pierre.

¡OH! Pierre, I have *sorpresa*, sorpresa disagreeable. I don't understand, No Pierre, amor mio. Mercedes don't understand. You tell me: You don't like destroy all photo of collection, you don't like to do that – big sorpressa Pierre. Mercedes is very sad.

I thought what all those photo it was the more, all it was a hindrance for you since what: "You in love with me." If it's true and if I'm the queen of your hearth, what pain (pena) can you to have? I think all it does to render turbid our felicity. Now I think with big bitterness you don't love at Mercedes. If you love at Mercedes you had what destroy without pain (pena) all photo and all souvenir of womans frivolous, and you don't maintain correspondence with none woman. If you don't like destroy, por favor Pierre, you keep all photo and souvenir. What does it matter Mercedes suffer and Mercedes die pain. ¡What does it matter! . . .

Pierre angel mio, I love you. I'm in love with you.

Tuya siempre,

Mercedes

Gillam 21 July 72

Amor mio Mercedes.

. . . I am anxious to see and speak whit your confessor, but my conscience is tranquil, why she will be no tranquil. That is question of philosophia. (Who is not with god is in again him.) Mercedes, I think it is a mistake to speak or think like that. We have to respect idiologia, philosophia, conception different of ours, because all that is question of conscience, and alma, that is universal.

Example: the Chinese or Indian have same alma, conscience universel but different conception, philosophia, ect. more important, and no body can cheat himself, because the conscience is universel . . .

I hope you listen me about the suggestion of you healht. Take care of you.

Hasta pronto, amor mio,
Pierre XXXXX

Bilbao – España
July 30, 1972

My dear Pierre:

. . . ¡OH! Pierre, I'm happy if you have conscience tranquil but many people to mistake for (or to confuse) conscience sleep (dormida) by conscience tranquil. It's two thing different. I think the philosophia is only for to can to live in this life but with god no is valid the philosophia. The philosophia with God it is deceive yourself. The philosophia with God you mean is to be too indulgent or to be unscrupulous. It seem to me you be wrong . . .

Pierre, vida mia, my sky, my treasure, I love you every day more . . . I dream of you from day to day. Alway, all the minute I'm with you. Pierre amor mio, I love you. I'm in love with you. I miss feel to you very much . . .

Tuya siempre,
Mercedes

Gillam 21 Sept 72

Amor mio Mercedes

. . . OH! yes I remember when you said the happiness of the marriage depend grand part of the woman. I believe is true. I have totaly confianza in you. I know we can build a new beautiful life together for always because we want the best for all and each other. Also you have good nature and facility to adopt any circonstances that important. The true love is there for give power for help us to face all circonstances.

Amor mio, . . . When you make a mistake in the life, not good solution to run after. We have take responsability face and accept and repair the mistake by the best solution possible . . . I don't regret I tell you all the true of my life, I have my conscience tranquille, that the best way to be happy in the life, be conscience tranquille . . .

Mercedes your eyes drive me crazy (loco). When I look you on the foto I concentration my mind inside your eyes all my body is electrify . . . Mercedes, Pierre think when the first night we be together for honeymoon I be realy crazy (loco) (loco). The happiness. You can't imagine how I need your affection, sex of you. I make the sacrifice to wait for you, not easy believe me . . . All this sacrifice for love. I wait for you that be fantastic. You can't imagine.

Hasta pronto,
Pierre XXXX

Malaga – España
February 25, 1973

My dear Pierre:
. . . Well Pierre we shall go to Guernica, we shall have a day to go at this important place town. We shall be fiance officially with our ring in this place, typical Basque. O.K. OH! yes Pierre that will be duro no sex before the marriage. But we can wait fews more days. We shall sleep in two rooms different and far be it from each other. Pierre, amor mio, I'm very pround of you, 15 months no sexual relation, I beleive you . . . We shall have a

naturel and satisfaction sexual life, with very profundo love. Our sexual life will be fantastic; . . .

Pierre say me, are you happy with Mercedes? Do you love me as much as I love you? I'm in love with you like you can't imagine . . .

Tuya siempre
Mercedes

VIVA PIERRE MICHEL TRUDEAU! VIVA MARIA MERCEDES ROMAN! VIVA CANADA! VIVA! VIVA ESPAÑA! VIVA! VIVA OUR LOVE FOR ALWAYS! VIVA! VIVA! VIVA OUR LOVE TWO IN ONE! VIVA! VIVA! VIVA PIERRE MICHEL MY HUSBAND FUTURE! VIVA! VIVA! VIVA! AMOR MIO, I LOVE YOU VERY PROFUNDO. I NEED YOU, YES PIERRE, I NEED YOU FOR ALWAYS.

Gillam 21 March 1973

Amor mio Mercedes.

. . . That correct for the date 3 May (Thudsday) for be married. That be important date for us . . . Well Mercedes very soon we be together for always 24 April 1973 (Madrid). Imagine only 34 days we the winner. These days will be long, I am very anxious to be with you . . . that be fantastic, since 1 week I don't work very well. I am always in the luna [moon]. I just thinks about you all the time. I am no more concentration on my work . . . I am in profondo meditation. I am in love more at never. I dream I see you and me all the time, all different place. Yes, amor mio, I am in love with you, I need you, I want your affection, your love, your sex.

Pierre also have electricity cross all my body, when I look you in your eyes on the photo. You are a angel, I am so pround of you.

Some time I wonder if is a dream or reality. I know it is the reality, a fantastic true love . . . God give me realy a perle. Pierre want give you more happiness is possibles . . . I love you profondo for always, my only love of my life . . .

Hasta Pronto,

Pierre XXXXX

Viva Mercedes Roman my only love of my life. Viva España Viva Canada Viva our love. Two in One.

Mercedes and Pierre married, as so carefully planned, on May 3, 1973. After a "memorable" honeymoon, they flew to Canada to take up residence in the Vanier, Ontario, apartment where they live today. They have worked together for twenty-one years and have never missed a day: he is the supervising chef in a nursing home where she is in charge of cold-food purchasing and preparation and arranging special meals and diets. Childless, they enjoying travelling and continue to discuss all manner of topics profondo.

THE POET AND THE OUTLAW

Susan Musgrave, born in California and raised on Vancouver Island, left school at fourteen and published her first poems in a literary magazine two years later. In autumn 1984 the brilliant, edgy poet and novelist was in her second year as writer-in-residence at the University of Waterloo when a criminologist brought her the manuscript of an autobiographical novella by a convicted bank robber named Stephen Reid. Susan's first husband had been a criminal-defence lawyer, and her second, with whom she had a daughter, was his client, an accused drug smuggler she married after his acquittal. Now she fell in love with the fictionalized character in Jackrabbit Parole *and wrote the convict author at Millhaven Institution in Ontario to say she wanted to edit it (and in one of the many letters she wrote that week added, half-jokingly: "PS Will you marry me?"). Stephen, one of nine kids, had his first hit of morphine at age eleven in northern Ontario from a doctor who was sexually abusing him. In the 1960s and 1970s, he had been a member of the Stopwatch Gang, so-called because he wore a timer around his neck as the trio took about $15 million in more than a hundred non-violent robberies of banks in the United States and Canada. Stephen and Susan wrote each other for two months before meeting. What follow are excerpts from the first two years of their correspondence.*

October 15, 1984

Dear Writer-in-Residence.

Hello. What a strange title. Would you tell me what it means? Is it like Beware-an-author-in-the-home?

Sending out my last draft was like sending a Victorian aunt a nude picture on a drunken whimsy, then waking up in the morning. Wobbly knees and white paunch offending the quiet, elegant parlour from your Aunt Polly's mantelpiece. Sort of vulnerable.

October 31, 1984

Dear Stephen

I'm feeling vulnerable, too. I wonder where vulnerable comes from, what's the original meaning of the word. I should have studied linguistics. The art of tonguing things? Once, in France, I was in a post office and I was licking stamps and the postmaster told my friend, who lived in the village, he'd like to hire me because I had such a beautiful tongue. When you get out I will only lick stamps in the privacy of our own bedroom.

November 12, 1984

Susan: I finished working. Served 128 breaded pork cutlets, green breaded pork cutlets. Ran four miles. I just came in, had a shower, and I'm sitting here in baby powder and pyjama bottoms. Would you like to have an oil-fondue party?

Stephen wrote her that a friend of his, a Native inmate named Danny, had died.

December 4, 1984

Stephen:

I walked out of the prison last night, it was snowing, getting dark. One of the guards, walking behind me, said, "I'll trade you coats." I had on my raccoon coat, I said, "Even this one isn't warm enough for me." He put his arm around me, hugged me tight. He was older, looked Irish. He said, "Maybe you need a drink."

I said, "You are Irish." He said, "My parents were." He suddenly looking ashamed for letting a little of himself be known. Another man, walking slightly behind him, was shackled, in leg irons and a chain around his waist. He carried his belongings in a cardboard box.

The guard said, "I'm looking after him." I nodded. He became distant and we passed through the gates that lock us out, lock us in, lock us everywhere away. I got in my car and thought of you doing three years chained in the hole having bean cake slapped on your face three times a day, breakfast, lunch and dinner, and I thought *that's the saddest thing I know.*

Carolyn Forché has a poem in "The Country Between Us" called "The Visitor", about a prisoner in Salvador . . . "it is his wife's breath/ slipping into his cell each night while he imagines . . ."

Slipping into your cell, I wander around lost. I love listening to your breathing. Each night I lie awake imagining it to be my own.

My heart's a rag. It's a rag in the wind. It's a soggy bean cake, a man carrying his only belongings in a box, it's leg irons for one and Danny being poisoned by cyanide . . . why? Because he was close to you?

There is nothing one person will not do to another.

And out of these nothings, all beginnings come.

Jan 10, 1985

Susan, I love you. All things begin there. Last night on T.V. a woman said she wanted two men. One to be her friend – tolerant, giving, someone to share her life with – then she wanted a more dangerous one, unpredictable, moody, a male animal. She said more. She was articulate and very intelligent – the only thing that bothered me was the impression I got that she wanted the two men in one – and to choose when he would be what.

April 20, 1985

Dear Susan:

Someone tried to escape last night so we were locked down. Breakfast was a luke-cold cup of coffee, slice of plain bread. Then they announced they had found the guy, so our doors would be opening at noon, but there would be no lunch. I asked if they could leave my door closed and feed me instead. I got a dirty look.

I watched an author's conference in Toronto last night. Ken Kesey, James Baldwin, Margaret Atwood. Will we go to author's conventions? Writer's meetings? The HIS and HER sides of the wild side of Canadian writing. A poet and an outlaw. Which do you want to be?

[April 1985]

Stephen. I love it when you gather up my clothes into a bunch and pull me up to you. You can tear anything. I don't mind. I love the sound of tearing. You're so beautiful. I love your face. I can't find words for how you are. You are beautiful. It hurts me.

I want you. Stephen, I only want you. For the rest of my life I want to write to you. I want to sit like this and write. Nothing more but letters to you. And nothing less. Susan.

Stephen and Susan were married in a maximum-security institution in 1986. He was released on full parole the following year, and for the next dozen years – as they lived near Sidney, British Columbia, where she gave birth to their daughter – he went straight. But in June 1999, back on heroin, Stephen and a partner robbed a bank in Victoria and exchanged gunfire with police. He was sentenced to eighteen years in William Head Federal Penitentiary on Vancouver Island, where Susan visits him regularly. In her poem "Razor-wire, Millhaven Penitentiary," she writes, "The heart is a gash/and the sky glitters, but all/That high wire coiled and ready to cut/can't keep tenderness out."

CANADIAN ON THE VLTAVA

*In 1993 **Carolyn Harris**, an American trying to escape an unhappy relationship and a dead-end job at Radcliffe College, found herself in Cesky Krumlov, a medieval town in southeastern Czech Republic, where everyone asked her if she was staying with the Canadian by the river. Eventually Carolyn found **Callon Zukowski**, a Toronto born artist who'd changed his plans to study in Berlin in favour of running a hostel in a five-hundred-year-old house on*

*the banks of the Vltava River. Carolyn stayed at Cal's hostel, and
then returned to the States, broke up with her boyfriend, quit her
job, and exchanged letters with Cal.*

[2 days after]

Hi Carolyn –

. . . I want to tell you what a pleasure it was for me to get to know
you. I miss people like you in my life. I still don't really understand destiny and all its workings, but I do know that happiness
seems to be its courier – Since you made me very happy, it stands
to reason destiny takes an interest in our meeting – time unfolds.
Your eyes are still with me – I'm sure they always will be. I also
(amazingly enough) got immense pleasure from reminiscing
American culture (wait! is that a contradiction in terms?) Actually,
right now you are on the flight home to meet, BOB – tell me how
that goes . . .

I'm curious to hear from you. How did Prague go? How was
the flight? How did America seem (as if it can only read in a
moment)? I'm feeling very unhealthy, and am determined to make
a concerted effort to be a little less so. Take care of yourself my
beautiful girl. Let's hope destiny listens to its couriers!

Love

Cal

PS: My back and bum are still very itchy from that romp in the
grass!

PPS: "whiff" in Czech is "bafnuti" – great name for a kid!!!

30 July 1993

Dearest Pen Pal –

. . . I've been back here for three weeks now, and I still don't feel
adjusted. I can't get rid of the feeling that I don't belong here

anymore. So, this past weekend I went to camp in the Adirondacks and did some serious hammock-swinging/thinking and I've come up with a conclusion: I'm going to move to the Czech or Slovak Republics by November 1. I'll take an intensive Czech language course for the whole month of September. I figure – hey, if I don't like it there I can always come back here. I'm just tired of being a fraidy-cat. My grandmothers, my parents, my friends, even my co-workers are very supportive of my rash decision. Of course, my ex, Bob, thinks I've gone off the deep end. And since I've made this decision I find myself unusually calm. I wonder about the interior dialogue you had when you made your decision to stay in Cesky Krumlov. Did you struggle with it, or did you just lay yourself down to the winds of fate? I know it won't be easy, but that's precisely the point – I want a challenge, and I want to survive doing what I love to do – teaching. If I can just get out of my own way the fun will follow . . .

I know our letters will probably cross each other with a nod and wink as they make their way over the Atlantic. I just find it too frustrating to wait for a letter from you before I can tell you all the stuff that's happening in my life. It seems I'm moving fast-forward to something greater – Do you think that my almost perfect handwriting is a sign of being anal-retentive?

Your memory is a bright day without a cloud to darken the ground.

Waiting,
Carolyn

August 24 1993

. . . How are you? Or rather, "Jak se mas?" I'm doing quite well and feel rather untouched from the day-to-day drudgery of life (mainly, work). I've got only eight days to go and an open calendar full of adventure awaiting. I feel like a horse at the starting gate, sniffing the acrid air of anticipation, ears perked, eyes rolling, hooves stomping, thinking of previous rolls in the hay (nay nay wink wink nudge nudge!) . . .

I've made a very important decision – from now on I'm going to live as a romantic sensualist. I'm not sure what it exactly entails, but it's opposite of how I lived my life before traveling to the Czech Republic and meeting you. Oh, if you knew me then, well – who knows? But I think you would have thought of me as a wasted, unrealized life waiting for something unknown. Good thing I met you when I did, because I have found a new honesty in my life and a new understanding of myself. I feel that I can accomplish anything and I've done it without the help of smarmy self-help books. I'm sure my housemates are finding me difficult to live with, but fuck it! When you're feeling big, you're BIG! And with this new-found bigness comes big thoughts that are tending to fly eastward, floating up the Vltava, towards Cesky Krumlov, and into your bedroom window. I know these thoughts could be arrested for breaking and entering, but they can't help it – thoughts are remorseless voyeurs. And dreams, of course, are the biggest looters of all. They've stolen selected, perfectly placed and pack-aged memories and relocated them in troubling and sometimes amusing surroundings. The other night I dreamed that I was walking that long hallway from your bedroom to the bathroom, but instead of ending up in the bathroom I ended up on the set of "The Partridge Family." This dream was brought on from my memory of the night the lights went out in U Vodnika and I had to feel my way to the bathroom (I was reading *Natural History of the Senses* at the time, and was quite excited to use them at that point) AND my memory of lolling with you and talking about our favorite TV shows when we were growing up – funny how the mind works. As a romantic sensualist, I just sit back and let thoughts and dreams happen – don't try this at home unless you're a trained RS. I've also found that in being an RS, one tends to drop things and bump into things more often, and I've also noted a real burst of excitement at night that makes me tend towards insomnia. It's just that damned silver disc of a moon that shines right through my bedroom window and onto my unexercised bed that drives me lune-y . . .

LOVE
CAROLYN

Carolyn landed a teaching position with a university twenty kilometres from Cesky Krumlov and was back with Cal within six weeks. They were married in 1994 and have two sons. Now they both run Krumlov House, where Cal's artistry has created interior spaces that cast a charm over visiting hostellers: Carolyn knows of ten romances that began in their house on the Vltava.

THE MARROW OF LOVE

*In 1993 nineteen-year-old **Sarah Haxby** was working in a music kiosk in a mall in Vancouver to pay for her fine-arts education. A co-worker often asked her to point out among the mall shoppers the kind of guy she found cute, and one day Haxby made her choice. As Jeff, a twenty-four-year-old Ph.D. student at the University of Washington, walked by, Sarah said, "I'd go out with him." "He had blond hair to his waist, faded blue jeans emphasizing his lean frame, and a bit of an intellectual wit gleaming in his blue eyes." By coincidence, Jeff was in the mall with a friend of Sarah's, and so they were introduced. They saw one another*

for a few days before he returned to Seattle. That was the begin-
ning of Sarah's first true romance – a long-distance relationship
that lasted three years.

July 19, 1994

Jeff, darling, dear,

Please! I beg you, stop calling me by terms of endearment that involve meat. It's getting overdone, and I feel it is very rotten of you when (as a vegetarian) you know my aversion to carcass. If you can not find something else that can tickle your ribs I fear your life may be at stake, I will have to flay you to the bone, or at least roast your rump. So there!

Now that I've finished butchering the language I will turn to a more moderate tone. I am in high spirits today; tired . . . but happy.

I received a battered box of exotic spice tea in the mail today, thanx my little blood-pudding. You did not send this gift in vein, for I greatly appreciate it, and that's no bologna, my'dear.

It is an ideal day, the trees stand straight and tall like pepperoni sticks, the ocean is smooth like a cut of lambchop, growing to look like bacon when a wind blows up from the great slaughterhouse in the sky. The clouds have the texture of fresh-plucked chicken breasts, and the sky – why should we remark on the color of the sky when we can mention its odor instead? Fresh. Like salted ham.

I am feeling better for being on Bowen [Island], and knowing you are willing to travel all the way to Bowen to see me in 10 days. It has been another long break, but your letters have been a source of entertainment, a diversion. Something to laugh at, deride, chortle, snicker at . . . but, my dearest, I grow too cruel! . . .

Enough!

Until we meat again,
Sarah

Sarah Haxby just before she met Jeff in 1993 (Self-portrait, facilitated by Dcc Partridge)

Feb 1 1996

Dear Jeff,

I have been thinking of you with great frequency, and wondering where you are on the great map of the world and glad you are at a pin point I can contact you at, however, briefly . . . I was relieved to receive your humorous post card. I like seeing images of where you are. Please send more if possible, of images that mean something to you, or try to describe them to me if you have the energy . . . Please talk to me, let me know. I am dreadfully ignorant and you are surrounded by a lot of grey in my mind. I can't imagine where you are and the lack of visuals disturbs me.

What is the weather like? Here we've been down to minus eighteen and this morning I watched the dial go from -8 to plus 2 as the sun came up and went to work melting the four foot icicles hanging in front of my picture pane window. I speak only of the weather so I can tell you my little anecdote of the first night it snowed. A whole foot of snow came drifting down from grey heavy clouds that had been moodily drifting in until that certain heavily imminent atmosphere clarified into that perfect feeling of: SNOW.

And for hours it fell, and the sun set unnoticed and the moon rose unseen and the stars were duplicated and sent down by facsimile. I went and had a very hot bath scented with a rather wood nymphy like scent and when I felt almost a little parboiled I went outside and lay naked in the snow. It was quite the feeling to sense every little snowflake melting into my skin, each one making a bit more of a tingling cold creeping fire as my skin temperature dropped and began turning to snow . . .

The second anecdote I have regarding the weather occurred tonight . . . I went to Killarney Lake in the dark, and walked out into the middle of the lake, given that it was frozen enough to do this.

Ice in moonlight and the haunting whalish sounds of ice expanding in the cool of the night and the stresses that puts on the great plates . . . of the ice cause a most haunting sound, I find most alluring. A wordless echoing sound . . . a sound I would attribute to a siren if there was ever one designed to lure me into the ocean. Do you know this sound? very haunting.

Alison gave me a sparkler before I left to go to the lake so when I was out in the middle of the lake I lit it and wheeled around under the great almost full-term waxing moon spinning madly with this sparkler until I was quite dizzy and the stars kept spinning . . . I have found too few people who share my notion of magic, or even the romance of going out on such a night. I find a solitary form of romance suits me better than listening to mundane comparisons . . . I am quite sure you would have been quiet and listened to the ice with me, even if perhaps you did not fully understand what I meant to myself when I said the magic, you would then surprise me at times with your intuition on the subject . . .

I wish to ramble to keep contact with you just a little longer, knowing, perhaps that your eyes will linger a little longer on these pages and sense a little bit of Bowen is still with you. And a little bit of me too, if I may accompany you on your journey. . . .

Please don't get lost to me Jeff, I do fear that I will lose contact with you and worry about you for a year or so . . . or until the next time I heard from you.

S.H.

HE- AND SHE-MAIL

They met on the Internet through a Canadian Web site called Quality Soulmates. She was the unmarried mother of a teenaged daughter; he was a childless divorcé. **Constance Wrigley**, *an association manager from Burlington, Ontario, recalls her decision to find a partner on-line: "A forty-three-year-old single woman says, 'Okay, that's it, I'm not going to get married, but I'll make one last-ditch attempt at finding Mr. Right.'" At the beginning of June 2000 she put an ad on Soulmates.* **John Thomas** – *three years older, a salesman for a local envelope company who was about to pull his own ad from the site – was among about five hundred men who responded, sending her a photo of himself holding a golden retriever puppy. Within a week of talking on the phone, they met and began dating. While clicking in real life, they kept fuelling their Net-born relationship through constant e-mails.*

Date: Wednesday, July 12, 2000
Subject: Countdown
John,
Not that I'm counting down or anything, BUT since you're wondering: only 63 hours and 28 minutes until we leave for Muskoka!

I just looked out the window – the weather is gorgeous – and am feeling a little giddy. I must . . . get . . . work . . . done . . . !

Date: Wed, 12 Jul 2000
Subject: RE: Countdown
Hi,
I had successfully kept it from my mind for about 10 minutes. We're so weak . . . in the knees, that is. Miss you. JT

Date: Wed, 23 Aug 2000
Subject: A Haiku
Good morning John,
Just in case you haven't got your daily dose of Haiku, here's one I wrote for you:
> Red shirt in my bed
> Evokes sensation of you
> Can't replace your touch

So now you can't say that I never write you any poetry.
Feeling romantic and missing you . . .
Constance xo

Date: Wed, 23 Aug 2000
Subject: Haiku to you
Hi!
I would never say that. You ARE poetry to me . . . it's in everything you do.
> Read last night
> Many cards of love
> Heart filled with more joy?

John xo

*The same day, John e-mailed Constance for some advice on build-
ing a corporate Web site and implanted a not-very-hidden message
in his request, to which she replied in kind.*

Date: Wed, 23 Aug 2000
Subject: Re: This is business – what an excuse!
Dear Mr. Subliminal,
Allow me to pull some materials together . . . here are some quick
tips for planning a website:

     Investigate ISP's [Internet service providers]
     Learn as much as possible about the available
         technologies
     Observe other sites
     Verify your mission
     Emulate the really great sites
     Yield to no one
     Open your mind
     Understand what it is you are trying to achieve
     Think like a customer
     Own your message
     Organize ahead of time

And, if you follow the cryptogram above, you will find my
response to your subliminal message.

Date: Wednesday, October 18, 2000
Subject: Your health
Good morning John!
    I am so glad that I could contribute to your good health this
morning.
    As always, I am thinking of you.
    ILY

Date: Wed, 18 Oct 2000
Subject: RE: Your health
Hi Hon,
You are wonderful and so giving, and I can hardly wait to soon contribute in kind to your good health! . . .
    ILYT

Date: Wed, 15 Nov 2000
Subject: Happy Anniversary
John-darling,
    November 15th – thank you for making this the most incredible five months of my life!
    As I said last night, I am convinced that our souls have always known each other – how else could it be that these past few months seem like a wonderful lifetime spent with you.
    You are my life and my love!
Constance xo

Date: Wed, 15 Nov 2000
Subject: RE: Happy Anniversary
I too have never been happier, sweetheart. Here's celebrating 5 months and hundreds more to come.
    Love You!
    JT

A month later they were engaged and the following September were married. "We still communicate by e-mail," Constance says, "and have our own endearments and our little code."

ETERNAL FLAME

*Like many couples today, **Peter Menlove** and Joanne Neufeld of Winnipeg worked for the same company and wrote e-mails, but during their year-long romance, Peter also penned letters and cards to the woman he called his "tall and graceful one."*

[2000]

T&G,

You're just a dream boat sailing in my head. You swim my secret oceans of coral blue. Your scent is like sweet incense burning. Your touch is silken yet it reaches through my skin. But it's when I sleep that I see you in my dreams. I hear you softly breathe somewhere in my sleep. It clings like a sea mist surrounding my body.

I've caught myself smiling alone. Just thinking of your voice and dreaming of your touch. So happy to have opened my eyes to see you in a brand new way. I now believe there was something different that I needed to see.

P

Nov.

Joanne,

Goddess from heaven, my inspiration, my uplifting soul, my voice of song and poetry, my slender Aphrodite. You vanquish all doubt that God created love and beauty and rested his tender hand upon you.

I pray you will continue to be the piece in the puzzle of life that is contentment. Not a moment goes by when the warmth of your voice or the sparkle in your eyes fails to fill me with joy and enchantment.

You are the fuel that burns the fire of life in me. I feel your passion envelop me and the knowledge that I can enjoy all you share with me fills my heart.

P.T.M.

Peter was drowned on August 5, 2001. Joanne treasures his cards and letters "more than life itself."

Friendship

—⊸⊷⊶⊷⊸—

"You shall hear all the bad and good
that happens to me"

Sheep's Eye and Cholera

"Bridget Lacy" was a family servant who emigrated with her employers to Upper Canada in 1832 from County Wicklow, in an Ireland battered by bitter religious strife between Protestants and Catholics. She was among the 27,000 immigrants who arrived that year and brought with them the scourge of cholera, which reached epidemic proportions. The family she was serving, members of the Church of England, ended their journey in York, in what's now present-day Toronto (where more than four hundred died from the disease). Bridget survived the long ocean voyage and the epidemic and thrived on the attention of a fellow seafarer – as she wrote in a gossipy letter to Mary Thompson, a girlfriend in Ireland.

[York, Upper Canada, August, 1832]
Dear fellow Servant, and fellow school-fellow, –
For we were edicated together, and printiced out together – and my blessing on the Committee of fifteen, and my blessing on them that taught us to read and write, and spell, that you may know all about me, and I about you, though there are rivers, and seas, and woods, and lakes between us – and my blessing on the mistress that taught us to work, and wash, and make ourselves useful, so that while

health stands by us, we may earn honest bread in any country. And sure enough, dear Mary, you shall hear all the good and bad that happens to me, and I hope to have the same from you.

And now that I am on land, it is only good natured that I should give you some account of my doings since I set out.

If I had you with me, I would have been easier in my mind; but still my mistress was very good, and I got on bearably, barring the shocking sickness, such as no one in the cholic, or the breeding way, or the billious fever, or after hippo, or after sqills, ever felt before or since.

If you were only to have seen how smooth we floated down the River, and out of the Bay, and away to Wicklow, where I was born, at the back of the murrough [a coastal wetland complex], near Tinnakilly, you would have said, away you go – eating, and drinking, and laughing, and cracking jokes; but my jewel, before the second day was over, we were all knocked of a heap; and then if you were to hear all around you as I did, groaning, and raching, and willy wombling, and calling for water, and nobody to bring them a sup, and wishing themselves at the bottom of the sea; in troth, Mary, you would have pitied a dog in the same taking. The hold was full of people, mighty snug and decent, with money in their pockets, going out to make their fortunes; and most of them Protestants, that found home growing too hot for them; and that they had better save their four bones, and their little earnings before it was too late, and sure enough, I believe they're right. There are mighty good people among them, and mighty pretty girls, that when they arn't sick, sing psalms in the evening, very beautiful; and there's one Jenny Ferguson, from the north, that I am very thick with, and she has a voice like an angel. In troth there are none of them bad, and its mighty sweet upon the sea,

Well my dear, when the singing is over, they're all very merry; and there are some gay lads, and great fun, and a little courting, but all in a civil way; and I sometimes make one; but between you and I, Mary, but don't say a word at all at all, I think there's a servant-boy of a Mr. Jackson's, one Benson, that's throwing a sheep's eye at me – but nothing certain, barring a sly pinch here and there, and other tinder tokens that may end in smoak [smoke] after all. They say a girl will soon get a husband in this country. Some will, and some will not. I'd be sorry to be trusting to them.

The boy I have told you of, may be settled near us, and if he is as sweet upon me then, as he is now, he may put some of their noses out of joint. To say the honest truth, I would not like to be beholden to them; though they say they're civil enough in Canada, not all as one as the States, where they have the impudence of Old Nick, in making free with their betters.

You would not believe, dear Mary, the forwardness of them Yankees.

Sure, I heard a gentleman, after coming from Philadelfy, in the Untied States, telling my mistress of there going some journey there in a cart, and the horses tiring and stopping to sleep at a farmers, and when he had got into bed, and was falling asleep, was roused by one over him, saying, "I guess I tumble in here," when the greasy carter that drove him, stretched his ugly carcass alongside him, and began to snore in three minutes. Now think of that, Mary. If it was my case, not a pin in my pin-cushion but he should have the full benefit of, the impudent mohawk.

That's liberty and quality as they call it – a nice bed-fellow indeed – instead of his own pretty wife, who was put to sleep with the young woman of the house, to make room for this scurvy Gee-ho-dobbin.

The only accidence we had on the voyage was an old woman that died, and a child born in the hold, and a little girl choked with a potatoe, and two doctors on board – but no blame to them – they weren't called till all was over – and the Captain, long life to him, put the old woman decent in a coffin, saying that the sherks [sharks] should have a mouthful of sawdust before they got at her old bones . . .

Well, well, well, – I believe this letter will never end; so that I'll say nothing about the journey from Quebec to York, only that it was mighty pretty; and beautiful steam boats, and rumbling coaches, and bad inns, and fine rivers, and plenty of trees; and here we are at York, and here we have been for a month, living as bad as in a cholera hospital, for the whole town was nothing else; and every day, every day, we never thought we would get over the next night safe. But we could not run away, for my mistress was brought to bed of a little girl, as fine a little crature as ever you see. But we are all well now; and when my master comes back from the waterfall of Niggeraga, (they say they were all Niggers here once,) we are to set out for the estate he has bought in the Huron Tract; and whatever comes across me there, Mary, you shall know the particulars of it, as it may be a temptation for you to come out yourself next year, with your own black eyes, to throw yourself in the way of the same good fortune. They say no girl, barring she is old and ugly, will stand two months.

My Mistress says an officer will take this free, with her own.

So dear Mary no more, (and I'm sure no more would be agreeable,) at present, from your loving schoolfellow,

And friend,

Bridget Lacy

My next shall be from our own place, and you shall hear all the ways of it.

Not long after, "Bridget" – a cook now, instead of a children's maid – had a pair of possible suitors ("two strings to one's bow my dear Mary"). Her correspondence appears in Authentic Letters from Upper Canada, *a collection of letters sent home by the Irish immigrant Magrath and Radcliff families, originally published in Dublin in 1833. Its editor wrote: "The name of this correspondent is the only fictitious one introduced. The facts, however, are correct." In an introduction to a reprinted version of the book, the late Canadian historian James John Talman remarked, "Bridget Lacy, the fictitious writer of two of the letters, probably expressed far better than her master and mistress the ideas of the great majority of settlers."*

WILLIE AND THE WOMAN IN WHITE

In 1897 **William Lyon Mackenzie King** *was studying economics at the University of Chicago when he became ill and was treated at St. Luke's Hospital. There he met* **Mathilde Grossert**, *an English-speaking nurse who had recently emigrated from Germany. The future Liberal prime minister was always inordinately fond of his mother. But as a twenty-two-year-old away from home, William fell for the caring Mathilde, who was as much as fourteen years older and (in his eyes) enshrined "all the goodness purity & greatness that God ever gave to woman." He pursued her in person and later by mail as he studied at Harvard University and then returned to Canada. She was a grandniece of the German poet Schiller and wrote William fluently in English, as she did in 1897, quoting George Eliot on women: ". . . it is not true that love makes all things easy, it makes us choose what is difficult." The following year, she described herself to him in humbling*

W. L. Mackenzie King's friend Mathilde Grossert Barchet in 1916
(Library and Archives of Canada PA-116911)

terms, addressing him with an indecipherable German salutation
in a letter that is missing its last page.

Wednesday.
Jan 22/98.

. . . I am heartily ashamed. I have no special gifts & possess no
particular attractions, nor am I accomplished in anything particular. But I am a woman and as such am born to nurse to soothe, to
help and to heal. I have always felt that I could do that well, that
I must make use of these modest gifts, that though my life might
never amount to anything great, yet I hoped that in this quiet,
unpretentious way I might be able to uplift some fellow-creature
of mine. if I had a voice, if I were a Jenny Lind, I could in this way
endeavour to make my fellowmen aware of the divine harmonic
above; if I could paint, I would endeavour to make my fellowmen
realize the beauties of nature and through it the creator, but since
I am none of these, since I possess no great gifts and genius has
not overshadowed my cradle, yet I may endeavour in my own quiet
way to make my fellowmen aware of the great heart that beats for
them above . . . I will let nothing attract my attention elsewhere.
It must be done and [if] you feel for me what you profess you feel,
you must help me . . .

You must be very tired after all this work of late. I am so
selfishly nursing my own griefs & trials and yet believe me you
are hardly a moment out of my thoughts. I seem to bear you in
my mind almost constantly. Excuse this hastily written letter.
Letterwriting affords but little satisfaction. There is much I would
like to say to you, but the thoughts come so rapidly and the pen is
so slow and by the time one thought is penned a dozen more have
gone. You have an advantage there. You are able to fashion your
thoughts quickly . . .

After William wrote in March 1898 to ask for her hand in mar-
riage, she sent him a telegram: "My answer, yes . . ." Unfortunately,
his family was shocked at the thought of his wedding an older
immigrant woman living in the United States. The long-distance
sweethearts began to lose heart, and later that year they ended any
thought of a romantic liaison. But they kept corresponding and
exchanging gifts; she sent him afghans, handkerchiefs, and books.
Although Mathilde married George Barchet, a doctor who pre-
ferred to farm, she and William remained friends throughout his
twenty-two years as Prime Minister Mackenzie King, from 1921 to
1948, and long after he retired. Just as Germany was invading
western Europe in the Second World War, he visited the farm in
Maryland where Mathilde and her husband raised dairy cattle and
grew vegetables. (They had a son who grew up to be a rear admiral
in the United States Navy.) A neighbour who worked on the farm
as a boy recalls, "Mrs. Barchet would bring German cookies and
talk to me about the old Black Forest that she knew as a child. She
was a great storyteller." In 1932, when the Barchets' frame house
burned down, William had sent Mathilde a gift of $250. After his
visit during the war, he wrote a letter of thanks and reminiscence.

May 6, 1940

Dear Mathilde,

I shall never be able to tell you and Mr. Barchet how very much I
enjoyed my little visit to Belfield Farm . . .

Most vivid of all in my mind will be the calm beauty of the
evening hour of sunset and the lovely scene, with all the wonder
of the springtime, intermingled with the glow of the setting sun.
The last glimpse I had of you was as you walked around the turn
of the cottage, clothed in white, the white shawl over your head,
falling as it did as a mantle across the white dress you were

wearing. It was a radiant picture of one arrayed in white. It brought back many thoughts of the St. Luke's uniform which you wore many years ago and which was so becoming to you.

Ere this letter reaches you I hope you will have received a photograph of my dog, Pat, and myself which I left with Gortham's of New York, to be framed and sent on to you . . .

[Mackenzie King]

Mackenzie King, who kept trying to communicate with his dead mother in seances, never married (although in his younger years he patronized prostitutes and tried to rehabilitate some). Writing in December 1946 after Mathilde sent him a letter marking his seventy-second birthday, he said, "It is difficult to believe that it is now almost a full half century since we first met when I was attending the University of Chicago, and you were on the nursing staff of St. Luke's Hospital. Those days continue to lend their happy memories to the present. In that interval of time, we have, I think, exchanged greetings at every Christmas Season. I hope there may be many more." There were at least three more such exchanges before he died in 1950. "As for letters," he wrote her that year, "they are a nightmare and must be treated as such. Otherwise they are certain to become intolerable burdens. If friends or relatives fail to understand not hearing from me, it is just too bad for them." Mathilde, his friend of fifty-three years, was an obvious exception.

Maud of the Island

Pen pals can often become close friends, even if they seldom, or never, meet. When she began a lifelong correspondence with a *literary pen pal in Scotland, **Lucy Maud Montgomery** of Cavendish, Prince Edward Island, was five years away from writing* Anne of Green Gables, *the first in a series of books that brought her international success. Miriam Zieber, a Philadelphia poet, was trying to form a writers' club and, in exchanging letters with Maud (as Montgomery called herself), put her in touch with George Boyd MacMillan, an apprentice printer and hopeful writer. In this first letter to the twenty-two-year-old George, the much-older Maud was open about her aspirations and limitations, but less than honest in revealing her true age – she lowered it by three years.*

> Cavendish
> P.E.I.
> Can
> Tuesday Evening: – December 29. 1903.

Mr dear Mr. McMillan: –

I must ask your pardon for not answering your letter sooner . . .

I shall be very pleased to carry on a literary correspondence with you and hope we can make it mutually helpful and interesting. I am particularly glad that you live in Scotland for I have no other correspondent there and think it is the most delightful and interesting land on earth. I am Canadian born and bred but my forefathers on both sides were from Scotland. Our family of Montgomeries claim kinship with the earls of Eglinton. My mother was a Macneill, which is even "Scotchier" still.

Like yourself, I will tell you a little about myself in order to enable you to visualize me a little bit and not leave you to think of me as only a vague intellectual proposition.

I am 26 years old and like yourself have been scribbling all my life. Six years ago I began to inflict my scribbling on a public that suffereth long and is kind. I have got on pretty well and make a comfortable living for one small girl by my pen besides finding a vast deal of pleasure in my work. Apart from my literary bent I am small, said to be very vivacious, am very fond of fun and good times generally. I write this because so many people have told me that from my writing they expected to see a tall, imposing looking girl with flashing black eyes and hair.

I don't know whether I call my verse my specialty or not. I know that I touch a far higher note in my verse than in my prose. But I write much more prose than verse because there is a wide market for it, especially among the juvenile publications. In 1903 I have made $500 by writing of which less than $100 came from verse. I am glad you like my verse and shall be pleased to send you some of them in each letter if you would care to see them. I shall also be pleased to see anything and everything of yours. I have never attempted essay writing because I do not think I could do anything in that line although I enjoy reading essays very much. My prose is all fiction – mostly short stories but I sold two serials this summer.

As you are trying to get into American journals I will give you all the pointers I can in any way. I have about 70 different periodicals on my list and will tell you about a few in each letter until I have gone through the list . . .

Do you typewrite your ms. [manuscripts]? I have done so for two years. I bought a good second hand machine taught myself to manipulate it and type all my ms. It has paid me, I think. Editors used to growl over my handwriting.

I sent you a couple of my "yarns" when I received your letter by way of letting you know that it had come to hand. Miss Zieber thinks my prose is poor and I do not claim any merit for it. But I am frankly in literature to make my living out of it. My prose sells so I write it, although I prefer writing verse. I know that I can never be a really great writer. My aspiration is limited to this – I want to be a <u>good workman</u> in my chosen profession. I cannot be one of the masters but I hope to attain to a recognizable position among the everyday workers of my time. That is all I hope or expect.

I am interested in many things and <u>love living</u>. I have a camera and enjoy taking photos. I enclose a few unmounted "squeegees" of P.E.I. corners. I love <u>fancy-work</u>, <u>cats</u>, horses, pretty dresses and feminine things generally. Revel in books. Don't care for athletics but love out-of-doors. This is all a very egotistic claim but such can't be avoided in such a correspondence as this, especially at the start.

Whereabouts in Scotland is Alloa? Near Edinburgh? Don't roll your eyes over my ignorance? Remember I'm 2,000 miles away and my ideas of Scottish geography are merely on broad general lines.

Well, I shall stop now for this time and shall look forward with pleasure to your next letter. I have a long list of correspondents but always try to answer each letter in them.

Very affectionately your
L.M. Montgomery.

A year later George became a reporter with the Alloa Journal, *where he stayed until retiring in 1946. Maud went on to write two dozen bestselling books, including* Anne of Avonlea, Anne of the Island, *and other titles in her beloved series about a feisty, red-headed young heroine. She married the Reverend Ewan Macdonald in 1911 and moved to Ontario. Over the next four decades the transatlantic pen pals kept corresponding, often expressing intimate thoughts, until she died in 1942. They met only once, for two*

*weeks. "What a wonderful thing our friendship has been," Maud
wrote thirty years into their relationship. "It seems to me something predestined . . . I realize how much would have been lacking
had this correspondence never materialized."*

A FEAST OF STEPHEN

*Strong intellectual friendships can often be nourished and even
deepened at a distance, on paper. In the 1920s, American-born
Leon (Leo) Edel, raised in Yorkton, Saskatchewan, had just turned
sixteen when he started to study at Montreal's McGill University,
taking the first steps to becoming an internationally known literary biographer and critic. He communicated his delight in college
life – mostly about matters of the mind, rather than young lust –
to his Yorkton friend Norman Caplin, who was studying art in
England. A theme that ran through several letters was Leo's excitement about observing Stephen Leacock in the flesh. The head of
McGill's economics and political-science department was then also
the world's most popular humorist (for such works as* Nonsense
Novels *and* Sunshine Sketches of a Little Town*).*

[November 10, 1923]

Dear Norman: –
To be frank with you I deserve to be kicked!

I haven't written for such a long time and my conscience was
so worried and troubled that I was nearly desperate. Imagine, for
the first time since our correspondence began, I haven't written
for some odd 3 or 4 weeks. Oh! what a terrible state of affairs . . .

I have now had 3 glimpses of Mr. Leacock. Quite a startling
figure! The first time I saw him was when I passed him on the

stairs of the arts building. It didn't take much to know that it was he himself who with long strides was coming towards me. He had his professorial robes on carelessly, half dragging on the floor. His hair, a dense black mass, intermingled with gray, couldn't have seen the comb for a week, and his rough looking reddish mustache was a picture to behold. I say I've seen him three times, and in each case he has been uncombed, and serious-looking. Nothing of the humorous about him that's in his books. He is quite an impressive broad figure, and one can't help noticing him. I think he is quite an important figure even when he strides around the building. All the students stop and gaze at him in awe.

Leo Edel

Fifteen-year-old Leon Edel (left) with his brother, Abraham (Center for Biographical Research, University of Hawai'i at Manoa)

Montreal, P.Q.
Dec. 18, 1923.
. . . As to Leacock and my previous sketches of him, I think now I can enlarge upon them. The other day I passed him in the hall. He was talking to someone, and he certainly has a loud boom in his voice. His voice could be heard all over the place.

The other day an ex-student of McGill, a graduate, now with the League of Nations, addressed the students. A few seats away sat Leacock, just a little in front of Abe and I. We could observe him at our leisure. He certainly is different from other Profs. His uncombed hair is a big feature, as is his bristly mustache. When the address was over there was a student discussion of the League. Abe sat up and questioned whether in trying to regulate war, the League was giving war a legal and moral right to exist. Whereas if war was prohibited absolutely it would be far better. And this prohibition Abe compared with liquor prohibition. Quebec, Abe said, by regulating liquor, was giving it a legal and moral right to exist. Whereas if it was prohibited completely it had no legal or moral right for its existence. At the mention of prohibition and liquor you should have seen Leacock prick up his ears and grin. One of his favorite topics I believe . . . By the way I've noticed Leacock's professorial robes – he wears them for all his lectures – they are unusually old, tattered at the ends, and he allows them to trail all over the floor. The other day he was bounding up the stairs 2 steps at a time. What an imposing figure!

Dec. 30, 1923.

As the year 1923 is about to pass away I shall use the remaining days in adding one more letter to our correspondence of this year, and thus round out a fairly decent "annum" although the latter part has been rather hard on our correspondence . . . let's make a new year resolution in common, – to wit: –

"We the undersigned do hereby certify that we, in accordance with all regulations, laws and certifications shall from the 1st day of Jan. 1924 correspond as regularly and often as time permitteth; at least twice in the lunar month, – or twice a month if the word lunar is objectionable."

(Signed) Leo Edel

Norman Caplin (per L.E.)

What of it monsieur? . . .

Today the 30th is Leacock's Birthday. I noticed this fact in his Sunshine Sketches, for he begins that book with a biography of himself . . .

I suppose the Old Dear is celebrating in good style this day that brought a regular sharp and witty intellect into this world.

Let that suffice for Literature at present. I also hereby sign off for to-day.

Leo Edel

Leo's own sharp intellect, if not his wit, impressed the world, as he went on to teach at Sir George Williams University in Montreal, New York University, and the University of Hawaii and won the Pulitzer Prize and the National Book Award in 1963 for two of the five volumes of his biography of author Henry James. Norman came home to study at the University of Saskatchewan, where he later became a librarian. He and his friend kept corresponding until Norman's death in 1984.

A WHISPER TO HIS HEART

In the early 1920s, the well-born Montreal artist Anne Savage met and was influenced by members of the prominent landscape-painting Group of Seven, including Frederick Varley and Arthur Lismer. She particularly befriended the storytelling, wilderness-roaming A.Y. Jackson, fourteen years her senior. Their friendship threatened to become more than platonic when Alex wrote in 1929, "What do you want me to do Anne? you are the dearest and sweetest soul I know and if you will be my wife I will try so much to make you happy." Anne, an art teacher at Montreal's

Baron Byng high school and later an influential art supervisor of the city's Protestant schools, dissuaded him. Three years later, on his fiftieth birthday, he hinted once more about deepening their bond in a letter written during a painting expedition with his friend Dr. Frederick Banting, the co-discoverer of insulin.

Fraser Hotel

Cobalt. Ont

Oct 3rd '32

Dear Anne

Your letter arrived just a few hours before I left Toronto and the little bird was right too. this is my birthday. you are probably the only person who thought of it. apart from your good wishes it has not been a very thrilling one Dr. Banting and I both picked up little colds. and it rained most of the day. I painted some shacks under a sombre sky. it's a higgley piggeldy little town. slowly disintegrating not a mine working. the great days when Cobalt was known as one of the great mining centres of the world are gone for good . . .

the autumn color is coming along at last but it has not much to work on. bush at second growth on the hills, out of which stick the gaunt mine shafts. it would be an exciting place in winter . . . or early spring. someday a fire will burn it up and the cheerful citizens will have to move . . .

You will be seeing Arthur Lismer and hearing all about his voyage to Europe. It is well we have some people of vision. there should be one to every hundred stoopids.

It is very thoughtful of you to send the electric pad to keep a body young and fit. I will use it and bless the sweet gentle donor

You have been a dear and constant friend even when I have been careless and forgetful your cheerful little letters have come

A.Y. Jackson in April 1959
(National Archives of Canada
PA-201338)

along. until now I would feel lost without them. Perhaps you remember years ago when I was rather obstreperous. you wrote just a little severely to make me understand that our acquaintance was nothing more than good friendship. and that friendship I have been very proud of ever since but this birthday rather bewilders me. I'm a complex individual. I have many friends and contacts. for some reason I'm popular socially without wanting to be so very much and here I am getting on in years. next door to me the horrible example of Williamson. soured, lonely and helpless. I am pretty happy. Eugene ONeill says happiness is only a byproduct, that people who search for it never find it.

I dont know what little Annie Savage will make of all this. and I wonder if she just wants to go on being good friends . . . until the end of the chapter. and I wonder if she realizes how pretty she looked in her green costume. or if she knows how many girls come to tea in my studio and tell me Im wonderful but she has so much to do her life is too full of good deeds to spend time in mere fancies.

> With all good wishes
> as ever.
> Alex

Although Anne Savage remained resolutely single, she did write Alex later that "[m]y heart stands still when I imagine existence without you." And in 1944, hinting about a deeper relationship, she acknowledged the struggle he faced as an artist, but "I also know that friendship which has stood the test of years if properly adjusted could become a bulwark against all ills and create a haven or shelter which could face any tempest . . . Don't try to answer this. It is just a whisper to your heart . . ." In one of his last newsy, opinionated letters that Anne kept, dated March 26, 1963 – after a correspondence of more than three decades – the eighty-year-old Alex closed poignantly: "All the best to you. keep up the good work. it makes me feel very sad to think of the old days in Montreal. Cheerio. as ever Alex." He died in 1974, at ninety-one, three years after Anne's death.

A FRIEND OTHERWISE ENGAGED

Long before becoming one of Canada's most popular humorists, Eric Nicol and his friend Howard Rigney, both lecturers at the University of British Columbia, went to Paris in 1949 to earn their doctorates at the Sorbonne. Howard soon fell under the spell of a Canadian-born woman living in London and bought an engagement ring there that he intended to give her later in Paris. But the course of love seldom runs smoothly and sometimes you need a good friend to run the course for you – as Eric explained in a punning letter to his parents in Vancouver.

29/1/50
La Maison Canadienne
31 Boulevard Jourdan
Paris 1-e, France

Dear Folks,

Yoo-hoo, I'm over here again. Room #9, Paris. Old Ants in his Pants is back in his manse. I won't say that I got back unscathed, because if you examine me under a magnifying glass you find that I am scathed here and there, and also need a shave.

The way I got scathed is closely tied up with my getting "engaged" while I was in London, and engaged to Rigney's fiancée, Margaret Benn, at that. In fact, what you are about to read is a chronicle of romance, treachery and bigtime smuggling such as you rarely find far from Humphrey Bogart. So pull up a jug of smelling salts and harken.

First of all, there was this engagement ring, see. While in London at Christmas, Howard paid for its cutting and setting in dollars on the export scheme, whereby you save money and pick up the goods at the port of embarkation. But on his way back to Paris, Howard missed the export desk at the Newhaven customs, and tried to get his ring from the ship's purser, who didn't have it. Thus Rigney arrived back in Paris fit to spit, because Margaret is coming over in April, he wanted to give her the ring then, and she could wear it back into England on her finger, since the English customs can't keep track of all the fingers that go through their hands, so to speak. Well, seeing Rigney fit to spit, in my room, I let my big fat mouth flap out the offer of <u>my</u> bringing the ring back on this latest safari into the darkest bungle. This was an example of unbridled generosity on my part, and I'm buying a new bridle, with teeth, first thing in the morning.

Anyhow, I met Margaret at the jewelers in London, where I filled out a form, and we all (Margaret, the jeweler and I) joined in gay badinage about her quick turnover in <u>fiancés</u>, fickle womanhood, etc. And I was quick to pick up the rock at Dover Friday morning. Okay. Well, I worried some about the French customs, wondering how I would explain having a diamond ring in my pocket, and a ring worth 200 pounds at that (the gem is a family heirloom). [Friends] Pat and Alex worried with me, Alex coming up every five minutes with a new place of concealment, such as stuck to the roof of my mouth with adhesive tape. I wasn't concerned about English customs at Dover, because I knew of no reason for their getting sticky, except that the jeweler had given the value of the ring on the form as 98 pounds, there being a regulation forbidding the exporting of jewelry worth more than 100 pounds (national treasure, Dept. of Onoyoudont).

So I arrived at Dover, handed the export man my claiming slip, and he said to the customs man next to him:

"Ah, here's our man. Mr. Mullins wants to see Mr. Nicol."

Now, when I picked up the trousers, on the previous trip, Mr. Mullins didn't want to see me. Nobody wanted to see me. They just handed me my pants, the customs man checked my passport, and away I bounded to the boat.

Not this time. I waited while the minor customs man hunted up Mr. Mullins, a major customs man, and an ingot of leaden fear hardened in my belly.

Mr. Mullins came up and asked:

"Is you <u>fiancée</u> an English citizen, Mr. Nicol?"

"Ohhh," I said. "I know Margaret to talk to and share tea with, but that's all. She has a Canadian passport."

"I see," said Mr. Mullins. "And where does she work?"

"Work?" I squeaked. The full horror of being engaged to a girl without knowing where she worked broke over me. I knew Margaret worked for an auto supply firm. "She works for an auto supply firm, I think," I said.

Mr. Mullins gave me a cold, hard look and told me to wait. Now thoroughly miserable, in a shed emptied of everybody but me and hundreds of customs men, and seeming to hear the ship's whistle blowing up the anchor, I waited ten minutes until Mr. Mullins returned with a plainclothesman, whom he introduced as his chief. The chief smiled encouragingly and asked:

"Why are you taking this engagement ring to Paris, Mr. Nicol? Why don't you give it to her here?"

"I can't," I said. "I'd have to go back to London, and she's coming over in April. She can't go anywhere near it. I'm a student."

The chief allowed a shadow of confusion to film his eyes, then smiled again and asked:

"Well, when are you getting married?"

"In the fall," I said, remembering Rigney's having said something about getting married in the fall. "We thought it would be nice in the fall."

"And will you be returning to England to live?"

Not knowing whether the customs wanted us to return to England to live with the goddam ring, or not, I said:

"Well, that's not quite decided. There's a bit of a tug-of-war going on at the moment, ha, ha, but I think it'll be Canada. If it isn't England, that is."

The chief nodded again, baffled. Then he held out the package containing the ring.

"We opened it," he said. "You had better have a look at it."

I fumbled off the packing, opened the ring-box and stared at the ring, which I had never seen before, and which I couldn't even be sure was the right ring. The customs men must have been further nonplussed by my looking at the ring without recognition, and handing it back with my mouth open.

"This ring is valued at only ninety-eight pounds?" asked the chief, tilting the diamonds so that their light momentarily blinded me.

"That's right," I said hoarsely. "Ninety-eight pounds."

After one final searching look, the chief took Mr. Mullins aside and they mumbled together. Finally they turned and handed me the ring, with evident reluctance.

"We'll be on the look-out for this ring," said the chief.

"Thank you," I said. Then I took the package and tottered to the boat. Ahead lay the Channel and the French Customs . . .

Eric

Eric passed through the French customs check without incident and delivered the ring to Howard, who presented it to Margaret in April in Paris. However, Eric was the first to live with her (and two other attractive women) when he moved to London to write a BBC radio series for comedian Bernie Braden. Margaret and Howard later married and lived the rest of their lives in England. Eric returned to Vancouver, where he became a humour columnist and the author of satirical novels and non-fiction, the latest being Old Is In.

The real her

Margaret Laurence met Malcolm Ross in the mid-1940s when she was Peggy Wemyss, a student from small-town Neepawa, Manitoba, and he was a professor at the University of Manitoba,

teaching her a course on the poet Milton and seventeenth-century
thought. Their paths would keep crossing over the years, and they
became close friends as she became a distinguished novelist,
winning her first Governor General's Award for fiction in 1966.
He was a champion of Canadian literature as a critic, the editor
of the New Canadian Library, and an educator on three other
campuses. While teaching at the University of Toronto in 1967,
he tried to convince her to become writer-in-residence there. At
the time, Margaret was living in England with her civil-engineer
husband, Jack, and their two children, Jocelyn and David. In
refusing the position, the wife and mother – and, in her mind,
sometime writer – bared her soul to her former professor.

Elm Cottage, Beacon Hill,
Penn, Bucks.,
England.
24 Oct 67

Dear Malcolm:
If you have not already written to Dr. Bevan, please do not do so
– I feel tremendously apologetic about this change in plans, as you
and various other people have been so kind about trying to help
me to go back to Canada, but now find I can't do it. Sat up much
of last night wrestling with the problem, and came to the conclusion that I would simply not be justified in removing the kids from
Jack. Also think that he and I are more fond of one another than
anyone else is about either of us, so it is time for me to quit acting
so immaturely and to accept the fact that things don't happen
exactly as one would want them to, and I have been extremely
fortunate in having been able to combine writing with family as
much as I have, but cannot this time put my own interests as a
writer ahead of the interests of three other people, or perhaps four,

if I count myself as a non-writer, which I also am. Too bad this dichotomy exists, but it does, and all the nonsense which writers spout about any sacrifice being okay in the cause of Art just is not true, or not for me. It's okay for Irving Layton to say it doesn't matter who you kill as long as you produce one good poem, but personally I do not buy that point of view. It's all very well to apologize for one's presbyterian conscience and to see all the loopholes and to know that what is probably behind it all is the unwillingness to see oneself as a bitch, but there it is. I really cannot return to Canada while Jack is working in this country. I have to try to work out things with him. I am so terribly sorry that I've put you to all sorts of trouble re: this writer-in-residence bit. I need hardly say that I would have loved to have a stab at it, but this may only be the 40-year-old syndrome (I'm 41, actually) – trying to do a lot of interesting things before it is too late, not realizing that it is too late. So – apologies and thanks.

Best wishes,

Margaret

It wasn't too late. Shortly after Jack informed her their marriage was over, she took the writer-in-residence post in 1969. As she told another friend, the poet Al Purdy, she had to make a psychic change: "Back to self-image of professional writer . . . Actually, that being, as they say, the Real Me." In 1982, after she had won a second Governor General's Award, for The Diviners, *Peggy Laurence recalled for Malcolm Ross her days as a student: "Frankly, I can't remember whether I ever felt 'intimidated' by you, all those years ago at the U of M, or not. I don't think so . . . What I recall most is sitting around (or along) a huge table and discussing and arguing, and you challenging all of us to support our views."*

WITH BLUNT SWORD AND OAK CHAIR

Morley Callaghan always feared he'd be mostly remembered as the scrappy Canadian who decked fellow author Ernest Hemingway in a friendly Paris boxing match refereed by F. Scott Fitzgerald. He and the two-fisted American novelist had been friends since working together as reporters and hopeful creative writers at the Toronto Star in the 1920s. Ernest helped him publish some short stories and the two later reunited in Paris. Morley's reputation soon grew well beyond his prowess as a literary brawler when the twenty-eight-year-old prodigy published his first novel, Strange Fugitive, *in 1928. The books and short stories that followed drew international acclaim and the attention of Edmund Wilson, the esteemed American critic who in 1960 wrote that he was "unjustly neglected" and likened him to the Russian masters Turgenev and Chekhov. The two men became fast friends. In one of numerous letters they exchanged, Morley comments on a revised version of* The Scrolls from the Dead Sea, *Edmund's book about the Essenes, a Jewish sect that preceded Christianity.*

20 Dale Ave,
Toronto, July, 10, 69.

Dear Edmund,

It was distressing to hear about your tropical hangover, and recurring bouts with the thing must surely drag you down. We pray that you will find in Boston a doctor with the right touch. We had looked forward so eagerly to seeing you. Let's hope that some magic is at work some where and in a few weeks time you will find youself feeling so much better you'll cry out, "Bring my horse, Have it saddled at the gate." A man has to believe that things can suddenly change for the better. And why not? I have been feeding myself on this slogan for years. I read your book, and, of course, all the old speculations come into one's mind. And by the way there's some very vivid writing, quite aside from the information given, in that book. For example, the few pages at the beginning of the chapter, The Monastery, I kept looking at them and admiring them for as description they seem to be so easily done, they are just there, as a thing, an object is there, not to be noticed as description, the thing just there.

And reading the book in one piece your own view, your own temperament in reaction to their beliefs, emerges clearly enough. You say you are not a religious man. Religion is a bad word. Where there is a sense of mystery and wonder, and an awareness of the inexplicable there is something better perhaps than the thing nominally called religion. The Essenes seem to be a case in point. They had a rule and a strong sense of exclusiveness, but after all isn't this kind of thing just discipline, a way of putting a saddle on the human spirit which in the end may be destructive of all spirituality. And certainly I enjoyed the way you made it clear that as you saw it Jesus, the rule breaker, the careless fellow about these ritual drills, wouldn't have had much luck as an Essene . . . It always struck me that the notion that the world was a battle ground for a struggle between the Children of light and the children of darkness was murderous fantasy . . .

The other day, looking through some old papers I found a few letters from Hemingway, and one in which he told me that he had met you, and Scribners had just given him an advance of fifteen hundred dollars for The Sun Also Rises. He sounds so eager and hopeful as he was in those days . . . My own condition as a writer? Well, I remember, when I was in college, hearing Lloyd George who had come to America, making a speech, and he said, "I will go trecking into the wilderness with my blunt sword in my hand." That's me now, Edmund, and I'll come out of the wild[e]rness with something good.

All our love,

Morley

Two years later he was within the civilized confines of his own home in Toronto when he heard a noise and walked downstairs in his dressing gown to confront a well-dressed burglar claiming to be a tax collector. As the author examined the man's calling card, the intruder started slugging him with a leather billy club. The bloodied Morley Callaghan, in his mid-sixties, weighing in at 171, defended himself with a stout oak chair until the burglar beat a retreat.

Edmund Wilson (left) and Morley Callaghan (Courtesy Barry Callaghan)

20 Dale Ave,
Toronto, April 19, 71

Dear Edmund,

Tomorrow we are to go to Rome and Paris and now I find myself thinking of you and wondering how you are. I licked my wounds till they healed and find I have a lot of writing to do. Your son, to our regret, did not get in touch with us. I would like to have seen him. As for the burglar who beat my head with a blackjack, they have not caught him and I am not surprised. He was a really competent workman. It's a very odd feeling, standing there numb while a guy keeps swinging at your head. It's unbearably humiliating, the strangest experience of my life. Of course the thug had seen too many movies. In every movie I have seen a man hit from behind with a blackjack is knocked cold. I remained on my feet. The funny part of it was that the pain of the repeated blows was so stinging and shocking it actually began to revive me. A strange business. The doctors at the hospital said my adrenalin must have started pumping furiously. Anyway, after being hit about eight times I was much stronger than I had been after the first blow. It must be that it's my heart that's soft.

I understand you won't be going to Talcotville. Is this true, for soon I'll be going down that way.

All our love,
Morley

Edmund died the following year. Morley Callaghan went on to write six more books, including A Wild Old Man on the Road, *which was not a memoir but a novel about an aging man of letters who betrays the dreams of his youth. It was published when the author was eighty-five, two years before his death in 1990. Four volumes of his* Complete Stories *were recently released by Exile*

Editions, the publishing house run by his son, the writer, educator, and publisher Barry Callaghan.

THE PRISON OF DEPENDENCE

*The fiction of **Jane Rule** deals sensitively with friendship and love, particularly between women. But whatever their gender, most of her characters are richly drawn. When she received an Order of British Columbia in 1988, the citation read in part, "She is an observer of social and emotional relationships, and she writes with warmth and candour." Her first published novel,* Desert of the Heart *(which became the film* Desert Hearts*), tells the story of a liaison between two women – a Reno casino worker and an English professor – that evolves into a lesbian affair. Jane moved to Vancouver from the United States in 1956 and was soon joined by her partner, Helen Sonthoff, who became an English professor at the University of British Columbia (and is the "Helen" in the following letter). Jane is known as a prolific correspondent with other Canadian writers, including David Helwig, who in the early 1970s was teaching at Queen's University in Kingston and hadn't yet become a full-time author.*

March 18, 1972

Dear David:

I haven't heard from C_____ since he got back, but I have had a letter from B_____, and it sounds as if the trip did them both, separately, good. C_____ finished a story while he was here, a good one, and I hope he'll stick by decisions to get less involved with some of his projects and carve some time out for himself, both for writing and more easy goofing off. B_____ says they're moving out into the country again, and that in itself should create more space.

I think we are all people landed with the negative truth about long established patterns of living. How to make positive sense out of change is the job before us ('before us' like dinner, not like the future). I brood, having talked at length with B_____, for instance, who was here some days before C_____ and E_____ arrived, about how much of her sense of identity and self worth is in C_____'s hands rather than her own, how much, therefore, she must see problems as 'conflicting needs' rather than needs expressed as conflict. For C_____ it is not so much a matter of identity and self worth as of security and backing, which very soon can seem a kind-of prison. When B_____ asked me where I got my 'support', I said, 'a tree has its own roots'. I don't see how identity or security given over to someone else can finally have anything but negative value. I can only give or take freely when I know these aren't part of the exchange, but that is often practically baffling, hard to keep clear. Dependence is the jealous jail so many people live in, recognizing it but blaming themselves or each other rather than the dependence itself. Lots of people, of course, shouldn't try to live in close association, no matter how fond of each other they are, but I don't see how anyone can live for long with anyone else richly in the conventional definitions given. In a way, Helen and I are fortunate because we start without a lot of the bad trappings of roles, and neither of us can, even if we were tempted, draw strength from the other's public identity. It is good, reassuring, to discover that living unprotected in those ways is not at all difficult, gives much more air to breathe. Identities unhooked, we don't have to be threatened by and therefore critical of each other's different styles and attitudes and tastes. But threatened or tired or troubled, either of us can be tempted into immitation of that apparently more secure 'married' state. And the taking on of a house, mutual social commitments, families all tend to create images and expectations not only for us but for people around us. Helen-and-Jane, Jane-and-Helen. Children often take months to remember which name belongs to which. To keep respect for one's own and the other's freedom, right to grow and change, to keep enough territory of time and space open for that possibility is sometimes very difficult. But people not committed to that value seem to me either to break apart or to grow narrow and negative in a tiny world. I try hard not to honor 'long term relationship' for its own sake. I try hard not to see separation as 'failure'. I am so weary of the wrong guilt of people being asked to do the impossible for no good reason. But it's hard to talk, never mind to live, in terms outside so many habit forming expectations and judgements.

. . . Jane

Years later, as if echoing her partner, Helen Sonthoff said, "Neither one of us has ever really wanted to make a relationship with anyone who didn't stand as tall as we do. You like to walk with someone who's got legs that are long enough to keep up." Helen died in 2000, having lived with Jane for forty-five years.

THE FORGIVING HEART

*Patrick Lane had apologized for drunkenly – and publicly – slighting his friend and fellow west-coast poet **Patricia Lowther**. A thirty-seven-year-old mother of three daughters and a son, Lowther was a high-school dropout whose poetry was dazzling readers across Canada. Meanwhile, her nightmare of a marriage*

Patricia Lowther, circa 1973 (Ian Lindsay, *Vancouver Sun*)

*to the mentally disturbed Roy Lowther, a much lesser poet, was
ruled by his rage and physical abuse. Despite her own desperate
situation, Pat Lowther gave Patrick one of the gifts of true friendship: forgiveness.*

April 6, 1973

Dear Patrick,

You are quite right I do know you well enough not to have been
insulted. I guess what happened is that being just slightly sloshed,
you didn't say quite what you meant. I understood but others
didn't. There has been talk about it, and whenever I've heard it
I've tried to set it straight. I think some people just like to have an
excuse for feeling indignant. . . .

My kids are fine – fascinating and exasperating like all kids I
guess. As for Roy, I see no way out of continuing to live with him.
I've finally escaped the emotional bondage, much much too late.
Leaving would mean having to be a full-time mother with not time
or energy for writing or simply being the person I have to be. Some
people could do it but I know my limits. I'd end up so neurotic
and bitchy I'd be no good to my kids either. But living as a family
is dishonest and harmful too. It's the kind of situation psycholo-
gists devise to drive white rats crazy.

What a depressing letter to lay on you. oh well nothing lasts
forever. And it is objectively Spring, which helps. I'm going to be
creatively domestic, and paint my little girls' bedroom.

Best to you and Carol.

Love,

Pat

*Two years later, Pat Lowther had been elected president of the
League of Canadian Poets and was teaching in the University of*

British Columbia's Creative Writing Department. One autumn morning, her husband murdered her with a hammer and dumped her body in Furry Creek, north of Vancouver. Although she had been having an affair with another writer, friends felt it was her flourishing literary success that inflamed Roy Lowther. He died in prison in 1985. His wife's reputation as a poet, and as a beloved friend of so many Canadian writers, has been honoured in the League's annual Patricia Lowther Memorial Award.

BUCKING UP MAX

*In the 1980s, author **Farley Mowat** was in his sixties, living in an Ontario town he called Port Hopeless. His good old friend the novelist and humorist Max Braithwaite was ten years older, living in Port Carling, Ontario, and writing letters to Farley about his holidays in the southern "Excited States." Max, a winner of the Leacock Memorial Medal for Humour, had already written most of his twenty-five books, his radio and television plays, and his scripts for theatre and film, but in the year of this letter would publish* Max: The Best of Braithwaite, *followed three years later by the autobiographical* All the Way Home. *Farley had twenty-five books behind him, including the 1956 Governor General's Award-winning juvenile novel* Lost in the Barrens.

Dec. twenny. 83

Max, old Mugwump.

You sound low. And since I empathize, I know how, why and all that stuff. Me too. For a while I thought it was the gallumphing years, a natural decline of internal temperature. But I don't think so now. I figure we are all victims of a new syndrome, as the bloody

Farley Mowat (Courtesy McClelland & Stewart)

Docs would say. Loss of faith in the future of this bedeviled species of which, for bitter or for wuss, we are parts. I see it at every age level, and in every nook and corner of the human house where I may happen to peer. Except amongst those blessed of the blest, the dough heads and dunder logs of the idiota who wouldn't know a threat to mankind [i]f it clobbered them on their beer bellies.

There is a kind of shadowed look in peoples eyes, masked usually by a kind of hectic frenzy. I am reminded (although I wasn't there) of the way medieval Europe reacted to the plague. There is a fear upon us too vast and diffuse to be understood, and it unmans us. The active participants are bounding about like random atoms in an incandescent ball of gas (which they will likely shortly become) but you and I are past that stage. We sit on the periphery in the coolth and watch the madness wax. Well, well, I do ramble on. But be of good cheer, old friend, you and I and ours have given the Old Man a good run for his fucking money and while we may not be totally without repreach, we tried . . . goddam it, we tried to hold the show together.

I feel as you do about going on writing. It is sheer agony to go on working at Slaughter. Only my anglosaxon guilt complex keeps me at it all – can't waste all that time and labour, you know. But when its finished I have grave doubts that I'll ever write anything again for publication . . .

Problem is, as you so clearly know, if you and I don't write, what the hell DO we do? Wanna take up anarchy? Better than crocheting! Or we could become guru-gurus and minister (verbally) to the pre-menstrual crowd. Or we could just learn to sit around and watch it happen.

Or. And I don't know if it'll even work for me, so why am I suggesting it to you? We could cast back to earlier, and better times, and tell the story of our own sweet little selves. Not necessarily for publication (but publish if neccessary, sayeth Mackenzie McClelland) but just for the plain old <u>hell</u> of it. We could compete, to see which of us could tell the biggest, boldest lies. A kind of literary conversation on a nice low plane! <u>Born Naked</u>. Escape from now and here . . . all the way back to the womb-room. Well, I'm going to give it a go anyway.

. . . Jesus, Max, the real trouble is that everyone is confused up to their floating upper lobes. It ain't just us . . .

Meantime, mucho lovo to Aileen, and you too, you old horse.

F.

Max slipped out of the reins on March 19, 1995. Farley still resides in that town on the northern shore of Lake Ontario. Despite the doubt expressed in this letter that he would ever publish again, Farley had by 2003 finished thirteen books – two of which he mentioned here, Sea of Slaughter *and* Born Naked.

JACK IN A BOX

Jack Shadbolt, *the influential Vancouver artist and writer, once wrote a friend, "I like the idea of a correspondence – and I don't really care if it ever gets published, though it would be nice to* *think it was kept and might stand as a testament if the evidence behind one's work were ever required – a sheer, vain hope, to be sure, but aren't all we artists a little vain in this basic sense or we wouldn't project ourselves as indefatigably." Jack was a tireless correspondent with friends, in letters that often revealed the mental agonies he faced in creating his innovative landscapes, which melded modernism with themes from nature and native art. At the age of seventy-eight, he wrote from his vacation home to Joan Lowndes, a Vancouver visual arts critic whose diminishing sight would eventually lead to blindness.*

Gen. Delivery
Hornby Island, BC.
VoR 1Zo
July 7 '87

Dear Joan,

Here (alone for the time being) on Hornby Island, after an intense winter of deadlines etc., I have been suffering one of those ghastly periods of emptiness where one's sense of self-worth suffers a severe bruising. One tells oneself it won't last but it goes on and on as the days pass in futility and a sense of valuable life being lost and that maybe one has lost the edge, etc. – which brings me to the gist of this letter.

Feeling very low yesterday, before going to bed I was pulling out anything around that might awake a spark or offer me a re-assurance about my work (for without it – the work, I mean, I am lost) and I happened on the earlier copy of Vanguard which con-tained the section of your aborted book which dealt with me. I was so impressed with it (all over again, in fact – I must have told you at the time) that I felt I must drop you a note to convey once more my thanks.

This statement is so damned well done. It is written from inside my approach rather than from the critics' external evaluative approach which one gets subjected to so often. It is lucid, clear, and to the point and it reads amazingly well; and furthermore it has the quality of summarizing so much of my progression of pre-occupations that it is probably the best thing done on me so far. And I am more than grateful for it.

Perhaps part of my state is conditioned by having had to go through my entire back work during last year to help Gary Dault sort it all out and decide on the reproductions for the book he is doing but which has been delayed for a year because his manuscript was not ready. So much exhaustive self-examination as this has forced me into is at first a little exhilarating and flattering but gradually grows into a prolonged self-questioning and the inevitable staleness which leads to doubt. Where does one really belong? What has one accomplished? – all that sort of thing one should never be thinking about. The process is what matters and whatever will get you into it.

And therein lies the rub. Since the "subject" has disappeared out the painter's focus and he tries to go directly, but abstractly, to the "content," where does he start? And can he get to the "content" without the sense of "subject" which is his immediate attachment to life. I sit here in front of blank canvas and can't, for the life of me, begin. Common sense tells me I should be out drawing, making notes, as in the long-departed good old days: but one tends not to draw that way any more. It gets harder to work instead of easier. One feels so empty of connection.

And the confused state of things "out there" is no help. Everything is unsettled and seething. And I refuse to feel "old" if I can help it. But not for the sake of "being with it" but for my own artistic survival. I want to go out painting.

Well, enough of this caterwauling: I meant merely to thank you and wish you well. Your burden and [her husband] Harry's put me to shame. Mine is simply emotional indulgence. Yours is real. But perhaps, occasionally, you too are not immune to being told you have done a good job.

With best wishes to you both,

As ever,

Jack

The year he wrote this letter, Jack and his wife, Doris, an art historian and curator, established ten-thousand-dollar annual awards for two local Vancouver artists and a fifty-thousand-dollar grant given every five years to a British Columbian for outstanding cultural contributions to the province. The indefatigable Shadbolt died in 1998, at eighty-nine; he went out painting.

THE CHRISTMAS LETTER

*It's a rare Christmas letter that is as interesting to the reader as it is to the writer, and an even rarer one that can be read with interest by anyone else but patient friends, but **Peter Calamai** of Ottawa wrote such a letter in December 2003. Peter is national science reporter for the* Toronto Star *and adjunct research professor at Carleton University's School of Journalism. During his twenty years with Southam News reporting from around the world, he won three National Newspaper Awards. His journalistic honours, however, are less relevant to his Christmas letter than his Sherlockian credentials. Peter is a Master Bootmaker, an honour conferred by The Bootmakers of Toronto, the oldest and foremost society in Canada devoted to Sir Arthur Conan Doyle's Sherlock Holmes. He has*

several times had the honour of being invited by Wiggins, the leader
of the Baker Street Irregulars, to attend the New York society's
annual dinner. And he has written many scholarly articles for
Sherlockian society publications. His story in the style of Conan
Doyle "The Puzzle of the Vanishing Laboratory" was published in
the 2003 volume of the best new Holmes short fiction.

[December 2003]

The Suspicious Closure of the Wig & Pen

"I fear, Watson, that your decision to linger in the company of
Miss Morstan robbed you of a visit with our friends from Canada,
Mr. and Mrs. Calamai, who have only just departed."

This speech issued forth from the figure curled in the basket
chair in front of the blazing grate even before I had the opportunity to hang up my muffler. The remonstration continued as I
advanced, my fingers outstretched to the warmth.

I took the chair opposite and, once my pipe was drawing well,
asked Holmes the question he was so obviously expecting.

"What leads you to believe that I was with Mary Morstan this
afternoon, as indeed I was."

Holmes sighed audibly. "Another of my parlour tricks is called
for. And then no doubt after I have explained my deductions you
will comment on how obvious it all is.

"A man takes particular care with his toilet on a Sunday afternoon while saying that he is merely going to play billiards at his
club. He returns several hours later than customarily. From his
coat pocket protrudes a program from the Royal Academy where
the current exhibition is of paintings I have heard him dismiss as
mere dabs. He is in such distracted high spirits that he neglects to

wear his gloves on the walk home, leading to hands that instantly sought out the fire. And to top it all off, he is now smoking a tobacco blend of a highly aromatic nature intended, no doubt, to appeal to feminine sensitivities."

Somewhat sheepishly I glanced at the smoke curling from my pipe and joining with his to wreath the hearth.

"I own that I miss my old Navy cut, but Mary said that she found it too harsh."

Holmes laughed: "QED, Watson. QED."

To change the topic, I asked: "What news of Mr. and Mrs. Calamai?"

From Holmes's account it was clear that that admirable couple had enjoyed yet another event-filled year. There was an orgy of play-going with no less than three visits to the Canadian town of Stratford for Shakespearean performances and two outings to a town called Niagara-on-the-Lake for George Bernard Shaw.

"I gather from Mrs. Calamai's accounts that these visits also afford the couple the chance to spend time with friends and family who live some distance from the capital city on which so much centres, as it does here in London. Over-awed by the importance of Ottawa, these relatives and others are loath to venture there. So the Calamais regularly travel to small towns where their provincial friends will feel more at home."

"That seems to be quite self-sacrificing of them," I noted.

Poking at the coals with a fire iron, Holmes proceeded to describe a dizzying series of sojourns made during the year by the Calamais, separately and together. Occupational duties had taken Mr. Calamai to Denver, a dwelling of relatives in the state of Tennessee called Happy Cow Farm and Saskatoon, Saskatchewan, a locale which experienced the thundering herd of bison with which readers of my accounts in the Strand magazine will be familiar. On one such occupational trip, to an establishment called The Jackson Laboratory in Bar Harbor, Maine, Mrs. Calamai had accompanied her husband.

"On that topic he held my attention entirely, Watson, recounting the scientific investigations there which use mice to reveal the very essence of humans, something called our genome. It seemed obvious to me that mastering such genetic knowledge will be essential to the private consulting detective of today."

Not for the first time did I observe that my old friend, although in his 150th year, still regretted his retirement from active practice. It was little wonder that he had abandoned the quiet cottage near the Sussex coast to return to our snug rooms at 221B Baker Street. Being here meant, however, that he was forced to pass almost daily a bronze statute outside the Underground station which purported to be his likeness. Fortunately it was nothing of the sort, so Holmes could walk the byways without being recognized. His voice tugged me from this reverie.

"You may imagine my astonishment, my dear Doctor, when Mrs. Calamai informed me that she had rebuffed her husband's invitation to view laboratory mice genetically altered to give off a green fluorescence. I had always considered her one of the more sensible of her sex, but I may be forced to change my opinion."

Mrs. Calamai had, it turned out, displayed common sense enough to join her husband on the current visit to Britain during which they called in at 221B. Much of her time seemed to have been spent attending the theatre, although the play names which Holmes rhymed off meant little to me – *Democracy*, *Happy Days*, *Mourning Becomes Electra*, *Jumpers*, *His Girl Friday* and something called *Jerry Springer, The Opera*.

"A strange event occurred while that good woman was making her way between theatres, from a matinee to an evening performance. Many roads were closed to omnibuses because of protests against the visit of the President of the United States, so Mrs. Calamai was forced to walk up Fleet Street from Ludgate Circus.

"As she passed the Royal Courts of Justice, she asked a constable if the way was clear to pass over Waterloo Bridge to the National Theatre. The constable assured her that there would be no difficulty, because the protest march was bound for Trafalgar Square. Imagine Mrs. Calamai's surprise when she had traversed the few steps to the turn for Waterloo Bridge, only to discover that the march also was crossing that bridge."

"What did the poor woman do?" I asked.

"What else could she do. She joined with the marchers of course," Holmes replied. "Many were of her stately years so she had no concern for her own safety. But the erroneous information volunteered by the constable is highly suspicious."

"Likely the constable was brought in from outside London and unfamiliar with the streets."

"That was my thought as well Watson, until Mr. Calamai gave me this." He handed me a blue rectangle of cardboard.

The faded cover proclaimed "Wig & Pen Club" and inside a Life Membership in the name of Peter Calamai was dated July 16, 1973. A line drawing depicted the well-known building that dates from 1625 and is the only one on the Strand to have survived the Great Fire of London. Since 1951 it has been a celebrated meeting place for journalists and jurists.

"No doubt Mr. Calamai has spent many enjoyable hours at the Commonwealth Bar in the Club and I understand that the Dover Sole of the restaurant is highly regarded," I said, handing back the card.

"But no longer, Watson, no longer. On this visit Mr. Calamai discovered the Wig & Pen was closing in a week's time. The reason offered was the expiry of the lease, but I fear there are deeper waters here."

"Surely it is just what it seems Holmes. After all, the journalists have all moved away from Fleet Street and the collapse of Lord Black of Crossharbour no doubt meant the loss of a substantial expense account patronage."

"But consider the geography, Watson. The Wig & Pen is at 230 Strand, directly opposite the Royal Courts of Justice. From the roof an airgun would easily cut down some of the most powerful judges and barristers in the land, not to mention litigants.

"As well, we have the curious incident of the constable ignorant of London streets who was directly outside the Wig & Pen. It is too much to be a coincidence, Watson. The constable was almost certainly a look-out. Unless I am very much mistaken we will find the new lessee of 230 Strand to be none other than Professor Moriarity. Kindly collect your service revolver, my old friend, for there is not a moment to lose. Once again, the game is afoot."

Mature Love

"It seems like we have lived lifetimes together"

Incessant intercourse

William Smith – America's loss, Canada's gain – was born in New York in 1728, graduated from Yale University, and followed in his judicial father's footsteps by becoming chief justice of New York. A historian of the British colony, he stayed loyal to King George III while the American Revolution raged. But after George Washington marched into New York in 1783, William fled to London. Sir Guy Carleton, the governor of Quebec, was a friend and offered him the post of chief justice there. Janet, William's wife of thirty-four years, and their daughters remained in the new United States during the three years he was in England. Just days before taking the oath of office in Quebec, he wrote Janet in the fulsome prose of the day.

Quebec 28th Oct. 1786

What a Delight, my dearest Janet, to be able to date a Line to you within 600 Miles from you, after writing so many at the Distance of 3000! Our Departure from England had been tolled on to the worst Season of the Year, but the Arbiter of all Seasons gave us a Voyage as favorable as in the best. Thanks to his Mercy, and Praise to his Name! Your daughter and we had our Parting in London the 27th Augt. Our Embarkation at Portsmouth was on 29th. and our arrival here, after visiting Guernsey and one of the Western Islands, on the 22 Inst. Not a single Moment of Apprehensional! Every Convenience that could be desired on the Passage, and a very hospitable and joyful Reception at our Landing.

It would complete my Felicity, to have been able to recollect my little Flock about me, but that, if it was possible, I ought in Kindness to oppose, till I have a House, and that furnished; which can't be till the latter End of May; by which Time if you improve the Opportunities you have, & I have not, our Supplies may be had from the other Side of the Water, in the ships that leave England in March or April. I am now and till then shall be in Lodgings, and diet at the Castle, as often as I shall think it decent to accept of Lord Dorchester's friendly Invitation to do so daily till you arrive . . .

I have heard of, but not seen the House recommended for our Mansion here – but however lodged, you will want a House Keeper & Cook in one Character, and a Female Hairdresser, with under Drudges & two Men Servants (in Addition to the one I brought with me) with a Boy. Think well of this, & if you cannot find them at N York, let Mrs. Mallet have Directions to send them out to me with your Furniture, & direct her to contract firmly with them under the Eye of Mr. Rashleigh or Mr. Watson; for as with you so here, the European Poor find so many of their own Condition, as to forget their stations and Engagements . . .

. . . Perhaps your Orders to Mrs. M may not rise to the Sum comitted, & this will leave you Scope for a little finery for the Girls of the newest Fashions of which Madam Mallet is no indifferent connoiseur. The Ladies dress here much as in England when I left it, except that their hair is not down yet into flowing Tresses . . .

Remember me affectionately to all our Relations and Friends. They shall hear from me very soon and very fully. Keep yourself

Janet Livingstone Smith, wife of William Smith,
circa 1751 (Painted by John Wollaston, courtesy Janet Beale)

warm, take care of your Fires, deny yourself and my dear Girls no comfort. Let me hear from you often; as soon as the Lakes are frozen the Intercourse will be incessant, and there may be chance Opportunities thro' Vermont besides. I hope my Brother will resume his Correspondence. I can never be indifferent to the Condition of my native country. I always wished her Felicity. She has made it my duty to render another so, if it shall be in my Power, would to God I could spread a spirit of Benevolence over the whole Human Race.

Commend me to every Man, to every Creature of the same Disposition and to all in Particular, who have done themselves the Honor, to show you and my dear girls, and any of my Relations, the smallest Kindnesses in my Absence. Thank them all in my Name, and give me the Catalogue that I may not die in Debt if it be possible . . . Ever, ever, my dear wife, most affectionately your's

WS

William lived for only another seven years, dying at age sixty-five. As chief justice of Quebec he became known for his concept that, under the Quebec Act, either English or French law could apply in a legal dispute, depending on the language of the litigants involved. Dearest Janet, who had eventually joined her husband in Quebec City, died in 1819, at eighty-nine.

DELICIOUS ARMS AND LETTERS

*In 1874, **Colonel James Macleod** was assistant commissioner of the newly created North West Mounted Police when he led a great trek of Mounties west to Fort Whoop-Up, built by American whisky traders near present-day Lethbridge, Alberta. At the time,* *he was the smitten fiancé of Mary Drever, a merchant's daughter he'd met during the Metis people's Red River Rebellion four years earlier. James was impressed by the seventeen-year-old's brave action of slipping a vital message in the bosom of her dress and delivering it to the Canadian forces' commander. They married in 1876, but Mary saw relatively little of her husband as he travelled from fort to fort, became a circuit-court judge, and then a member of the North-West Assembly. Yet he was a faithful correspondent and a passionate one, as in this letter from Fort Walsh in what became Saskatchewan.*

[August 1879]

My own darling love, –

I am not going to date my letters any more for fear of getting scolded in the very dreadful way I was in one of the letters I got when I returned from Fort Macleod. You naughty old girl to use such dreadful words towards you[r] poor devoted old husband. That letter is carefully marked and when the others are read over carefully avoided, <u>unless</u> I am in a particularly spooney mood. Well never mind I suppose I deserve all I get and I daresay a great deal more, but you must remember all I have to contend against between annoyances connected with the Force and all sorts of things including the fact that my old <u>stumack</u> [stomach] will go back upon me sometimes and put me out of temper with every thing in the world – except you – Well dear darling pet since I last wrote you I have paid a visit to our dear little home.

We had such a hot journey with bad thunder storms almost every night and the mosquitoes were very, very bad. Poor Mr. Dewdney was annoyed almost beyond endurance . . . He used to wonder how I could travel along with out any protection only now and then wiping them off my neck. He got so irritated – but you know my placid temper is proof ever against the attacks of mosquitoes innumerable . . . Do you remember the place where <u>we</u> camped the night before we reached Macleod where we had such fun with Clark and Williams? I stood over the place where our tent stood and thought and thought of that pleasant night when every body else was suffering like the very mischief from the flies, and our happiness was not marred by the abominable pests. About 300 yards above this – where we crossed in 74 – I was determined to try so I sent Jerry [Potts, the scout] across first and then Wilson with his four went over, and all the wagons were across in half an hour without any difficulty.

Arriving at Fort Macleod I found that Mrs. Winder had fitted up a room in the Cottage so nicely for me. I found <u>our own</u> sheets on the bed and longed from the bottom of my heart everytime I got between them that they enveloped some one else too!!! . . . I used to take every opportunity of going into the old place and whenever I <u>possibly could</u> would extend my visit into the dear old room behind, where I have been happier than any where else, in my life, in the whole whole world. <u>Dear dear</u> darling girl who would not be happy with you? . . .

I went to the Blackfoot Crossing with Mr. Dewdney and didn't we just delight the heart of our old friends the Blackfoot with the meat and flour tea sugar and tobacco we took them. They have suffered awfully this last Winter and it is wonderful how well they have behaved. Crowfoot appears to have kept them all in check. We went thro' their camp and I rec'd a perfect ovation. Men women and children flocked round to greet me and shake hands. The women brought their children on their backs to shake hands and held out the tiny little skeleton hands for me to shake. I had I am sorry to say to submit to be kissed by old and young not only by the ladies but by a lot of <u>men</u> ugh!!! One old hag was not content

James F. Macleod, circa 1880
(Glenbow Museum NA-684-1)

Mary Macleod, circa 1880
(Glenbow Museum NA-684-2)

to touch my cheek but tried to get at my <u>lips</u> crunching her teeth as she did so. It nearly made me sick. Of course she did not succeed and they all laughed when I told them it was only my pretty young wife that kissed my lips. – I asked Dewdney to take a walk with me and led him up to where our old camp was. There were a lot of Indian lodges all about but just where our tent was there is a perfect bed of wild roses. I plucked a couple of them to send to you and just near by I picked a pretty white one. They are all in a jumble now, but still retain some fragrance. Darling it made me so happy to go back to this place but still I felt most awfully lonely and as if I would give the world to fly in a moment back to your dear delicious arms which I know are always open to receive me.

Mary darling I can't tell exactly why but I have been <u>wretched</u> ever since I left you, and I feel that you only can make me happy again . . . I hope you will come to [Fort] Benton like a good girl and await me in patience there, altho' I know you don't like the idea.

What a sweet almost overwhelmingly delicious letter I have just got from you. My sweet wife it gives me such endless pleasure to have you tell me <u>all</u> <u>all</u> about yourself. Won't I be glad to see you as you are. You know my opinions about this matter and that I would never have you otherwise than as God intended in the nature of things that you should. My only anxiety is about your suffering and I pray to Him night and morning that he may watch over you. I am so pleased to hear such good accounts of our little pet [their daughter]. I do so long to see you both and may Heaven grant we may never be separated so long again. With endless loves and heaps of kisses.

Your loving and devoted Husband
Jim

[PS] I send the roses in another envelope

They had been married fourteen years when he wrote to Mary from the North-West Assembly.

Regina Nov 16. 90

My own darling Mary
I can't tell you how delighted I was to get your dear, delicious letter this morning when I came down to breakfast. It was so much more cheery than the last one . . . I [received] the photos all right . . . I never saw a more perfect picture of a perfect woman. It is simply you (the full face). How often have I seen you look just like that when I have drawn you into my arms. It is before me now & I feel an almost overwhelming desire to clasp it & hug it as I have so often done with the darling original. Mine I suppose

is like me. I like the ones with the gown on best. The children are simply perfect. Every time I come into the house I get out these pictures & place them on the table as I walk up and down, but it is yours and yours only that catches my eye every time I pass & not only my eye, my pet, my lips have some way caught the fascination and don't they now yearn for something warmer and sweeter than this pretty picture!!

I was rather tickled at your saying that I only had Julia [a servant?] when I felt naughty. Pretty good old girl. She has not sat on that sofa with me yet.

. . . There is nothing particularly new about the Assembly. I took the chair all Friday afternoon but nothing of any consequence transpired. I have a very strong desire to resign. In fact my resignation is written out but I will sleep over it, would to Heaven it was to be with you. With fondest & best love to my sweet wife and her three little beauties.

I am as ever

Your own

Jim

Four years after writing this letter, Jim died of Bright's disease, a kidney ailment. In another letter he'd told Mary that he had no inclination to tickle any other woman than her under the table: "My fingers tingle to be able to do it now. Alas I can't!" The couple's voluminous correspondence was so intimate for the Victorian era that she ordered him to destroy all her responses, which he did.

GOOD-BYE, SWEET FRANCES

Mature love often means having to say you're sorry. **Dr. Norman Bethune**, *born in Gravenhurst, Ontario, would become revered for his selflessness in two major wars of the 1930s. He created the first mobile blood-transfusion service for republican troops during the Spanish Civil War. He was later a heroic battlefield surgeon for Mao Zedong's army during the Japanese invasion of China. In between he was famous in Canada as a thoracic surgeon treating tuberculosis (TB) patients. But he was less successful with the women in his life. After developing TB and believing himself doomed, the doctor insisted on divorcing his Scottish wife, Frances Penney. He recovered and the two had a second tumultuous marriage – only to divorce again. When Frances later wed the "R.E." of this letter, Norman wrote to apologize for his treatment of her and to announce his resolve to end their relationship forever. His letter was obviously designed to be shown to her jealous spouse.*

Sunday, Feb. 11/34.

Frances: –

Thank you for your letter. I see your confusion of mind, body and soul and since, within the past 3 months, my ideas have clarified, today I think I may be able to put into words what I believe to be the truth.

Truthfully and sincerely I believe I want nothing more from you. Not I as a man, physically nor as a soul – spiritually. I believe we have had all the profitable commerce between us that is possible, and nothing more is to be gained by prolongation of our relationship. It never at any time completely satisfied either of us – let us make no more attempts. I regret nothing of the past that has

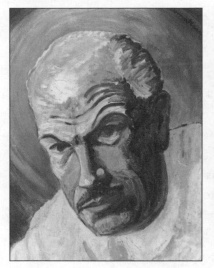 

Norman Bethune, a self-portait painted circa 1935 (Library and Archives of Canada PA-160629)

Beth's portrait of Frances Penny Bethune (National Film Board of Canada/Library and Archives Canada PA-116911)

happened between us except one thing – my essential masculine stupidity on the non-recognition of reality – and my fumbling attempts to change a fantasy into a fact.

Forgive me, if you can. I am truly sorry for the unhappiness I have caused you. I was like a clumsy and furious gard[e]ner, hacking away at a tree, a living tree, in an attempt to make it conform to a preconceived and fantastic design of his own. I tried to bend you, to re-make you, not recognizing you as you are, but only with the sort of genetic, stupid male idea of you as woman. Any women – and not as a woman, a special kind of woman called Frances Campbell Penn[e]y. I know now you must be taken only as you are. You are not to be changed. Either a man must take you as you are or he will destroy both you and himself in the attempt to change you.

Well, I am not going to do that. Because of my love for you, I am not going to do that. I believe you must be left alone and then you will flower in peace and quiet and give peace and quietness to those about you. But no persuasion, no aggression of others, and on your part, most important, no attempt to change yourself to please another.

There would be no need for us to part completely if R.E. would abandon his suspicions – suspicions of both you and I. I am not the cause of the disharmony between you two. I am no rival. He has nothing to fear from me. He has only to fear himself. He said at your marriage he accepted the idea of the spiritual relationship between you and I. He must accept it, or it will destroy him. He must accept what you and I have been to each other in the past. It does him no harm. Only egotism forbids acceptance of that.

And you must spend your life acting in [t]he true, internal deep compulsion of your own spirit. You must give up trying to conform to another's idea of you. Do as I do – if I can say that – be yourself and <u>don't try to please people.</u> For you that only results in self-mutilation. If they do not accept you as you are – remove yourself, let them go, – or go yourself. Only live with those who respect the spiritual and physical necessities of your nature.

The tragedy of it all is this – that between the two of us – R.E. and myself – two men who protest they love you – we have torn you, violated you and will, if we persist in our present course, distort or destroy one of the sweetest natures that God ever made. Well, I will do my part – I will leave you alone.

I accept gratefully what you once gave me, and now ask you nothing more. That is the only way I can show I love you. I can do nothing for you except leave you alone, entirely. We must die to each other. For peace between you and R.E. You and I must die to each other. Let us remember it only as a dream.

Good-bye, my sweet Franc[e]s. I loved you once and to prove it, I will leave you now. Let us part. Good-bye.

Beth.

P.S. Show this letter to R.E. I have written it as truthfully and sincerely as I am able. A truthful and sincereley soul will accept it as such.

B

In 1937, Norman wrote another letter of farewell to a woman named Elizabeth, in which he expressed "fear for myself that you penetrate my defences once more, as you did once," and said prophetically, "My road ahead is a strange & dangerous one. You can not come with me." The following year he went to China to become the Red Army's medical chief in their war against Japan; he died there in November 1939 from blood poisoning.

Clown and lover

Northrop Frye may have been one of the world's great literary theorists – for his studies of Shakespeare, William Blake, and the Bible, among many others – but this Canadian intellectual giant considered himself a rudderless incompetent without his wife. She was Helen Kemp, who met him at Toronto's Victoria College when he was nineteen and she was twenty-one. They became lovers, and Helen had an abortion in the summer of 1936 (he sent her fifteen dollars to help pay for the procedure, arranged by her mother and performed by a doctor). Twenty-four when he wrote the following letter, Northrop was studying in Oxford while Helen remained

in Canada. Although they didn't marry until the following year,
he referred to her as his wife – their five-year relationship had
become mature and loving.

Paddington

8 October 1936

My little girl:

Two days ago it was your birthday, and I wanted very badly to
write to you, but I took a warm bath in a cold room, and it's been
headache, wretchedly sore eyes and a vacant mind, so no letter
got itself written. I think of sending you greetings on your birthday rather than a week or so before it, because naturally celebrating your birthday comes more appropriately from one who gives
thanks every day that you got born than from you yourself.
Besides, it's as much my birthday as yours. Exactly a year ago –
again a delay of two days! – you came back to Toronto, and by
doing so made yourself my wife, and by becoming my wife ended
my adolescence. I mean by adolescence the period in which I collected materials for building the sort of life I was cut out to build.
I had the materials; I knew in a general way I was a pretty froggy
sort of tadpole and would never turn into anything different, and
I knew I would do the sort of things I had to do no matter what
happened. But the point is that a life to be any good has to mean
something to the person who lives it as well as to other people,
and I couldn't find anything that would give my capacities any
value or meaning to <u>me</u> until I was sure of you. Now I'm all right
– I can go ahead building and planning. You have the power to
destroy that building at any time, if it pleases you, but until then
at any rate I am secured by knowing that everything I can achieve
in contributions to "culture" or "the intellectual life" or whatever

abstraction you please, as long as I can keep pouring them out, has another name, and that name its real name, Helen.

So, while I am desperately lonesome for you, I am not lonely. I don't mean only that I have enough people to talk to and enough to occupy me, though that enters, but also that what I am doing here grows naturally out of my love for you, as well as out of my own urge to advance, the desire of Victoria College to have English-trained professors, or the will of God or the pattern of twentieth-century thought. All these other things are admirable enough, but I shouldn't care to be left alone with them. It's bad enough to have to sleep by myself, without taking a Purpose to bed with me, personal or impersonal. But you're part of the scheme now, and everything that happens, if it fits in with the fact that I love you, is all right.

Why do I protest so much? Partly because I am a little nervous at seeing you holding my happiness in your volatile and temperamental little hands. Partly because I am one of those people who have to give some form of expression to their feeling or burst. And of course I may be simply dramatizing myself, overwhelming you with flatulent words and egotistic emotions over a comparatively simple matter. That is your own opinion – or at least it has been your opinion – so I have gone into it more carefully and from more points of view than you ever did. And what emerged was: it is quite true that I sound like an intolerable prig and am making an abject fool of myself continually. And I don't care; and I shall never care. I don't mind if you laugh at me and say to yourself: "That's Norrie hypnotizing himself again." Because a love which is dignified can never be more than liking or respect: love itself is ridiculous and grotesque, like the sex act itself. I could hardly be a lover without being a clown first. That is because I am blissfully and completely in love with a very real woman. Why do they say "head over heels in love" if they don't mean that a lover will do absurd things, like writing absurd letters to bore his sweetheart with?

I go up to Oxford tomorrow, travelling light because I love you.

Norrie.

Helen was working at the Art Gallery of Toronto and was a live-in don at a women's residence at Victoria College when she responded to Norrie's renewed avowal of love.

October 22. 1936.

My dearest, your letters are coming right along now, and I am so glad you are writing to me often, it does help the separation a little . . .

[After giving a roundup of her activities, she writes] I am awfully tired and must turn in soon. There is no use, this year I can not

Northrop Frye and Helen Kemp Frye, wed on August 24, 1937
(Victoria University Library, Toronto)

afford to get too exhausted because each day is as strenuous as the one before it. I wish I could hold your hand and go to sleep peacefully. I don't stop to think much of how far away you are, I don't dare. I just go around with you on street cars and go for walks with you along University Crescent in the evening and think of how much you would like it. And I'm always very happy thinking about you and how nice you are. BUT BY THE WAY – how DOES the lemon yellow sweater look??? It sounds just a bit weird to me, but perhaps Oxonians dress that way. Also – PLEASE be careful of your haircuts – I really do mean that . . .

ANYHOW, I'M SENDING YOU A LOT OF LOVE

I SEEM TO BE GETTING INTO THE WRONG
SEASON, BUT THEY'RE ALL THE SAME SO FAR
AS YOU'RE CONCERNED. BESIDES, YOU'RE NOT
A CLOWN. WHAT IF I SHOULD CABLE THIS, –
I'M JUST A LITTLE NUTS. HELEN.

Helen Frye continued her work in education at the Art Gallery of Toronto and later became an editor with Canadian Forum *and the* Toronto Star Weekly *before overseeing women's organizations at Victoria College when Norrie became its principal. She died in*

1986 and he five years later, renowned as one of the twentieth century's pre-eminent English scholars and literary critics, and a valued observer of Canadian society and culture.

WARM HEARTS, WARM TOES

Gérard Rochon, a pharmacist in Tecumseh, Ontario, first met and fell in love with Eulalie Langis when she was eighteen, a piano and violin teacher, and a pianist with a band called The Acme Five. Six years older, he decided to wait a little and then proposed to her when she was twenty (on the same night his rival, a podiatrist, unsuccessfully asked for her hand). Their passionate relationship almost ended when she cut her long, black hair. The couple hoped to have ten children. They had been married for sixteen years when **Eulalie Rochon** *was in hospital in Windsor, Ontario, and wrote Gérard after the birth of their seventh and second-last child.*

In the hospital
Christmas Eve. [1943]
7. p.m.

My dear husband,
Our first Christmas Eve apart, but what a beautiful separation! Neither of us are alone. I have left you our six darlings and I have with me the new one God has sent me. She has just left me, having partaken of a hearty dinner, followed by having her little feet held in my hands till they were rosy pink. Sometimes I find her toes cold and have the pleasure of warming them up. She's a sweet cherub dear, I am very anxious to be taking care of her.

And how are you feeling my darling? Anxious for me to be warming your toes too? A week from tonight I shall act in that

Eulalie Rochon with baby Pauline, born in December 1943 (Courtesy Pauline LeBel)

capacity. What a New Year's Eve that will be! As I write, I have your picture before me, holding Pierre as a baby. I musn't look too long. It makes my heart ache a bit, it is so like you, the very dear lovable you!

You should see me now, practically surrounded by flowers. Everyone has been so kind, considerate in every way. It seems almost too much to be done for one person. I had offered [Sister] Bernadette any of my flowers or plants she might like to have to adorn her altars, and she has sent for the beautiful basket of red carnations. I think it is going to be very impressive here at midnight. There will be Mass in the chapel, after which Holy Communion will be brought to our rooms, and I am told the Sisters sing Christmas carols in a body, walking through the corridors. I went to Confession and am Receiving for poor dear Grand Mother Rochon.

Well my dearest, I have reached the end of the page, and have not yet told you how much I love you! But of course, you have estimated it as you were reading, and you are right, <u>With all my heart and soul, all my life!</u>

Your wife,

Eulalie

On the flap of the envelope she added: "I.L.Y. Just for old time's sake, I had to write this here. And I have heard it said, one can not write a love letter after several years of marriage. That is not meant for a love such as ours is it dear? I am so anxious to be with you." Their baby was Pauline, who remembers the first sound she heard was her mother playing a George Gershwin tune on the piano. Eulalie died in 1975, aged sixty-nine, Gérard in 1994, at ninety-four. Pauline Le Bel, as she came to be known, grew up to be a prominent singer and writer based on the West Coast.

COUPLES

Barry and **Nina Callaghan** met at a Toronto nightspot, where she was bearing a Christmas turkey on her shoulders. Afterwards they played chess and she let him win. They got married and had a son, Michael (Mischi). Nina worked in radio for the Canadian Broadcasting Corporation (CBC). Barry, the son of celebrated author Morley Callaghan (see page 146), was a writer, books editor for the Toronto Telegram, and a journalist for CBC Television. He was reporting from Jerusalem when he met and fell in love with an American actress named Saya, who had moved to Israel and done her required military service in the navy. On July 20, 1969, their sixth wedding anniversary and the day the first man landed on the moon, the Callaghans were on Cape Cod with friends, artist Bill Ronald and CBC producer and director Paddy Sampson. That night, Barry and Nina agreed to separate after a twelve-year relationship and, he recalls, "We made love in the moonlight on the wet sand for the last time." Soon after, she wrote to his parents from their vacation home.

[1969]

Dear Morley and Loretto –
The situation here has been and is one such that not even John
Updike would touch [his novel, *Couples*, appeared the year
before]. In one half of the house are Barry, myself and Mischi and
Bette [a friend]. And you know what our situation is like! Next
door Bill has been depressed and despondent since our arrival –
partly because of his artistic career and partly because of the
impending arrival of his mistress and her husband. Before they
came, Barbara (Fefferman) arrived for a ten-day stay. At the same
time Paddy Sampson and a female acquaintance drove down.
Paddy's companion was a striking girl with a face which was edged
in great sorrow most of the time. We discovered that she had to
give up her 2-year child some four years ago to her ex-husband
and now had visiting rights twice a month. It was sad to see her
watch Mischi with such hungry eyes and at times reach out to
caress his cheek (much to his annoyance & embarrassment). But
Paddy was great fun and a source of much energy.

As for Barry & myself, it is very difficult to describe. For the
first week here, he was very withdrawn and moody, but writing
like mad. I would fluctuate between sorrow and some sense of
relaxation. But as I came down here with no hopes of winning
him back, I've been feeling quite lost, not knowing what I was
supposed to be. There was a period where Bette did all the cooking
and catering for him. Most of the time I can reconcile myself to
our separation, but at night time, especially after a few drinks, I
find the thought so unbearable and cruel that it's hard to keep
myself under control.

I kept wanting to leave for home before the 20th of July
because that's our sixth wedding anniversary and I felt that I would

completely collapse on that day. But as Barry and I had been getting along quite easily for the previous days, we decided to go out on the 20th. It was a lovely evening, touched now and then with tearful memories. But it ended drastically as I tried to keep up my spirits with mixing the drinks. I have felt great sorrow for Barry in having to leave a woman who made him happy and felt that he must resent my being here instead of her. How could I fight to hold him after knowing about her, and his telling me that he can't live with me and must break off. I imagined that he knew what he wanted and how to go about getting it. I found out tho, that he is in as much pain as I about the separation but he has to do it. But oh how hard it is for me to give up 12 years – only the will says, go ahead.

Enough of my woes. Let me tell you about Barry, the son you seem to have misunderstood these past few years. Barry is almost the opposite of you, Morley, and Michael [Barry's brother]. Whereas you two are reasonable men, Barry is not. Witness his manoeuvrings of his careers at the Tely and University. Against yours and Michael's sane directions, Barry did what he had to do and won the positions he was after. What wounds me, and who knows how much greater is Barry's sorrow, is your complete rejection of Barry's writing this year in the paper. Instead of judging his pieces, you are more concerned with what the readers will think of them. But then you are a reasonable man. He has written some beautiful essays and memories, which you, as an artist, have stubbornly refused to accept and see. And your comment on the [poet John] Montague work was most deplorable. For heaven sakes, don't look at it in terms of a newspaper article, but as your son's development into the kind of literary artist he feels he is and must become. I know you are imprisoned with your novel, but must you be so blind to Barry's sense of his achievements. But

Morley is a reasonable man. I remember what Kosso said about you and Michael. 'They have cultivated the appearance of outrageousness, especially Michael. But Barry is the mad one.' And as one who is tormented and just surfacing over his black moods, he must be looked on with different eyes . . .

I think you would be most surprised and pleased with Barry here. He is just writing, writing and writing all the time.

I have waited many years for this onrush and am thankful to be here at the onset. I am proud of him . . .

. . . Please excuse me for berating you too much, but I can't stand by and watch your relationship with Barry dissolve because of lack of understanding.

Bette remains constant and content, Mischi demanding and happy & things really aren't so bad. Write if you can.

Love, Nina.

When Barry and Saya ended their relationship not long after, Barry moved in with a television colleague, a visual researcher and artist named Claire Weissman Wilks, the mother of two sons and two daughters. In 1998 Barry published his memoir, Barrelhouse Kings. *The acknowledgements begin: "Nina Callaghan, whose editorial intelligence, humor and devotion to this text has exceeded anything I have known."*

Afloat on Love and Tears

They met in wartime Canada, on a troop train from Winnipeg to army camps in Ontario in 1944. Tom Hubbard, a tall, blond, quiet fellow, was on his way to take tank training, and the blonde, blue-eyed eighteen-year-old Jean Brims to do basic training with

*The 1947 wedding day of
Tom and Jean Hubbard
(Courtesy Jean Hubbard)*

*the Canadian Women's Army
Corps. They corresponded for
the two years he was overseas
and were married after the war,
when he earned a forestry degree
at the University of British
Columbia. The Hubbards had a
son and two daughters. "Life
was good," she recalls. "Then a
hip operation in 1969 ended in
cancer and Tom having his leg
amputated. He surprised all of
us by getting right back on his
'feet,' returning to work and the
daily family routine." But the
following May, he was back in
hospital as cancer reached his
lungs. Fearing the worst, **Jean Hubbard** wrote him a letter on old
ship's stationery from the Japan Line.*

June 1970

Darling:

I'm writing on "ship's" paper because looking back over the years
I realize my ship has come in many times. Our trips to Manitoba,
your folks, Yellowstone, Niagara Falls, Disneyland, etc., are all
happy "cruises".

Life has been good since I met you. You committed yourself
the first time on the train. You asked "Can I buy you a cup of
coffee?" and you tightened the knot when you wrote to Kitchener
shortly after I got there.

The years since we have been married have gone swiftly and happily. Our children (fighters three) have been a part of you I could cling to when you were away.

Now it's time to test our strength and love. I know the roots are deep and strong, nourished by love and companionship. They will weather the storm.

Take my hand in yours, hold tight. You'll never walk alone – I'm by your side.

I'll get by as long as I have you.

Always forever

your

Jean

XOXO

After Tom read the letter, she noticed the ink was smeared and asked him if he'd spilled water on it. "No," he said, "I cried when I read it." He died that July. Although she remarried in 1981, "I look at the tear-stained letter," she says now, "and know we were blessed to have twenty-three happy years together. My words and his tears and our children are our legacy of love."

As the song ends

"When a man despairs, he does not write; he commits suicide," wrote George Monro Grant, the Canadian educator and Presbyterian minister. "K," a well-known western Canadian writer approaching seventy, was so physically and mentally debilitated that he no longer wanted to live. He warned his wife, "C_____," of his decision, leaving only the time of his death unspoken. Before

taking his own life in the 1970s, he prepared a detailed typewritten note for "C" offering advice about what to do when she found his body and some words of what he hoped would be comfort. If a suicide note can be loving, his was. (Some details have been changed to protect his identity.)

C_____

Though I have, as you know, done my best to prepare you for the action I've taken today in order to lessen the shock, I know shock is inevitable. Especially for you whose "Hope springs eternal in the human breast." While my "Hope oft deferred maketh the heart sick." Probably I have for some time been "sick" physically, mentally, emotionally.

Looking back on our 29 years of partnership, I would not want any other spouse than you. For me you have been the best possible partner. Our marriage has, from the beginning, been a partnership; an unusual one, but great!

Your innate resilience will at this time come to your rescue. Good. Continue with your love of life which to me has been so helpful. Do not mourn. If the mourning doves return next Spring to nest in one of our trees, welcome them for me too.

Though, as you know, I did give away my Plan Ahead button to M_____, I have done my best to plan my departure in an orderly manner.

In this regard I suggest that you:

1. Phone the RCMP as the Force is concerned with enforcing the Criminal Code of Canada and in the code are several sections to do with suicide. This should facilitate the issuance of a death certificate . . . To the member of the Force who appears as the result of your request, hand to him one carbon copy of my signed statement: "A final note to C_____, my wife and colleague . . ."

2. Retain the top copy and have Xerox copies made to hand to, or mail to, those individuals who may be interested in the "why" of what to them may seem to be my sudden departure. This is to save you from having to make repetitive explanations . . .

As I write this there is running through my head the melody of that somewhat nostalgic and lovely Russian folk song, You are always Beautiful. And this is how I think of you.

K

A final note to C_____, my wife and colleague, for whom I have love and respect, and who, I think, understands me better than anyone else, and who may wish to make use of this brief explanation of the action I have decided to take.

At the age of 68 my physical condition has deteriorated, in certain ways, beyond repair.

Perhaps not entirely unrelated to this condition, my mental-emotional attitude is such that I have no further interest in staying around as one more contributor to a misuse of science and technology – a misuse that appears to be headed for mass suicide on a global scale, possibly to be preceded by a disintegration of relatively orderly human affairs due to unprecedented psychological pressures.

Yet more depressing is the irreparable damage being done to the balance of nature. In this regard, each Springtime and Summer, I have seen and heard less and less songbirds – the songbirds I have long loved.

However, what I have so far said may be no more than a rationalization. So perhaps I simply should have said I no longer have the will to live and see no purpose in lingering.

If, after the incident of physical death, it becomes revealed to me that there is a personality survival, there may come a time of reunion with those I have been close to when they too, in the course of time, find themselves disembodied.

K

K's wife sent a copy of this note to a friend, saying, "I could not ask K to alter his decision. And while it was not a surprise, the shock was still a shock and I am missing him . . . We scatter the ashes here on Sunday when old friends will gather and possibly exchange some good thoughts." The notes from K and his wife are in the National Archives of Canada.

THE MAN BEHIND THE MASK

In the world of hockey, where the unusual is not uncommon, goal-tender Jacques Plante may have been one of the most extra-ordinary characters of all. He was the National Hockey League (NHL) goalie who pioneered both roving out of the crease and regularly wearing a mask. But he was also a different drummer on the road, where he read literary classics, did embroidery, and even knit the famous wool tuques he wore. He also enjoyed ballet and was part owner of a hairdressing salon. And at night, in the loneliness of hotel rooms during the three decades of his career with four NHL and two World Hockey Association teams, he wrote love poems and letters to his second wife, Swiss-born Caroline Raymonde Plante. The seven-time winner of the Vezina Trophy as best netminder retired as a player in 1975 and split his year between living in Sierre, Switzerland, and coaching in North America. He kept penning romantic odes to his wife, as the fifty-three-year-old did in this letter written while travelling.

The Hilton Hotel of Philadelphia

Monday February 2, 1981
Past midnight

Hello dear,

Do you love me? As much as I love you? . . . You know who I am; do you recognize my handwriting; and my ink? And yes, it's me who wrote you soon after the film "Little House in the Prairie".

Since that letter, my love has grown. The evening is over and I am still thinking of you. You believe me, I hope.

I even have your photo on my night table at the head of my bed, not on the dresser in the middle of the room. Why? Because I want to see you close by just before turning off the light and to find you again all smiling in the morning when I open my eyes.

In this way, I dream of you all through the night and I think of you all day long. What's more, I have several photos of you in my wallet and one of them I have in the first sleeve, so that I see you each time I have to open it. I change the photo from time to time. You are so beautiful in the three photos. The smallest, the one from the trip to Lake Louise, attracts me the most. It reminds me of a beautiful trip which took me far from the Nordiques and their problems [in the World Hockey Association's 1973–74 season] and marked the beginning of a new life for the two of us. You stopped working and spent the winter with me after having sent our furniture to Switzerland.

And yes, in Switzerland where our trip continued for five beautiful years and where we had a small love nest in a small, out-of-the-way corner of this big place which is the world.

Unbelievable, when I think of it. We found each other in this immensity where more than four billion people live. On an artificial island, you were waiting for me and opened your heart to me. The seed germinated slowly and our love has produced two beautiful flowers that smell sweet and are never parted. They were well transplanted, these flowers, several times to Toronto, Boston, Québec, Edmonton, and to Switzerland without being separated. Their roots have been intertwined through two rings and they are inseparable.

I adore you and . . . good night.

I am happy. Thank you.

> Your little husband,
> Jacques

In January 1986 Jacques signed on as special goaltending instructor for the NHL's St. Louis Blues. A month later he died of stomach cancer. Caroline continues to live in Switzerland, where she keeps his ashes. She plans to have them and her own ashes cast from a Swiss mountaintop after her death. Meanwhile, "I live as if he is here beside me," she says. In her mid-sixties, she has been living a full life, recently leaping by parachute from an airplane in Tunisia – "Jacques would say, 'This is my wife.' "

JOY AND SHOCKING BEAUTY

*In early 1993 **Jane Eaton Hamilton** was giving a reading of her short story that won a prize in a contest sponsored by the Vancouver-based literary journal* Prism International. *An Ontario-born writer of fiction and poetry, she was a single mother of two daughters aged eleven and fifteen, and an out lesbian. That evening she had a drink with the journal's editor, who confided that his wife, **Joy Masuhara**, thought she was a lesbian. As the* *three of them became friends, the two women fell in love, "as awkward and alarming as these things are," Jane recalls. The trio continued their friendship even when the then-childless Joy, a third-generation Japanese-Canadian medical doctor, moved in with Jane and her daughters less than a year later. During their courtship and cohabitation, they have put their love in writing through notes, cards, letters, and more recently e-mails.*

Feb 1995

When I breathe in, taking your exhaled breath back inside my lungs, I can feel our love physically, through the barrel of my chest, as if an angel has me down on the floor and is puffing bits of divinity into me, warm and rich and healing. The air I breathe is carrying spoors of pleasure. The sensation isn't quiet. It's big and rackety. This is no goody-two-shoes angel – my chest expands and churns until it feels like I have a mass of whirling stars under my ribs. I have you under my ribs.

Mom called from Key Largo. I said it was raining all the time here, but that I didn't mind. She said, "You don't need sunshine. You have Joy."

11/1/96

The last thing I should be doing is writing to you, Joy, when I am only in the break between novels and it's nearly two. But I can't stop thinking about you . . .

Why I think about you, of course, is the plethora of gifts you've given me these couple of weeks. The dozen white roses, the bagel chips pinned to my bulletin board, the books, the angel sconce, the mirror – which, by the way, is absolutely exquisite – and I think about how happy I am to be with you and I think about the great good fortune involved in the simple, complicated act that was falling in love with you, and I am left speechless. Lucky, lucky me. And no one knows. No one else is inside this good and nurturing relationship. No one can know. I think of K – and B – probably on the rocky shores and what good women they both are and how still they're on the rocky shores and I think, oh God, why? Why me? But then why not, for once?

Thank you, thank you, from the bottom of my spongiform heart, Joy, just for being the woman you are, and looking after me while I do this intensive [work], and just for being yummy. I feel spoiled and like I'd like to spend the (sunny) day curled up in bed with you. just relaxing into what we feel.

But alas.

J.

Joy later sent Jane a card with a photo of a very old woman stretching.

Hey honey bunny, bull bunnykins, ding-dong d'amour etc etc:

This is what we'll both be like when we're 80 and living somewhere south and swinging with the best of them. I will likely be addled enough to call you things like "Foofie". We'll bomb around on our matching scooters giggling like schoolgirls and when everyone's looking I'll grab your boobs (somewhere near your waist) and plant a big slobbery kiss on your dentured mouth. Your smile will be perfect and I'll still be perfectly in love with you.

Yours forever,
♡ Joy

In early February 1998, tests showed a lump in Joy's breast. Jane wrote her a Valentine's Day card.

I know Feb. is a long, tough month for you, made worse this year. But I want you to know, if it helps, how much I care for you. Not just the love part, which is extreme, but the regular, everyday admiration. Because you're such a good woman – intelligent, funny, generous, thoughtful, kind. A good partner. No matter what happens, Joy, know that these five years with you have been the most invigorating and satisfying of my life. You've taught me the meaning of partnership – of love.

All my love now and forever,

J

Joy recovered after having a mastectomy and chemotherapy. In May that year, in a message marking their fifth anniversary as a couple, Jane wrote, "I love you as a one-breasted amazon warrior more than I did when you were a 90-pound heterosexual weakling, and you can shoot your arrows my way any time of the day or night. I am simply smitten." On Mother's Day 1999, the second May after Joy legally adopted Jane's biological children, Joy sent a letter to Jane.

For my amazing co-mother. Happy Mother's Day. It is an honour to share parenting with you. You have given me the gift of children. Daughters to admire, to laugh with, to worry about, to be proud of, to be angry with, to hope for, to share with, to love. I always wish I could have started parenting with you earlier – the experience has been so rewarding and I'm sure it has made me a better person. I remember when parenting was on my fret list. It isn't anymore. It's just another wonderful part of the incredible richness of our lives together. I hope we remain this wealthy for a long, long time. I love you, co-mom. Thank you for everything.

xoxoxo Joy

HAPPY 6TH ANNIVERSARY OF THE DAY YOU MET ME AT THE AIRPORT IN TORONTO IN AN INCREDIBLE DOWN-POUR, AND WE WENT TO BADLANDS [a gay and lesbian bar] AND FELL IN LOVE OVER AND OVER, AND WE MADE LOVE AND FELL IN LOVE CAUTIOUSLY AND TENTATIVELY OVER AND OVER, AND THEN I HAD TO LEAVE YOU AND I WAS SO SAD AND YOU GOT CAUGHT OUT NAKED WHILE YOU WERE TALKING TO ME ON THE PHONE BY THE HOUSE'S OWNERS UNEXPECTEDLY RETURNED, WE HAD ONLY BEEN SEPARATED A FEW HOURS, BUT IT SEEMED LIKE LIFETIMES, AND NOW IT SEEMS LIKE WE HAVE LIVED LIFETIMES TOGETHER AND AT THE SAME TIME ONLY MILLISECONDS, AND I LOVE YOU SO MUCH MY SHOCKING BEAUTY.

♡ Joy

Date: Fri, 14 Jul 2000 12:45:05
To: (Dr. E. Joy Masuhara)
From: Jane Hamilton
. . . I know what you mean about this incredible love. It doesn't matter how furious we are with each other – look how we light up when the other person comes in the room. Our eyes are aglow – ridiculous – and then one of us (usually me) smiles, and the other can't help smiling and then one of us (usually you) says, "Jerk! You jerk!" and the other one says, "Jerk! You jerk!" and then somehow, even if the fight goes on, we can't help laughing and we've got some perspective . . .

Seven years and still this helpless melting, all our emotional insides turning to syrup just thinking about each other. And even when we're firmly ensconced in the everyday, as long as we're together we're so happy. I mean that without exaggeration: Happy! I know what the expression filled with happiness means, because it feels like that – pleasure tip to toe. Satisfaction. Contentment. But also glee.

I think that I have never been as sweet on you as when I told you I'd bought chocolate ice cream to go with the raspberries and you wagged your tail. Just like a dog – your whole body wriggling in pure strains of pleasure. And I thought: Yes. Just yes. Yes yes and yes all through me. Yes to you, Joy. Yes to you who have brought me such joy.

J

Jane Hamilton (left) and Joy Masuhara after they were married (Brian Howell photo)

In the late 1990s Joy switched from general practice to mental-health work with Vancouver Community Mental Health Services and Vancouver's Mid-Main Community Health Centre, while Jane altered her creative focus to include photography. In early 2004 she won first prize for her short story "The Lost Boy" in the CBC Literary Competition. Their grown-up daughters were living on their own. Jane and Joy are among the eight B.C. couples involved in challenges to change Canadian law to allow same-sex marriages and, when the law changed in June 2003, they travelled to Toronto and got married.

AN EXPLOSIVE SECOND CHANCE

*Some people of a certain age believe that, as the song says, "love, like youth, is wasted on the young." Among them are **Margaret Crawford** and Aloise (Al) Firek, who in 1950 met in their workplace at an explosives facility in Nitro, Quebec. There was a mutual attraction, but while she was single, he was married. At twenty-two, Margaret, a Scottish-Canadian from Campbellton, New Brunswick, wed another workmate, Québécois Renaud Caza, and they moved to his small hometown, where they ran their own construction and farm-equipment business. She wrote a humorous account of their marriage, three children, and divergent styles of doing things in* Walk Alone Together. *When Caza died in 1990, Margaret was resigned to living alone – until Al resurfaced a decade later. In a restaurant he'd overheard a group of women talking about her book and found her number in a telephone directory. All these years, they'd been living only ninety kilometres apart. She was seventy, a prolific magazine writer and the author of two published books; he was an eighty-two-year-old widower. They had lunch together, and, as she recalls, "Ignition!" After Margaret left to winter in Florida, Al phoned her often (logging 2,164 long-distance minutes in one month alone) and she wrote him almost daily.*

9 March, 2001.

Dearest Al: –

We talked the other evening about sharing. Companionship.

About how important it is to have someone with whom to share the days. The nights. Life.

You struck a chord of recognition there. I have missed sharing.

Not "surface" sharing – with just any person. Sharing with someone special. You are special. I am glad to be sharing with you.

I waited for you – not knowing for whom I waited. But it was you. I have been "running on empty" far too long now. Empty of that special feeling that takes place between people of like mind. Emotion. Appreciation.

And now, I have that very unique experience with someone I truly care for. Beyond any expectations. Beyond imagination. Amazing, that we should discover each other. And find in each other this delightful empathy.

Sharing

What can we share, my darling, on this new life's journey?
We can share soft evenings of velvet darkness.
We can share morning sunrises, as we stand on the deck,
    arms around each other.
We can share the sight of fresh, green cedars, trembling
    with beaded, dew-laden spider webs.
We can share the cleanness of freshly laundered skies;
    misted horizons, thunder and lightning.
We can share distant mountain tops and quiet vistas,
    picnic baskets, and waves lapping at the shore.

We can share art, museums and concerts.
We can share perfect notes of beautiful compositions.
Familiar rhythms of favorite melodies.
Touching words of love songs – old message, newly clear,
    now with special meaning.
We can share majestic anthems; delicate sonatas; wistful
    nocturnes; joyous rhapsodies.

Life's treasures, not so rare, but appreciated anew,
    through both of us. Together.
Melodies, lost on one alone; swept along with
    someone to share.

We will appreciate these delicious miracles
    that surround our senses.
I cannot return to those empty days, when there was no
    hand to be held;
no one to bless with sweet and tender kisses;
no strokes of gentle caress while looking deep into caring
    eyes.

We do not experience life's wonders in solitude.
We see them together. Hear them together.
Feel the happy magic of it all.
And now – everything we experience will be special,
because the joy has been multiplied by caring.
And I care for you. So very much.

Margaret and Al married in February 2003 and moved to L'Original, Ontario, where she continues to write. As she noted in her first book, "Though each person walks alone through the strange lot of experiences that comprise life in general and marriage in particular, walking alone is far better done in good company."

I AM THE TREE

Peter Clarke has been professor of modern British history at Cambridge University and, until recently, master of the university's

Trinity Hall. He is also a distinguished historian whose works include Hope and Glory: Britain 1900–1990, *which the* English Historical Review *called "a major publishing event." In the late 1970s, Peter met a Canadian graduate student, Maria Tippett, at University College, London University, where he was a lecturer. Both were married, "so even though we were attracted to one another, there was no hanky-panky," Maria recalls. When their marriages ended in divorce, she agreed to spend much of the year at Cambridge as a senior research fellow and a member of the history faculty. By then she was a noted art historian and biographer, winning the Governor General's Award for* Emily Carr: A Biography. *After many stays with her on the west coast of Canada, Peter took Canadian citizenship. In September 2003, while Maria was undergoing a tricky eye operation, he wrote a whimsical poem on the back of a paper bag and delivered it to her when a patch was removed from her eye.*

> For Maria
> I am the tree
> the roof on the tree
> the tree on the roof of the world.
> And I am the flag
> the pole on the flag
> the flag on the pole that unfurled.
> I am the mouse
> the desk on your mouse
> the mouse on your desk that rebelled.
> And I am the hand
> the arm on your hand
> the hand on your arm that I held.
> I am the hair

the head on your hair
the hair on your head that is curled.
And I am the tree
the roof on your tree
the tree on the roof of the world.
24 IX 03

The eye operation was successful. Maria and Peter have since moved to Pender Island, British Columbia, where they continue to write.

HELLO FOREVER

The first time they said hello, in 1981, **Randy Bachman** *had just heard Denise McCann sing an Aretha Franklin rhythm-and-blues song at a pre-Christmas benefit show in Vancouver and felt "a chemistry that had been missing for several years." The Winnipeg-born Randy was the legendary catalyst of the Guess Who and Bachman-Turner Overdrive – some called him rock and roll's greatest guitarist – a Mormon convert who had never indulged in drugs or groupies on the road. He'd recently emerged from a bitterly fought divorce with legal custody of his six children. Denise was an American, now living in Canada, who had sung rock, disco, and later punk as Denise McCann and the Dead Marines. The bohemian single mother was involved in a relationship at the time, but Randy persisted in his pursuit of her and they were married early the following year. Twenty-two years later, on Valentine's Day, he expressed his love to the woman who had become a surrogate mother to some of his children and Mom to the daughter they had together.*

February 14, 2004.

Dear Denise:

From the moment I saw you, I knew you were the one. After all these years, I know it even more. You are my anchor, my lifeline and my sunshine. Thank you for being there everytime I needed you and for carrying my burdens with me. It's a joy to be with you in this life and I look forward to an eternity together. I'm so sorry for the times I've hurt you and hope you forgive me for my insensitivities.

Thank you for the love, the laughter, the companionship, the understanding, the joys, the music, and for just being you. You inspired this song and it's for you:

The First Time You Said Hello
The first time you said hello
It seemed as though we'd met before
Somewhere else in a different time
In a never ending dream of mine
Tomorrow seemed to start so long ago
The first time you said hello

The first time you said hello
And I felt the glow in my heart
Knowing in that moment something changed
And life would never be the same
I knew I couldn't ever let you go
The first time you said hello

My skies of grey all turned a lighter blue
It was because you brought the sun
To chase away the stormy skies

Love is such a crazy thing
And it's true I'd do most anything
Because I saw the same look in your eyes

The first time you said hello
I never felt this close to my dream
Now my melody and story line
Has harmony and perfect rhyme
I felt your magic in my heart and soul
The first time you said hello

©2003 Randy Bachman

Love forever,
Randy

With their last child moving away from their home on a Gulf Island in British Columbia, Randy says, "You find yourself alone with this person you married. We decided to change our lives, spend more time together – Denise comes on the road with me now – and re-fall in love with one another." In 2003, at a show in Oak Bay, Ontario, he had called his wife on stage, presented her with a bouquet of roses, got down on one knee, and asked her to marry him again. On his sixtieth birthday that September they renewed their vows in a formal ceremony – vows that they wrote themselves and a copy of which he keeps in his wallet. While his wife played for fun in a local band called Rosehip Jam, Randy continued to write songs, produce albums, mentor young musicians, and record new CDs. One of them was Jazzthing, his first venture into a new idiom for him, which includes vocals by Denise and songs the couple composed together. Among the tracks is "The First Time You Said Hello."

Family Love

"What a wonderful source of Happiness
you have always been"

Dad's little homily

*Affectionate father **Herman Witsius Ryland** had no love for Canadian nationalists. Born in England, he came to North America first with the British army in the American colonies and later in 1793 as the civil secretary of Sir Guy Carleton (Lord Dorchester), governor of Lower Canada. In 1810 Governor General of the Canadas Sir James Craig sent Ryland back to England to promote his repressive policies against French-Canadian nationalism. While Ryland was in London, he installed his wife at Cockglode in Nottinghamshire and enrolled ten-year-old George at a boys' academy in Southwell. The postage for Ryland's letters to his son, transported by coach from London to Southwell, would have been eight pence, which George had to pay, as did the recipients of all letters until postage stamps were introduced in 1839.*

London May 25th 1811

My dear George

Your well written little letter from Cockglode reached me several days ago; and yesterday I received one from your Mamma, informing me that you behaved vastly well all the while you remained with Lady Milnes, and that you went to School on Monday last where I hope you will continue to be a very good boy and apply yourself with all diligence to your learning. I have no doubt you will there meet with several boys not older than yourself, but who are much further advanced in their education, and I hope you will have sufficient spirit to endeavour to get before them. I am told you met with a Gentleman who filled your pockets with rich plumb cake, which I dare say you were eager to distribute among your new acquaintances. As soon as you have formed your little friendships I shall expect you to tell me what boys you are most intimate with, and how you amuse yourself, as well as what you learn. Learn as much as you can in school hours, and play as much as you please out of them. This is all I require of you – and you cannot think this too much. I have not time to say more to you now. I beg you will present my compliments to Mr. Falkner and his sisters and tell him I really very much regret it was not in my power to accompany you to Southwell that I might have had the pleasure of making a personal acquaintance with them. I have this moment

Herman Witsius Ryland
(National Archives of
Canada C-069942)

received a letter from your Mamma who is still at Cockglode and does not think of returning to town before this day se'nnit [se'nnight, meaning "seven nights"]. She will call to see poor William on her way back. I desire you will write to him from time to time, and to your Mamma or me once a fortnight at least. We shall be satisfied with a very short letter provided it is well written. Little Sophy is vastly well, and just now playing beside me with some of the pebbles you left behind you. If she could speak well enough, she would send her love to you, as your Grandmamma and aunt do. I fear you will be obliged to ask somebody to read this letter to you, which really is a shame for a boy of your age. I understand you are very rich, so you will not grudge paying the postage of it, and it is more like a man to pay it yourself. I make no doubt your Mamma requested Mr. Falkner to furnish you with such Money as he may think proper for you when your present stock is out. Farewell my dearest Boy. I earnestly pray God almighty to bless and preserve you. I think of you constantly with the tenderest regard . . .

You truly affectionate Father
H.W. Ryland

In 1818 George Herman Ryland became his father's assistant clerk with the Executive Council and succeeded him in the position of clerk when his father died in 1838. After Lower and Upper Canada were united, George was registrar of the City of Quebec and of Montreal.

CONSIDER THE LILIES

At the time he wrote this letter to his married daughter, **Egerton Ryerson** *was superintendent of education for Canada West, a religious and moral man who set the standards on which Ontario's education system was based. He was also a minister in the Methodist Episcopal Church and a leader in the reform movement that achieved the secularization of public lands long reserved for the maintenance of the Church of England. He would later be president of the Methodist Church of Canada. His daughter, Sophia, born in 1836, was the first child of his second marriage. In 1860 Sophia married a barrister, Edward Harris, a second*

Sophie Ryerson Harris in fancy dress
(Harris Family fonds, University of
Western Ontario RC-1497)

Egerton Ryerson (Ryerson
University Archives)

cousin on her father's side, and went to live with his family at
Eldon House, an elegant residence, now a museum, in London,
Ontario. Sophia was nearly thirty in 1865.

Toronto, Sept. 5, 1865

My dearest Sophie

I confess I read your letter of yesterday with some surprise. Not
knowing that it contained anything <u>peculiar</u>, I was going to put
[it] in my pocket & read it in my study after prayers; [but] your
Mamma wished me to open & read it before prayers; so I read it
out. To my surprise, your Mamma wishes me to comply with your
request & send you the money – though she does not approve of
the proposed expenditure. I must say I regret it myself. A passion
for jewelry should rather be resisted than cherished, as it gains

strength by indulgence, & is sometimes attended with very painful consequences, especially when one is not rich.

You have done well, & made your way hitherto, without so costly an ornament. Col. Lowry & the officers of the 16th invited Ella last week to a "garden" party in the old Govt. grounds; and one of the officers referring to you, said you were the most charming woman he had met, & spoke in a manner to indicate that this was the opinion of <u>all</u>. I was <u>gratified to hear this</u>, & could not but think how superior are the diamonds of the mind & heart – a cultivated & refined mind, pure, generous & cheerful feelings & affections – to the diamonds of the hand. <u>I</u> think you are more charming in simplicity, than in the most splendid ornaments.

As Edward has so kindly furnished you with pin money, I think you ought not to make such a purchase without his knowledge & approval. Perhaps this suggestion is superfluous, but I have thought I would make it. I have no doubt he would value the ornament more highly if his knowledge & consent were united to your wish in the purchase of it. A diamond is always worth something, but seldom brings what one gives for it.

Having thus said all that is in my heart on the subject, I herewith enclose you a <u>cheque</u> for $30, as I have no money from the Bank; & I hope you will be guided aright in your decision. . . .

I beg you will regard the cheque as a <u>free</u> gift, not as a loan.

Your ever affectionate Father

A week later Ryerson wrote, "I think you came to a proper decision in regard to the ring – one that will afford you much more satisfaction tha[n] if you had bought it . . ." Later he wrote that he has "always leaned to the side, perhaps to the extreme, of indulgence," but he urged Sophia to forgo her "endless gaities."

BE A FATHER TO ME

*Eleanor Papineau, the granddaughter of Parti Patriote leader Louis-Joseph Papineau and the grandmother of Talbot Papineau (see page 278), was married in July 1875 to **John Try Davies**. The young couple left in August on a honeymoon tour that took them by steamer to Ottawa and then to London, England. John's note to his in-laws suggests that his wife was not in good health.*

Ottawa

19 August 1875

My dear Father & Mother,

Eleanor has just asked me how to spell lovely which argues well for the tone of her letter. I do not flatter myself that the adjective is applied to me. She sent you a telegram this morning to say that she was well. I can only say that though very tired yesterday she is looking most lovely today. She really is. We took a little drive this morning and I felt so proud of her. I did not mind being thought a very new Benedict at all.

She slept for two hours & a half this afternoon and has drunk several pails of milk. I shudder to think what the milk bill will be . . .

I thank you very very much for my share in your affectionate little notes which arrived this morning. I cannot tell you how very earnest my desire is to be a good son to you. Will you call me in future by my old name of John which my other Father & Mother used. Please ask Pap & Marie Louise to do so too.

With very much love to all believe me

Your affectionate son

John

In London, Eleanor's health began to fail. One of her physicians was William Jenner, formerly Queen Victoria's doctor and famous for his investigations of typhus and typhoid fevers.

4 Clarges Street

London 4 Nov '75

My dear Father,

My sad telegrams to you and Dr. Macdonnell have already told you that our darling has entered in rest.

It only remains for me to tell you the particulars.

After sending my first telegram to you, Eleanor sank rapidly and breathed her last in my arms at 5 minutes before 5 this morning.

She suffered very little at the end.

The cause was organic disease of the heart.

I have had little hope for some time past but it was possible that she might have lived for some time longer.

Now it only remains to bow to this awful choice of the almighty and to care for the living.

I telegraph[ed] for Papineau [Eleanor's brother] and he was present with us. My heart was with you all through.

I cannot attempt consolation just yet my own heart is too bruised.

Mother [Eleanor's mother] is as well as can be hoped and a married lady cousin of mine will be here in a few hours to take care of her.

I shall have the dear remains preserved and will bring them out when you arrive to take charge of Mother. I shall probably take Mother and Marie Louise to Paris as soon as possible but I have not time to settle all plans yet as today is mail day.

You may rely upon my caring for dear Mother as her own son would.

Dr. F. Roberts and Sir William Jenner were in attendance. We had two skilled nurses and everything possible was done to make dear Eleanor's suffering as light as possible.

Friends here are very kind and the people of the house have been most kind & considerate.

Oh my dear Father, my heart bleeds for you. Will you still be a father to me? I am so alone.

Mother is much better than I had hoped. She was able to weep freely & the blessed tears brought relief. . . .

God bless and comfort you.

Your affectionate son

John

John continued to write loving letters to Eleanor's younger sister, Marie-Louise Papineau, always signing himself "Your very affectionate Caterpillar." In May 1878 he wrote from Montreal, where he was a lawyer, "I hope you do not give yourself airs because you are eighteen years old. If I were near you I would brush your head against the wall a few times just to keep you in order. In the meantime I beg you will give Mother a good kiss from me and think of us often & always . . ."

HIS ORPHAN FAMILY

*Evangelical work in the Canadian West in the nineteenth century was almost exclusively conducted by the Oblates of Mary Immaculate, a society founded in France in 1816. **Constantine Scollen**, born in Ireland, joined the Oblates in England and came* *to Canada in 1862. He taught at the first elementary school in the North-West Territories at Fort Edmonton and worked with Oblate priest Father Albert Lacombe on his Cree dictionary and grammar. After being ordained in 1873, he was the first resident priest among the Blackfoot, a parish priest in Edmonton, and director of Notre Dame des Sept Douleurs in Hobbema, Alberta. Father Scollen wrote to his father in Ireland in January 1882 and then came the news of his father's death.*

Bishoprick of St. Albert
Saskatchewan
June 17, 1882

My Dear Brother Joseph –
I[t] was yesterday evening when our Revd Superior announced to me the awful news contained in your note, the death of our poor father. Seperated as I have been from the family for so long a time and by so great a distance, the news paralyzed me. What must it have been for you, my dear boys, who were eye-witnesses of this sad event! I know what a kind Christian father he was and what pains he always took to raise his family in the fear of God; and I know from the feelings of sorrow which fill my own heart what must be the grief that reigns amongst you all by this sudden privation of so vigilant a guide!!! Such, Dear Brother, is this poor, miserable transitory world, the closest bonds of affection are often times suddenly torn asunder when least expected. Today, the feast of the Sacred heart of Jesus, I had the happiness of offering the holy Sacrifice of the mass with the Blessed Sacrament exposed in our Cathedral of St. Albert, and with all the fervor of my soul, I applied this tremendous Sacrifice for the eternal repose of our dearly beloved father. Oh! My Dear Brother, let us unite in constantly praying for one to whom we owe so much, you in your

Father Constantine Scollen,
circa 1890s (Glenbow Museum
NA-3022-2)

frequent communions, as I will in the holy Sacrifice of the Mass. Now, Dear Brother, you are left alone to watch over and care for your younger brothers. My mind is so troubled I scarcely know what advice to give you. However, I have the greatest confidence in your experience and wisdom to conduct things for the best. I will propose a plan of my own to you, and will wait impatiently for an answer. I hear that Ann is about to marry. I think she does well; i[f] so inclined. Father told me also that you were to marry after Easter; well you have every right to do so and I pray God to bless you. But this needs not be any obstacle to what I am to propose. First then, my intention is that David should enter our order of Oblates and study to become a priest. For this purpose he should come over to Ottawa, Canada and enter the juniorate under the direction of our Fathers where he would be trained for our Bishop here in Saskatchewan. I know that David has made good progress in his schooling, has a good deal of talent and is virtuous besides. I have already spoken of this to my superiors and they approve of the plan. But I must have a few words from David himself on this subject. He must choose freely whether or not this would be according to his taste. Therefore let him write to me at once and let me know so that the question may be decided immediately.

Now regarding yourself and the other two boys Thos. and Patrick, I would like to see you out here. Our country is opening and there is a vast field for industry. If Patrick and Thos. were here, either one, or both, might have an inclination to become brothers in our Order; if not, they could settle in the country and become good members of our Catholic community and so with yourself. Even if you are married this would not hinder you from coming. Now Dear Brother do not loose a moment after you get this letter, but write at once and let me know what you think. As to the rest of the family, Hugh, John, Rose and Annie, I will write to each one as soon as I feel less sorrowful. At present the tears blind me. My heart is filled with grief for father, and anxiety for his orphan family. In the mean time give them my kindest love . . .

Your very aff. bro.

C. Scollen prst. O.M.I.

Nearly five years later, Father Scollen had not been able to arrange David's admittance to the Oblates. In one letter he suggested that their stepbrother, William, who was farming in Alberta and not attending church, might have affected David's chances.

NEPOTISM FOR A NEPHEW

There may be few more delicate tasks than trying to find employment for a relative's delinquent son. Irish-born **Henry John Cambie**, *who came to Canada as a boy, was a federal government engineer assisting Sir Sandford Fleming in his first reconnaissance for the pioneering Intercolonial Railway line from Halifax to Montreal in the mid-nineteenth century. Cambie then oversaw construction of the challenging Fraser Canyon portion of the Canadian Pacific Railway (CPR) during the early 1880s and later supervised the survey and layout of the city of Vancouver. Years* *later, as head of the CPR's Pacific division, he had to deal with a different kind of stress – family pressure – when he wrote this imploring letter to a friend.*

Vancouver March 19th 1897

<u>Private</u>

My dear Perry,

I have a nephew who has been very wild and caused his mother in Ottawa a great deal of trouble & expense. He was in a bank and had to leave it. She wants me to try to get him a job out here! and the sooner the better – He is a fine active young fellow – a good accountant – a regular athlete. What his particular vices are I don't know but believe wine & women.

Can you get me a job for him on the Slocan River line? Accountant – Chairman – anything so long as his mother is relieved of his expenses. Don't imagine I want him petted! make him Cook's assistant if you like. In my opinion no job would be too menial for him till he shows he has reformed –

Drop me a line quick – and if you can take him I won't forget it.

In haste yours very truly
H.J. Cambie

MATERNAL INJUNCTIONS

*After her lawyer husband died in 1888 (likely of a combination of a sleeping medication and alcohol), **Mary Baker McQuesten** was left with six children and little money. By careful management and scrimping, she managed to educate her children, hang on to*

Whitehern, the stately McQuesten home in Hamilton, Ontario, and maintain the family's position among the elite of the city. Strict in her moral beliefs, she was a leader in the missionary movement of her church and campaigned for temperance in the 1902 city referendum on alcohol. She wrote hundreds of letters to her family. These to son Calvin reveal her manoeuvrings regarding the suitors of her daughters Hilda and Ruby.

1902/08/10
Montreal Quebec

My dear dear boy,

It seems a very long time since I wrote you, when I did Ken [Trigge] was just here and his visit was the occasion of most trying experience for all concerned. Of course, I had to have a very plain talk with him and when I spoke to him of his not being an abstainer, he was very frank and open, but simply said that for him to be an abstainer meant that he must throw up his position and then I discovered that it was all far worse than I imagined. It is his business to be most agreeable to the firm's customers and to this end Mr. Beardmore gives him and instructs him to go to any expense in treating, asking men to lunch or dinner and when he does so of course he must drink or smoke with them. Well, of course, I said it was far worse than I had any idea, that I always heard a traveller's life was one of great temptation but I thought it meant that others would ask him to drink but in this case, he was asking others, in fact was making his living by tempting men to do wrong. What an awful position! So I said I could never consent. On explaining the state of affairs to H. [Hilda] she agreed with me, but it was a most distressing time and really made us ill. . . . But Hilda I must say was wonderfully brave and conscientious and

Mary Baker McQuesten and children, including Hilda (left),
Calvin (right), and Ruby (next to Calvin) (Whitehern Historic House
and Garden, www.whitehern.ca, IMG007)

though she had quite determined to take him, she withstood him
and said no, she would not marry a man whose living was made
in such a way. He himself said, that no one had ever put it before
him as we had, that he was given liquor at home from [when] he
was twelve years old and never knew it was any harm. But now,
he said, he saw, that he was committing a sin every day of his life.
But where to find another situation is the difficulty. It does seem a
most iniquitous thing, this treating system, Ken had been pretty
well disgusted I think with what he saw at Chateau Frontenac at
Quebec. I do trust this may be a turning point in his life and that
he may have strength to give it up and if only some good opening
would present itself, I think he might become a really good man.

. . . I am very very sorry, for I think he would have suited H. very well & she seemed quite heart broken but we must hope that it may all be overruled for their lasting good. . . .

> With much love my dear dear boy.
> Your loving Mother
> M.B. McQuesten

> 1906/08/20
> Bayview Farm Dorset

My dearest Cal,

I was glad to see by weather probs that it was cooler in Alberta, for you would feel the heat very trying; it was extremely warm here on Saturday but is somewhat cooler. On Wednesday we had a great surprise in the shape of David Ross. His story at first was that he had been at home with a sore leg and before going back to his surveying job on the C.P.R. had come up to recruit. At first I quite enjoyed his visit, he got a canoe and we went out paddling and one day I actually started to paddle having got on a stream so shallow that we were in danger of grounding. But alas! it was all a sham. Would you believe it he had come to propose to Ruby! It was last night she told me, and you can imagine I scarcely slept a wink all night. It was a complete surprise to her too, for she had never dreamed of it, he is only 24, Tom's age, is three years younger than R. Of course I know that he is a fine tempered Christian lad, and as R. says they have much in common, she is fond of all the Rosses, but we both think he must wait a while till his prospects are more settled.

I feel rather cross with him thinking about it at all with his mother and sisters all working for a living, but of course he tells R. that he would not be ready for two years. He is working with the head engineer on the new double track of the C.P.R. between

Fort William and Winnipeg gets $100 a month and expects soon $125. Has a man working his homestead, which is 50 miles north of Regina: his plan is to build a home there for his mother and Jean, they expect also to have Bessie's children to bring up. But it seems to me that R. ought to do better than this, she is a very attractive girl and it has always been a grievous disappointment that she never seems to meet any one worth looking at.

Then too I do not know whether David's view of things is to be trusted, the Rosses are as a family easily satisfied (I fancy) for they have been brought up very plainly and what D. might consider a very comfortable home I would not at all. R. is not worldly wise enough either. He looks such a boy too and has a weak face sometimes . . . The more I think of it the less I favour it. Sometimes I know I am thoroughly irked, for R. suggests that they might do much home mission work there and I know that is true but it seems as if R. were fitted to take a fine place in a higher sphere . . . In the meantime D. is to be told to wait till his prospects have developed . . .

Your mother
M.B. McQuesten

Not one of the six McQuesten children ever married.

COME HOME, FATHER

After the completion in 1885 of the British Columbia section of the Canadian Pacific Railway, on which fifteen to seventeen thousand Chinese men had laboured in conditions that killed many of them, anti-Asian sentiment in Canada prompted a fifty-dollar federal head tax to restrict immigration from the Far East. Around *the turn of the century, as many as 4,700 Chinese paid the now-doubled hundred-dollar fee, but when Parliament increased the tax to five hundred dollars in 1903, only eight Chinese were admitted. Nothing is known about the man named **Dian** to whom this letter was sent. His three sons wrote on the envelope: "Important family letter. Please bother you to submit it to Saltwater City," the Chinese name for Vancouver. Years later, the letter was found unopened in a Vancouver store with a bundle of other letters for Chinese people.*

May 10 1904

Dear father:

The entire family are deeply concerned upon hearing from Li Yinghi that you are under the weather overseas. He also said there is no way out there for you, your health is getting worse, and debts accumulate. As such, we beg you to borrow money for your travel expenses back home as soon as possible, so that you can recover at home. We, your sons, would like to take care of you so that you can have a happy life in old age. You are almost 50 years old, and with many children you deserve a better life at home. So why remain overseas and suffer so much alone! Your sufferings made us, your children, sad and cry, and upset the elderly grandparents. We are writing now, begging you on our knees to <u>start planning journey home immediately</u>.

Meanwhile, <u>we are anxiously expecting you home</u>. You don't need to worry about us, everyone is fine, old and young. We only hope you keep fit, and wish you good luck,

All the best,
Your most humble sons,
Dian Quan, Dian Fang, Dian Hua

P.S. Grandpa Chong Jiu [not a relative, but an old person close to the family] on May 3rd departed this world to roam with the immortals.

Their father's fate remains unknown.

COUPLETS FOR TWO

Thomas Phillips Thompson was eighty-three in 1927 when he composed these rhyming letters to his grandchildren Lucy and Pierre. Thompson, a journalist and early advocate of Canadian socialism, wrote political satire as "Jimuel Briggs" for Ontario newspapers, launched a weekly paper devoted to political commentary, and later also launched the radical Labor Advocate.

Oakville Sept 20th. [1927]

Dear Lucy. – As you're one of those,
Who poetry prefer to prose,
And I can write without much bother
One most as easy as the other,
I'll have Aunt Maude work the machine,
And tell you what we've done and seen.
The weather has been clear and fine
We've much enjoyed the bright sunshine,
The squirels hop from tree to tree,
The birds are sin[g]ing merrily,
Even the tom cats try to sing
A tom-cat's song's a fearful thing.
Yet why should they not raise their voice in
The general chorus of rejoicing.

The Exhibition has been here
Bigger and better than last year,
And people come from near and far
By steamer, railway bus and car;
There visitors could see displayed
Most everything that's grown or made,
Machinery, dry goods, cows and hogs,
Pumpkins, potatoes, cats and dogs,
I won't repeat the catalogues,
Not being there you will not need them
And it will tire you to read them. . . .

Oakville [Feb. 9, 1927(?)]

Pierre and Lucy
Your letter made me very glad
To learn what a good time you had
With the entire community
Around the merry Christmas tree.
And then the present that you got
Ah that reminds me I have not
As yet returned the thanks now due
For those nice slipper sent by you.
So comfortable, warm and neat
Which beautifully fit my feet.
Pierre I am glad to hear that you
As Orator made your debut.
Keep on and cultivate your gifts,
And by and by you'll get a lift,
Perhaps some day you may be sent
To hold a seat in Parliament,
Or win a name both near and far

Earning big money at the bar.
And Lucy need not lag behind
These are the days when womenkind
Has equal chances with the men
To strive with brain and voice and pen
And with her charm of form and face
She'll hold a leading social place.
I really have no news to tell
Except that we are keeping well
The winter has been very cold
But that's no news because it's old
With spring already on the way
The break up may come any day
Wishing that luck may you befal[l]
I now conclude with love to all.

Your loving Grandfather
P.T.

A few months before his death in 1933, Thompson began a poem-letter following his birthday party: "Dear Pierre and Lucy, I feel fine/ Now that my years are eighty-nine . . ." Pierre grew up to be neither a Member of Parliament nor a lawyer but Pierre Berton. Lucy Berton Woodward is the author of Kidnapped in the Yukon, *an adventure novel for pre-teens.*

A CHAMPION BABY

*Patricia L. Watts was one of the many babies **Charles B. Hill** placed in Alberta homes in the years he worked for the superintendent of*

child welfare. Hill's love of his babies and reputation for finding
the right homes for them survived for decades in the department.
Watts found Hill's letter in a tin box on a beam in the basement
of her parents' home following her father's death.

Edmonton
Dec. 5, 1932

Mrs. F. Watts,
P.O. Box 222,
Champion, Alberta
Dear Mrs. Watts,
I have your letter of Nov. 24th and note what you say regarding a
brown-eyed girl. I have searched everywhere, but have failed in
my quest. In my last letter I had to ask you to reduce the age, and
you agreed, but now I have to ask you to change the color of the
eyes. If you will do this I can send you one of the dearest little
babies that it would be possible for you to imagine. She has dark
hair and wonderful blue eyes, and was born on the 22nd of
September last. To see her is to love her, and if you really want a
darling baby you had better 'phone me at 916258, collect, and tell
me so, otherwise, I shall place her elsewhere.

Yours sincerely,
Chas. B. Hill
Director of Child Placement

BE A GOOD BOY

*Ordained in 1933, Toronto-born **Samuel Cass** began his career on*
the West Coast, serving as the rabbi of Beth Israel Congregation in
Vancouver and of Herzl Conservative Congregation in Seattle. In

*this period, he corresponded individually with his many siblings back home in Toronto, including the deftly deflective **Eliezer Cass**.*

November 17, 1933

Dear Brother Eliezer:

I am very sorry to tell you that I heard some very bad news about you, and that is that you are not the good boy that I left at home when I saw you last. And really I cannot understand it. In the first place I hear that you are not attending Hebrew School regularly. Now that is very bad. I heard that you have been put down to a lower grade in Hebrew School by the new principal. Well I think that he is right. You probably don't know as much as you think you do. And you probably played too much ball instead of paying attention to your school work.

Now I want you to make up your mind that you are going to go to Hebrew School and that you are going to like it. And let me hear from you right away. Let me know what grade you are in and who your teacher is and what you are studying.

In the second place, I hear that your behavior at home is not too good for a boy of your age. You had better correct that too. It will do you no good to be a badly behaved boy.

I am expecting an immediate reply, so get busy and explain yourself.

[Sam]

Toronto, Ont.
Nov. 28/33

Dear Brother Sammy, –

I received your letter after having written to you the night before. I'd like to know who wrote you the letter because the one who wrote it is telling lies. I was put back in Chader because I was sick for a week and missed my exams, thats why, and I'm not half so bad as is written in that letter. Now let's quit arguing and talk about some interesting things. I would like to know what you have been doing and what you are going to do because it interests me to know what you are doing. How are you feeling these days? Are you getting along all right in Vancouver? It's pretty nice now but it was nicer in the day time to-day. Your having plenty of rain right now it says in the papers. Well I'll have to say good-bye now as it is time to get the mail.

So good-bye again
From your brother
Eliezer Cass

Samuel was the senior Jewish chaplain in the Canadian Army and Navy from 1941 to 1946. He then became director of the McGill University B'nai B'rith Hillel Foundation and later worked for the Miriam Home for the Exceptional, a school for mentally handicapped Jewish children. In 1975 Rabbi Cass and his family died in an automobile accident.

A FREE SPIRIT

In 1935 thirty-year-old Saskatchewan-born journalist Gladys Arnold left her job at the Regina Leader-Post and set up a base in Paris from which she travelled throughout Europe, reporting to the Canadian Press on the political events and ideas that were pushing the world to war. She was the only Canadian reporter covering the German invasion of France in May 1940. In this letter to her mother in Regina, she gave credit to the woman from whom her courage sprang.

March 24, 1937

Dearest Mother:

Do not worry about me thinking that you do not think of me and that I am not dear to you – never think that. We understood all that when we were in England last year. We may have ideas about modern life, about politics and religion that are not quite the same, but fundamentally, Mother dear, you know that we are in accord, and that even when I do not see you I feel that security of your love and affection for me, and that it sustains me in my work; your faith means much in my life, for I am not brilliant; I have ideas, but it is difficult for me to put them down in a way which satisfies me, and for that reason I am very slow. I do not know if I will ever write anything of real importance, but I am trying – I want to write something really good, something, not to pass with a day, but to be some day, called literature – a literature for Canada. You must not fret or be lonesome, for although we are separated by thousands of miles, the spirit traverses that with ease – you are near me – and I feel you about me – and surely you must feel that I am there often in my thoughts. I am wrong not to write oftener – and I promise you that I will – so much so that it will seem to you that I am really there. No, in this life there are separations which we must bear it seems – and be happy and contented. When I look about me here – at the unhappy men and women, because they have no confidence in one another, because life is so hard, so difficult to gain their bread – living in immense cities when they would think it paradise to live where you do and have such a life as you have there – I thank my sort of God that it is so for you. Also I was happy to learn that your doctor said that you are in good condition physically. There is no reason why you and Arnold should not have a life full of beauty and happiness – only put aside the little things – forget the irritations – all people have their faults – and we must love them – in spite of their faults – even for their faults – we must learn to look for the things that make them loveable and I assure you there are many. You must not live for the day when I return – for that day – may be any day. Who knows what the future holds? In case of war or – in case of many unforseen things I might return any time – on the other hand – until I have satisfied that thirst which I have and while I have the time and chance, I must profit by it, for it will never come again. You know that dear Mother – you

Gladys Arnold visiting her mother,
Florida Mae Arnold Sutcliffe
(University of Regina Archives)

must therefore not live for a day in the future – but live for today, enjoy each day to the full as it goes by. Be able each night when you go to bed to say, "If anything happens to me tonight – I am satisfied – I have had a full, joyous life, full of richness, beauty, blessings." No regrets, no vain longings. Fill each day. That is what I try to do, of course I would prefer to have the world smaller so that I could go over every weekend and spend it with you – but that is impossible – so we must cut our desires to possibilities. Just remember that one day I will return and then we will have a happy time together, but in the meantime we must each and all of us learn to have our happiness from a source within us – that is not selfish or egoist – it is normal and sane. It is the people who seek to quench their thirst from outside sources who never find peace.

Thanks so much for the dollars you have sent . . . but Mother dear, do not deprive yourself of anything . . . be kind and generous around you – and that will do much more for me – I have always known that you have been good to other women's daughters for other women have always been so kind to me. It is indirect, but it arrives just the same. I believe in that kind of influence in the world. Love – it is the only thing which has a direct and sure effect.

. . . in the meantime, be happy, and remember that even if I am not demonstrative with you – very much – that I never cease to love you and to think you are the best mother in the world – for you have given me a free spirit – you are brave and never reproach me for following what seems to be my fate, even though it has left me over here so far away. Those are the things that fill me with pride and for which I shall never cease to honor, and never forget my Mother.

All my love,
Glad

THIS MAN'S SON

*In a note included with his papers, **Hugh MacLennan** explained why he wrote six letters to his late father: "My father died in February, 1939. I missed him very much and apparently wrote these letters to him afterwards [in] that half year when we waited for the war." Samuel MacLennan, a medical doctor in Nova Scotia, insisted on his son's becoming a classical scholar, and Hugh dutifully complied: after his B.A., he read classics at Oriel College, Oxford, and completed a Ph.D. in classical studies at Princeton in 1935. But Hugh was also following his own star. At Oxford, he had written a novel, which was not published. In 1937, while*

Hugh MacLennan in Halifax harbour in the 1960s (Bob Brooks photo; Hugh MacLennan fonds, University of Calgary, Special Collections, MsC 14.10.1)

teaching at Lower Canada College in Montreal, he finished a second novel, which also did not find a publisher. Then, at the suggestion of his American wife, Dorothy Duncan, he set a novel in Canada, choosing the background of the 1917 Halifax explosion, which he had experienced as a boy of ten. While the manuscript was making the rounds of publishers, Dr. MacLennan died.

Montreal

March 18, 1939

Dear Dadden:

It was just a month ago yesterday. It seems to have been such a long time. You are as much alive to me now as you ever were. It is a strange thing, yet very true. Not yourself, not the You that could perform operations, but the You that has always stood in a part – perhaps in the central part – of my mind.

Last week I got a letter fom my agent in New York, completely unexpected, saying that <u>Longmans' Green</u> were thinking of publishing my book. They considered me, to use their own words "a find." I could have wished that you might have at least seen that letter. In my heart I do not expect that book to be published at all. Last week, when the prospects for peace this year seemed better, I had some hopes, but this last move of Hitler's has dashed them.

I am largely what you made me. In a society at peace – even in a society in the throes of a great struggle towards a better world – I would be able to take my place. I would be able to fulfil your best hopes of your son. Now, with Caesars within & without, there is only a small place for the individual. It seems to me, therefore, that ambition is largely an illusion. To do a small job such as I have, to do any job at all, as well as I can, is about enough.

What frightens me, Dadden, is not Hitler, not the German Army, but the reactions created by them in society at large; even in myself. Hitler is a blind instrument of destiny, but he is a man of destiny as truly as Napoleon was. By what vile means history fulfils her ends! It has always been so – Alexander, Caesar, Napoleon. God knows the urban capitalists, with their morning coats & smug faces, never could have solved the problem. And the end is clear – the problem <u>goes</u>, with it Hitler will go, & the old world you knew will be changed forever. It is in one sense (with Europe) the same as it was with the city-states of Greece, when first Philip, & then Alexander, crept in & subdued them one by one. One hates Hitler. Yet the problem is: can anyone claim that the English & French had the responsibility necessary to keep the peace & produce prosperity? Obviously not. Yet Hitler has so far shown no sense of responsibility at all. And it is fatally evident that a continent frantic with fear, with no policy, run by incompetents, will fall to a madman just because he has a policy & cares not how many lives are lost on his path towards supremacy . . .

I am glad, Dadden, for your sake that you are not here to

witness the <u>denouement</u>. The rest of us must bear it as best we may. At least, we can have no choice in the matter.

Much love,
Hugh

Dr. MacLennan missed not only the 1941 publication of Barometer Rising *(by Duell, Sloan & Pearce) but also its huge success (one hundred thousand copies sold in Canada, England, and the United States by 1945) and of course his son's subsequent success as a writer of fiction and non-fiction, which won him five Governor General's Awards and an international audience.*

MOTHER OF THE CHIEF

John Diefenbaker, Canada's thirteenth prime minister, was first elected to Parliament in 1940, where he represented the Saskatchewan riding of Lake Centre for the Conservatives, who formed the Opposition. From his backbench seat, Diefenbaker questioned the government's actions and policies in a style applauded by his mother, **Mary F. Diefenbaker.**

[1942]
Saskatoon Feb 8th

Dear John

. . . Well John if I got writing my home life now it would not be a pretty picture. my new maid is going to set me wild. her name is Gwen Jones. what she dont know will fill a book. Mrs. Ivanfield told me about her she thought she would be all right. she is a big strong girl. red headed and not a bit good looking. she lives about 17 miles from Langham, but unfortunately she never did any house work. just helped her father to work the farm. she cant cook. cant even cook meat. has no idea in the world how house work should be done. . . . I never worked so hard in my life. but no use I could not teach her anything. after she made my bed yesterday I asked her if she saw anything wrong with it. she said it is very untidy. now what can you do with her. by spring there will be no maids to be had. So we will all have to work.

You sure gave those babies the right kind of dope. They dont seem to be able to answer questions do they? It was sure a good speech you give them. and the press wrote you up in great shape I was just proud of you once more. you seem to have a way of putting things so different from most speakers you sure hit the nail on the head every time. more power to you. . . .

. . . why should the world be in such a shape. nothing but kill, kill. The war dont look so good. day after day I look for a change. it is long in coming but I am sure it will come sooner or later. but Canada must do a lot more than she is doing now. Those french-men in quebec should have a bomb or two to wake them up. . . .

love to you both from us both xxx

In 1957 when he was prime minister, having led the Conservative Party to a surprise victory over the Liberals, **John Diefenbaker** *wrote two letters to his mother. This first was handwritten; the second was typed by a secretary.*

HOUSE OF COMMONS
CANADA
Oct 22/57

My dear Mother: –
You are getting close to <u>Oct 26</u>th which is the date of the birth of Canada's No. 1 Mother!

How does it feel to be approaching 85 years old – certainly your family has been a long long-lived one! How I wish I could be home but there is no leaving here while the Liberals keep kicking me around. One of these days there will be another election!

This week end the PM of England (MacMillan) and [?] will be here. That means an almost all night session on Friday night for me. I need not tell you that when I was a boy and saw my way to this position, I didn't know how much work there was (and worry).

Give Elmer, Austin Crosses best wishes.

Love to you

Ottawa,
November 18th, 1957

My dear Mother:

In looking over Friday's Hansard I noted that you had been referred to in the speech of one of the Members.

Mr. Taylor, M.P., spoke of you at page 1192 of Hansard, and I am sending you herewith a copy.

I hope that things are going reasonably well with you. Naturally I am very busy and this week particularly will be a heavy one as the Dominion-Provincial Conference begins a week from today.

With all good wishes,
I am, with Love,
John

From Hansard: "Mr. J.R. Taylor (Vancouver-Burrard): There is another person whom I should like to see in the gallery of the house. I refer to the mother of the Prime Minister. It is my understanding, sir, that she is the only mother in Canadian history who ever saw her son become prime minister of this country. Perhaps in the near future she can be present to see her famous son lead the government."

In-law love

*Adrienne Bruynings (whose grandmothers called her Jenny) met Maurice Leduc, a soldier from Montreal, on Christmas Eve 1944 while she was decorating the tree in her aunt's pub in Herentals, Belgium. The following December, Adrienne and Maurice were married in Herentals, and six months later twenty-two-year-old **Adrienne Leduc** was in London with other war brides, on her way to join Maurice in Canada. Not knowing much French and having limited English, Adrienne tried to tell her unilingual francophone mother-in-law what she was feeling and hoping.*

somewhere in Londen. 26-6-46. P.M. 930 evening
My dear Mother!
Comment allez vous? Je suis trés heureuse ma mére. I will come soon now. I guess we will leave England next Sunday or Saturday, from Southampton to Halifax, with the Queen Mary. We are here with 12 Belgium girls and about 25 Dutch, to-morrow we will have here a 1000 more English girls and also about 1000 baby's. I was a little sick on the boat from Belgium to England. I eat all day nothing then bread, I hope it will go better on the Queen Mary. We sleep here with 12 girls in one room. I had a hard day, last night when I leave my parents. I was crying very much. I bring them to the station at 10 o.clock. Mother told me to be good for Maurice and everything like that, so I am coming with the hope that everything will be going good and I will try to be a good wife and a good child for you.
27 Juin – PM 12 o. clock. Well dear Mother, you see it's another day. Last night I went to bed, we sleep with 12 girls in one room. I have taken some pictures of it here, so you can see my bed after.

I am writing now in my bed. I have a headache, to much noise here, plenty trouble, not good food and we are all very nervous. But I cannot write very good in my bed. How is everything going over there? Excuse me for my pencil but my pen is finnish. We will go out this afternoon to visit the town of Londen. I don't like it here very much, it looks all so dirty. Next week at this time we will be in Canada I guess. It's something I cannot believe, I cannot believe that I will see you all sooner then I'll see my parents. I am believing now there's something going on, but I was waiting 5 months for this, and now it will come, today we are just a half year married. I cannot explain what I feell now. But I will be very happy to see all of yours, and my boy, I hope he is O.K. now and also Laurent. It will be a big day when we meet again, after such a long time. I hope that you will be a good Mother for me, because I need it, and if I cannot [do] something, you will learn that to me, eh? I guess I'll meet you Maurice, on the station in Montreal but you will get a telegram from me I think, so you will know it, don't worry. . . . We will leave here tomorrow morning I guess to Southampton, the other girls are telling me we leave at 6 and 8 o.clock. So I think we will be going at 6 o.clock.

Well my dear new Mother, I am sure I gonna like you very much, so with everyone. I also hope I will like Montreal, because I never will be use to live right in the city, but were we live it is better, eh? Now my Mother and sisters, don't make [any special] trouble for me, when you get this letter it won't be long before we meet. All my love for you Maurice and be a good boy till I come. I know you are very happy and me too I am.

So God bless you darling, and keep smiling, we'll meet again, we know in Montreal and next week! I cannot believe it, it gonna be a nice moment, it would be nice to have a picture of it, but I guess it's to dark in the station. And you better clean your eyes good before you come, you know why? And don't be angry if I cry. Good night now and greetings to all.

Your daughter Jenny xxxxxxxxxxxx

Nearly sixty years later, Adrienne forgets the details of that meeting in the train station but recalls that Maurice's mother and one of his sisters were there, while the rest of the family, including some aunts and uncles, waited at home. Despite the language barrier, she connected with her mother-in-law and got on well with her.

YOUR BRIGHT FUTURE

Frederick (Ted) DeMille Knowlton was born in Cambridge Station, Nova Scotia, and came in 1920 to Standard, a small town east of Calgary, which had been settled by Danish Lutherans from the United States. Ted Knowlton was employed as the station agent for the Canadian Pacific Railway in Standard, and in a community where most people spoke only Danish, he was also, because of his skills in English, the notary public and secretary of various organizations. Ted insisted that Gwynneth, his first-born, get a university degree before marriage. Gwynneth enrolled in nursing at the University of British Columbia. She had completed her first year at the university and the initial four months of a thirty-two-month hospital training program when her mother, Faye, and four-year-old sister travelled to Vancouver to attend her "capping" ceremony, leaving her father and brother, Gerry, at home.

December 14/1948

My dear Gwynneth;

Mother and Judy left Sunday Evening, on the Local Bus, for Calgary. This was on account of the weather being so cold and uncertain, and as it is about 20 below

CONGRATULATIONS, Little Girl, on your Wonderful Work, and the Results of Your Examinations. Gerry and I had a little cry, swallowed hard a few times to keep feeling of Joy where it normally belonged, and then called Mother on the 'phone, so she could join with us in our outstanding happiness. I am sure that Mother was terribly excited and Happy, and we all join with you in extending our Congratulations, dear, and wish you every success in the Months that lie ahead. Your Record of Exams is one hard to be beaten – Your sister has a hard record to equal – yet, I'm not so sure that she will lag far behind; you may agree with me when you see her and realize what she already has in that brain of hers . . .

As an investment, Little Girl, I consider you one of my best. Given your Health, and Strength, I would wager my right hand on your ability to successfully complete anything you undertook to do, and in a manner well above the average expected of you. What a wonderful source of Happiness you have always been to Mother and me, dear, and your determined stand on that which you know to be right has placed you head and shoulders above everyone else in your class. You have proven to be everything that Mother and I have prayed that you would be, and that will give you some idea how very satisfied we are with you, and the wonderful work you have always done.

I sincerely trust that Mother and you will have a very lovely time together during the days with you. I am sure of one thing –

no Mother, who ever witnessed a "Capping Service", was ever nearly so proud of her daughter as Mother is of you, dear. It is a source of great satisfaction to me to know that Mother can be right there beside you, Little Girl, as this is as we had planned it all along.

And now, your Future. I do not want to look ahead even one minute of that. Little Girl, I only know that your judgement is excellent, and I am positive, given Health and Strength, your life will be one of Happy Service in your Months of Training, filled with daily new experiences – and the wonderful experience that you will witness in the realization that the result of your training has given you the ability to relieve the suffering of others – what a wonderful future is yours, Little Girl, and now, with your proba-tion period completed, actually in the palm of your hand. A person with the Christian Character you have, Little Girl, need only follow the course that right dictates to complete a future brighter than anyone would dare to predict, or anticipate yourself. Your First Thought at all times must be, GUARD WELL YOUR OWN HEALTH, for, without that, no dream you may have ever had can materialize. . . .

Now I shall away to bed, Little Girl, but I wanted to talk with you for a few minutes this evening, and what ever else I may have had that needed my attention is of much less importance than a letter written to my Little Girl, in whom I am so well pleased. . . .

All my Love, dear, and Love to all – from both Gerry and I,

Dad

After her university graduation ceremony, Gwynneth went directly across campus to her wedding rehearsal. Two days later, she married Robert Wallace, whom she had met six years before on a

blind date. Ted Knowlton retired from the CPR and set up a travel
agency in Calgary, from which he re-retired when he was eighty.

See daddy fly

*As a lad of four or five, **Homer Dean** saw First World War air-*
planes rising in the mist over the Mulmur Hills near Shelburne,
Ontario, where he grew up. He dreamed of being a pilot but chose
the ministry and was ordained in the United Church in 1940. Ten
years later, when Canadian forces were mustering for the Korean
War, a chaplain came to the Dean home in Kirkton and asked
Homer to join the Royal Canadian Air Force. During his basic
training, Homer flew from Trenton to Ottawa, a trip he described
for his young daughter.

[1950]

Dear Loral:

Just to think: my little girl is able to write a letter after only three
months at school. There wasn't one word spelled wrong, the lines
were straight and the printing was good. I would like to be home
and hear you reciting "Now that I'm six," but since I won't make
it for the concert, I want you to have it all ready.

When I was writing mother this afternoon in Ottawa I told
her that I was going to describe the airplane trip to you. It isn't
the first time Daddy was up, but it is the longest trip he ever took
. . . All arrangements were made to leave at 6.30 and we were to
report at the no 2 hangar at 6.15. When we arrived it was dark
and the wind was blowing hard from the East. We could see a
shiny two motor Expediter getting gassed up and sitting all ready.

A Group Captain and a Wing Commander were going too and so we waited until they arrived. Then we climbed up a little aluminum ladder leaving our brief cases at the back of the plane. There were just six seats – with two pilots sitting up in front in the first two. They started the motors and all the dials glowed greenish white in front of them. They tested all the gadgets, pushing levels and unwinding and winding cranks all over the cockpit. The plane was insulated inside and had fabric cloth, the seats had leather behind but were metal and hard where you sit down. There were six windows and I sat just at the back of the big wing. The pilots warmed up the motors for about ten minutes finally taxiing away down to the west end of the runway so that we could take off into the wind. Then they tested everything again and waited for a signal from the tower that no other airplanes were in the way. At about 6.10 the lights went out inside, the motors roared louder and louder, we picked up speed and then suddenly we began to lift. The lights of the buildings flashed past our right wing tip and we were away rising higher every second into the darkness. I could feel the pressure on my ears, then that cleared and we straightened out. The motors by now had settled down to one steady roar and fire flashed out behind from the exhausts. Then I looked down and there were lights everywhere, just as though I were looking up at the stars instead of down. I could see cars traveling along a highway – just little stabs of light slowly moving. It looked as though the ground was covered with tiny shining jewels – and I knew that each one was somebody's house and in it there were little girls like Loral and boys like James and Tommy and good Mothers like yours. Stretching for miles in every way I could see here and there little strings of light like diamonds and each one was a little place like Kirkton, with sometimes a bigger town showing up. When we came over Ottawa the pilots brought the plane down closer. We crossed the river and then I noticed a cloud right by the wing tip – I followed it down and down and saw that it was smoke coming straight up from two tall chimneys. We had just crossed the river and I think it was the pulp and paper plant. Mother will know it. The city was dazzling with millions of lights – lights strung out in straight lines

Homer Dean with daughter Loral and son James (Courtesy Loral Dean)

marking the streets, red lights grouped in squares and circles, headlights of thousands of cars moving every way. The air was clear clear and Ottawa never looked so lovely. It was a little bumpy – perhaps wind currents coming up from the concentration of heat which escapes from buildings in a city and makes it warmer than the country. Then I realized that we were down very low and that again the buildings were flashing past. There was a bump, then another and we were rolling along the cement runway toward a hangar. We unbuckled our safety belts, the pilots ushered us out and a minute later five chaplains met us, among them two Roman Catholics who were very friendly. We were shown up to the officer's mess – oh by the way, we landed at about 7.05, a little under an hour for the trip which is 115 aeronautical miles – get Jamesie to figure out how fast we made the trip – the plane travels about a hundred and eighty miles an hour but I don't think we could have gone that fast all the way. I then called Uncle Bill and Celia and spent the evening with them. This afternoon it has taken us six and a half hours from the time we left the officer's mess at Rockcliffe to the time we arrived at the mess at Trenton, and so you can see that it is faster by airplane . . .

Every time I see a little boy it reminds me of James or Tommy and every time I see a little girl I think of you. But none of them would take your place.

Love,

Daddy

Tough critic

Born in Belfast in 1921, Brian Moore emigrated to Canada in 1948 and became a citizen in 1953 when he was living in Montreal and supporting himself and his wife, Jackie, and infant son, Michael, by writing paperback thrillers under the names of Bernard Mara and, later, Michael Bryan. Moore disowned his six pseudonymous potboilers, saying he wrote them "with my tongue in my cheek," but these genre books allowed him to work on his first literary novel – Judith Hearne. *Rejected by ten American publishers, who admired the book but felt it would be too depressing for their readers,* Judith Hearne *was published in 1955 in England. A year later, it came out in the United States as* The Lonely Passion of Judith Hearne, *and it is still in print. While British reviewers lauded the novel as "a triumph," Brian's mother,* **Eileen McFadden Moore,** *was critical, especially of the sexual content.*

17 Cliftonville Ave.

Belfast

2 – 6 – 55

My dearest Brian,

The only Review I have seen since I sent you the one in the Observer is the one in the New Statesman, and as you already have got that one I need not send it to you.

As long as this rail strike lasts we are not allowed to send anything over 6 ozs by mail.

I enjoyed reading your book very much, but I was rather disappointed with the sex parts. I think you should keep these parts for the Bernard Mara books, also your choice of names for instance Miss Friel given as a teacher, & Kevin O'Kane as having a bar in the Falls Rd. [both?] perfectly true – none of your characters were lovable, but you meant it to be so, however I am glad to find you were kind to the church and Clergy. I would have liked your book much better if you had left out the part about Bernie and the maid. Also Mr. Madden in some of his moods. You certainly left nothing to one's imagination, and my advice to you in your next book leave out parts like this. You have a good imagination and could write books anyone could read. Perhaps you will think me rather hard and critical, but this is exactly how I feel no matter what anyone thinks.

As far as I know your book is selling alright here, and I will send you any review you come across.

Although I have said all this about your book I will be looking forward to the July one that is if you send it to me. . . .

With best love to you, Jackie, Mike and Sean [Moore's brother], and hoping to hear from you soon

Love

Mamma

Before he died in 1999 in California, where he had lived for more than thirty years with his second wife, Jean, Moore told an interviewer that he was very fond of his mother and was one of her favourite sons, "if not her favourite son."

A RETIRED NONENTITY

*Nearing his eightieth year, **Arsène (Tim) Goyette** was very much a fatalist, as his letters reveal. He saw himself having to "trudge along willingly" on "the one and only road" possible. That road began in Quebec about 1884. In 1902, when he was eighteen, Tim began working for La Banque d'Hochelaga in Montreal, which in 1905 transferred him to its western branch to substitute for six clerks who were hospitalized with typhoid fever. Tim's brother, Albin (known as Chéri), joined him in Winnipeg the following year, getting a job as a railway mail clerk, sorting letters and parcels on trains travelling daily between Emerson, on the U.S. border, and Winnipeg. After a stint in the hotel business, Albin returned to Montreal as superintendent of the Quebec Liquor Commission. In 1919, Victoria Starr, a Winnipeg girl from a Polish family, joined him in Montreal where they were married. Tim – "the exiled one" – stayed in the West, working in the bank – renamed La Banque Canadienne Nationale – for forty-seven years. After Albin's death in 1950, Tim wrote almost monthly from Winnipeg to his sister-in-law in Montreal. Sprinkling his typed letters with hyphens and rows of periods, he recalled the events of their past and shared his ever-darkening ideas about life. His letterhead was the crest of the Goguets (a branch of the Goyette family) with the motto "Chacun le sien" – to each his own.*

WINNIPEG – Manitoba.
June fourth – 1961

Madame C.-A. Goyette,
3951 avenue Van Horne,
Montréal – Qué

Chère Vicky,
Glad to hear you are back safe and sound after a wonderful trip down South – way down South I should say – something to take the cobwebs away – with a chance of scenery – and a visit with your dear sister – and the nephews – and Blanche and her hubby – a real relaxation – the one you needed, – in order to face the music once more – on your return where a package of worries was waiting for you....these don't fiz on you, when you have the strength & the vigor to take care of them – one by one – it is a cinch. You had some trouble with one of your trees – being unrooted – but you managed to have it done. So, everything is hanky dory – once again . . .

Gradually we have to submit to the changes – For the first time I had to get someone to take off my storm sashes this year. I must realize that I am getting old and feeble – I don't dare tackle a few large windows – they are getting too heavy – for my old frame – I submitted....without a struggle – I know when I am beaten – it is better than running the risk to drop one of these windows – and break them into smittereens – Better confess....early in the game – and save your strength – for worth while matters – I can still accomplish fairly well – If I say so myself....as a retired non entity. Life is a strange adventure – in youth, in middle age – and even in old age – little by little a slow transformation is being a reality – that we must accept readily – just like a punishment –

that we deserve no doubt. – We are less subject to influences good or bad – Our future is being shortened daily – but it is clearer in our minds – we seem to know what we can expect from life – most of our illusions disappear – we become wiser without any training whatsoever – we become hard boiled – and we don't expect miracles any longer. – It is all a game played on the checker-board – of days and nights – we are the pawns being – pushed right and left at the pleasure of the player-Master – just to be taken off...some day...to be put into dreamland. These are the circumstances – the main factor in every life.

Take in my case for instance – what would have happened – if in 1905 – there would not have been an epidemic of typhoid fever in Winnipeg – taking five employees of the Bank to the Hospital. I would not have been sent in exile – Chéri would not have come West neither – Your life would have been changed – materially – Would you have married a Frenchman like your sister Olga? Circumstances – are the governing factors – in life. We have nothing to do with them – they are the ones to rule our destinies – and we follow humbly – without a whimper – whatever road is shown to us to travel on – and this is how we get to the end of the trail – We have no great merit – for all this traveling we call our own – we were just shown the way to go..... and we obliged... like little children we are....dutifully obedient all through lifetime.

We didn't choose our surroundings – even our parents are chosen for us – we are not consulted about anything at all – circumstances decide for us – what will happen in our lives – we just follow directions – every time. And yet we believe that we are free to do – and act – as if we had perfect liberty of action – It's all fake – camouflaged – from beginning – to end – of the life we live on the checker-board – of days and nights – all through life. We often act as substitutes – nothing more – as we go on – in life – we learn of the little importance – we have in the whole picture of the universe. We are next to nothing – just a little shell – on the ocean waves until we capsize – and write finis.

This is one of my black days – forgive me. Take good care of yourself

Goodbye – Aloha –
Tim

Bridging the gulf

*When he wrote this philosophical letter (translated from French) to his eldest son who was working in cinema in Quebec, **Louis Martin** was living in Jonquière, then an industrial city on the Saguenay River in Quebec known for producing newsprint and aluminum.*

29 March 1969

My dear son,

I don't write to you often, and what's more I don't speak to you often. It's because I don't much believe in giving advice – I believe that you become a man on your own and that a father must very early on respect his son's personality. It's more important than ever, as Bertrand Russell said, that each man represents all of us; all the same I often regret not having been closer to you and your brother. It's because I fear sentimentality between men, and unfortunately I was often away. Anyway, ever since your childhood I have had a great deal of affection for you – you have always been agreeable – even in growing up you never caused us the least difficulty. You were good at learning music and at your trade, you now practise a trade that you love and for which you are well prepared and I believe that you are skilled as a film producer – unfortunately I don't know how to judge this art – and I'm distressed about that because I cannot appreciate your work and I would like to, but for a long time I have seen you work and I have confidence in you because you are an honest workman. I am grateful to you for the care you show to the two youngest members of the family. Your mother and I are very happy about your relationship with your brothers, as well as with your older sister. You perform a great service for the other children in the family and you are better able than we are to help them. I realize that our time and the values of our society hold no excitement for young people, but you and others are in the process of building a more humane and brotherly society, one that we want to see realized – everyone must work according to his talent, his temperament, his qualifications, and the depth of his engagement is more important in the long term than momentary, sporadic activism, without the quest for a deep transformation.

I will speak to you about this again.

I kiss you, say hello to your friends that I know. . . .

Here, all goes well. . . .

Your father

LITTLE ORPHAN KELLI

When Dale Johnston turned three, his parents, Allan and Linda Johnston, of Lac Du Bonnet, Manitoba, decided to take him flying in a plane that Allan, an experienced pilot, had recently purchased and overhauled. Allan had test-flown the plane and the weather was ideal for flying, but inexplicably, over open water, the engine failed. Allan managed to turn the craft and guide it back to land. Only a few feet from shore and a safe landing, a wing hit trees and the plane crashed. All three died, leaving the Johnstons' eight-year-old Kelli orphaned. At the funeral, Allan's mother, Eugenie Johnston, asked an old friend to try to comfort her granddaughter. **Walter Keller,** *a Swiss forester, knew the Johnston family during the years he worked for the Manitoba government. Keller flew to Canada from Switzerland to be a pallbearer. Unable to find the right words to help Kelli, Keller sent her a letter that she was to read when "the time was right."*

Horgen, Swizerland

25.1.1989

Dear Kelly,

I am writing to you because I hurt so much over the tragic loss of your mom and dad and little Dale. Because I knew them well and because your daddy was one of my closest friends, who in many ways was a lot like myself, I would like to share some of my thoughts with you. We cannot see a reason why they were called away from this earth so suddenly, and it seems that we can never stop hurting!

Still we will have to accept that they are gone. And some day, when all the crying starts to ease and the feelings of anger and hurt in our hearts begin to let up; it is time to remember the good and happy times you spent together. It is time to fill your heart with memories of your mom and dad and Dale.

I know that you will never forget them and that in your heart you will carry their memory forever.

Your daddy was away on business a lot of times in the past years and I know that you had felt lonesome for him, he was in some faraway place stuck with an awful lot of work, wishing he could be home with you. I know what that feels like because I'm a daddy too!

Daddies worry about their families a lot and they often work extra hard to make sure that there is enough money to give their wives and children all the things they need. Finally when he could stand being away so much no longer he decided to quit the flying business to be home with the family. That must have been a hard decision, because we all know how much he liked to fly his helicopters!

To us your daddy was the Wayne Gretzky of the pilots, he was a champion and a gentleman at the same time. He was a kind-hearted friendly outgoing person who's chuckling laugh will forever ring in my ears. Although I do not understand the reason for this senseless tragedy I learned one thing: If such a terrible accident can happen to a champion, then it can happen to anyone! So I'm going to lead my life from now on being kind to people while there still is time.

Dear Kelly, I know that you are a brave girl and I wish you all the strength and courage to continue your life the way your parents had wanted it to be. I know at times this will be hard and at times you will not know which way to go. Then just think back on how momy and daddy had taught you and how they would have wanted you to decide. Even though we now live far away from you, we are still your friends and you can write to us at anytime and perhaps some day you will come and visit us in Switzerland. I want you to know that in our thoughts and prayers we'll always be with you.

Your friends

Diana, Sarah, Christa & Walter Keller

Big brother

Lorraine Wynes *of North Vancouver wrote this letter for her brother, her only sibling, on his sixty-fifth birthday. Marvin Tandy worked for almost forty years for Pacific Press, the publisher of Vancouver's two daily newspapers, and lives today across the lane from the house in Vancouver where he and Lorraine were raised.*

March 17, 1990

To Marvin Tandy:

Once upon a time (September 14, 1934) in the village of Vancouver a little girl was born to the Tandy family. Everyone was glad to see her until they got her home from the hospital. This little girl knew how to cry!!!! It could have been the side trip her mother took on the way to the hospital that upset her planned coming out party. The Burrard Street bridge had just opened and her mom wanted to sight-see. Anyway this kid wasn't pleased and was going to make everyone pay for the delay. Luckily she had a brother who could rock and push a buggy and knew how to stop the crying. She must have known he cared and it wasn't his fault she was a little late so she latched onto him. It is documented in photos that he really liked this little monster so she became his slave. He took advantage of this adulation by flushing her head down the toilet and holding her by one foot off the porch while rocks below waited for his arm to fail. She

*Marvin Tandy
holding his sister, Lorraine*
(Courtesy Lorraine Wynes)

waited patiently for him to return from the airforce just so she could try on his uniforms. He returned and they spent many weekends in matching (ugly) yellow Jantzen swimsuits laying on their backs watching his pigeons fly. This was interrupted by water fights through the neighborhood with this little girl enlisting the help of her friend Shirley. He watched her after her appendix was removed waking her up to make sure she was sleeping OK. He also tried to make a track star of her but she seized up under pressure, to his chagrin. She finally graduated from high school wearing an orchid corsage he picked out. Of course he had picked the subjects she completed. The years went on with him overseeing her life. His car was the first she would drive. They shared her first "take-out" Chinese food and they actually survived on this for many weeks while the mom was at the logging camp with the dad. He took her to her first football games and even paid. When she left home for the first time to go to Calgary to work he came to visit her and to-gether they toured the Calgary brewery where she became an amateur brewmaster while they sampled the beer. He even took her to a Calgary football game that lasted almost to halftime when the weather convinced them this was not the town to live in!

After all the years he has always been there for her and her husband. She doesn't have a living father anymore but she does have a loving brother who has been as close as a father could be all her life and at times just as bossy.

Anyway to make a long story short, I looked and looked and couldn't find a suitable card so here you are!!!!!!! It is only Wednesday so I may find one yet and I may even win the lottery and give you something nice.

Lots of love,
Your sister

Praising Bronwen

*In the summer of 1997, **Mavis P.J. Butlin**, who was then living in Guelph, Ontario, looked after her four-year-old great-grand-daughter. When the visit came to an end and little Bronwen Schultz was on her way home to Renfrew, Ontario, Butlin wrote to her granddaughter, Ceridwen Roberts.*

[1997]

Dear Ceridwen:

I have just driven home from bidding Bronwen 'goodbye'. I cried all the way home and am still bawling my eyes out. Some deep love, I have never felt before, has been unleashed within me, by her. She is one gorgeous person. I feel so privileged to have been able to take a small part in her upbringing. She learns so fast – it is awesome to think what wrong feelings I may unwittingly convey and she would pick up.

My fridge is full of little pots of this and that – that she was saving till later. She knows when she has had enough and doesn't overstuff herself. My mirrors and glass doors have various finger and popsicle hieroglyphics – all very meaningful to one certain small person.

She seems to understand the difference between things that are 'not done' because they are hurtful of another person's feelings and those things that are 'not done' because of expediency or cleanliness. She carries her head high and marches around as if she owns the world.

Bronwen is trusting and fearless in the water – knowing Grammie will hold out a hand to grasp, or give her a boost when necessary. She tries and tries to swim a certain length, increasing the distance between her jump in point and the steps each time – and is so happy when she triumphs.

She has boundless energy! 'It's not dark yet, time for another trip somewhere' anywhere that might prove interesting, even peruses my shopping list on the fridge as a possible excuse for an excursion or a treat.

However – she is also very forgiving when I got her there too late to ride the carousel (tickets sold till 7:15 or we got there at 7:16).

Bronwen is very capable and resourceful. The video tapes flick on and off at her slightest whim – and her music tapes take precedence in car or van over all else that may be on!

She knows what she wants to wear – picked out very good colours and styles for herself – then wore them with pride and pizzaz.

She absolutely entranced the audience that had come to hear the band concert in the park – by marching up and down and swaying or moving in perfect time. The conductor actually asked her to conduct for him – but she just couldn't handle that – and sweetly declined.

Thank you for letting me have Bronwen for a while – this house seems empty without her. I love her so. You have a hard row to hoe, terrible decisions to make and such precious lives hanging in the balance. Whatever you have to suffer, however hard you have to work, you are blessed with two wonderful little people to make it all worthwhile in the end.

My love to you.

Grammie P. J.

Before moving to Victoria, B.C., in 2003, Mavis Butlin enjoyed several extended visits with her Bronwen.

Pas de deux

*In 1989 in her early forties, leading ballerina **Veronica Tennant** retired from the National Ballet of Canada after giving perform- ances of John Cranko's Juliet, the role in which she had made her debut with the company when she was eighteen, and after dancing in a gala tribute with guest artists. Before the gala, Veronica's mother, **Doris Tennant**, wrote her a loving note.*

My dearest darling Veronica,

They have called your Gala performance tonight – Tuesday, Nov. 21/1989 – a celebration of the TENNANT magic, – 25 years!

For me, it will be more than that. As I sit in the theatre, watch- ing you with pride, trying to capture & memorise every moment of the evening forever, I want you to know that you have brought me so much joy & happiness from the moment you were born, when I called out "Hello, Veronica, I'm a mother, I'm a mother!" And then onwards, so many extraordinary marvellous moments of pride & joy. You are so gifted in so many ways & I always am amazed at what you can do. You know I love you with all my heart. God bless you,

Mumma

Following her retirement, Veronica demonstrated her many other talents – as a choreographer of dramatic dance, author of chil- dren's books, teacher, and television producer. In 2001, she marked her mother's eightieth birthday with a typewritten letter of acknowledgement and admiration.

Four-year-old Veronica Tennant and her mother, Doris
(Courtesy Doris and Veronica Tennant)

November 16, 2001

My darling Mumma –
How do I distill into the written word – into the limits of this card, what you mean to me?

I think of how you took me to ballet class when I was 4 in England – how you established from that age, how important my education was. Within a week of our arrival here in Canada in 1955 – how you took me to ballet class – fathoming that this – DANCING – was of such urgent importance to me – education again, making great sacrifice – enormous decisions of personal forfeit, so that both Gillian and I could have the very finest of schooling at Bishop Strachan. And for me subsequently The National Ballet School – how you drove me to and from ballet class – which in those earliest years were in the grungiest parts of town – how you supported me through that persistent back injury in my graduation year – never once – as others did – suggesting I "not" dance – How you arranged for my exams to be written in bed – to go to Jersey and then London to rehab – & consult other doctors – how you "covered" for me when I finally gained entry into the National Ballet Company and then sprained my wrists so badly that I couldn't attend my first rehearsals for Romeo & Juliet – "Oh she's just fine Miss Franca – yes – yes – she'll be back soon –" meanwhile you were dressing me, brushing my hair – I couldn't accomplish anything without your help.

How you nurtured, loved, supported and believed in me – encouraged, and yes – pushed – but only taking the prompts from me – always allowing me to "call the shots" Strong personalities – 3 flowering in the same house – my not understanding until I was much older – how truly extraordinary YOU are. Doris Tennant is the fountain of youth, proof of positivity, orginator of generosity, – the inventer of a Mother's love – Doris Tennant is my Mother –

she is a modern woman a dreamer a creator an original – it's because of *My* MUM's talent that I gained entry in to my 2nd career at the CBC – she was there first – she opened doors always putting her 2 children first. My MUM has JOIE – SHE HAS SOUL – she loves LIFE – she bubbles and gives and it's perfect that amongst her closest friends – all who have been touched by her – we can share our gratitude, our amazement our love – DORIS – MUMMA – you have no equal – you are the best.

[Veronica]

GLORIOUS GOLDEN AWE

Terri Luanna Robinson was born on October 25, 1974, in Nova Scotia's Annapolis Valley. Early in the morning, twenty-eight years later, her father, the celebrated science-fiction writer Spider Robinson, wrote Terri the following letter about the morning of her birth.

25 October, 2002

Terri,

I know, you've heard it before – like all my best stories – but that's okay, I feel like telling it again.

Four sevens of years ago, at this hour, I was in a relentlessly soothing room – soothing layout, soothing decor, soothing ceiling even – soothing ceiling especially – having the small bones of my right hand crushed into paste by the merciless grip of a woman who was trying very hard to become your mother, and listening to her scream her head off. Nearly a full day she'd been in labor, by then, and she was as exhausted as anyone I've ever seen survive. I guess it was about this hour that she finally surrendered on Doing

It Natchurl, and let them give her drugs to dilate her cervix and to hasten your arrival. She would not let them give her anything for pain, though she was in so much agony that both Mary Corrigan and I begged her to. No need: soon the drugs would kick in and you would show up for your party . . .

Something like five or six hours later they said to her, it's not a matter of choice any more: the cervix just will not dilate for some unknowable reason, and the kid just will not drop for some unknowable reason, and after so much hard work trying, both of you are approaching clinical distress. We are going in there after the baba, and your only choices are to be relieved at that or to be stupid; say goodnight and count backwards from one hundred . . . don't be an asshole, Mr. Robinson, of course you can't come into the ER, go have a cigarette . . .

On the way out to the parking lot, I bummed a pack of matches from a nurse. It was one of a series then ubiquitous all over Nova Scotia, with Tarot cards printed on them. Like many hippies, I had been absently collecting the set, without thinking much about it. Somebody had counted mine and said I was only short one, but then we got sidetracked before he could hunt through the stack and tell me which one. But I recognized it instantly when the nurse handed it to me. Death.

Well, they say the card you pick often means the exact opposite of what it says. Certainly I said it – then, about a million times, to myself, in the time it took me to smoke that cigarette. Then when I could tell by the smell and taste that I was smoking the filter, I speedwalked all the way back into the building, ran upstairs rather than wait for the elevator, sprinted down silent darkened halls until I reached the door to the Maternity wing . . .

. . . stopped in my tracks, and stood there like a cigar-store dummy for how the hell do I know how long, knowing that when

I opened that door, somewhere down the hall ahead I would see a face, any one of several faces, and when I did it would see me, and when it did it would react, and if the reaction was not a smile I would need to become unconscious very quickly . . .

. . . opened the door and a nurse looked up and smiled at me and made a peace sign. Reboot heart –

She took me to a room, and carefully noticed only my broad grin, and not my tears or my uncontrollable trembling or my heavy breathing, and she said, wait here, and was gone. A minute later she was back, with other irrelevant carbon-based lifeforms, and you and your mother. Both as sound asleep as drunks, you sprawled on your belly between Jeanne's breasts, and I had about four or maybe five glorious golden awestruck seconds to contemplate and try to comprehend the new concept of the two of you, of something being that beautiful without it cracking the universe . . . and then both of you awakened at the same instant, as if somebody had rung a Zen bell somewhere, and your eyes opened and met and locked on to each other, and current started to flow between you, and I became just another irrelevant carbon-based lifeform, albeit one in a uniquely privileged position. You just stared into each others' groggy bleary eyes, for at least thirty seconds, information flowing in both directions.

Well, you've seen the expression in photos. The world did not impress you a lot. Way too bright, way too cool, way too loud, not cozy at all, and full of all manner of uncouth riffraff, like that hairy dork with all the teeth. (You hadn't recognized me yet as Belly-Singer; everything sounded different without liquid in your ears.) What I'm not sure the photos fully capture is the expression that Jeanne was beaming back down at you: trust me, girlfriend: It gets WAY better than this. You're gonna love it! This from someone who had just spent twenty-eight unbroken hours doing exercise equivalent to Navy SEAL training while in root-canal-level pain, and then got knifed. One look at you and she knew it had been a bargain.

A steal.

Happy birthday to you, darling daughter. For every second of every minute of four sevens of years, I have been very glad you decided to come out and play. You make me a very

Proud Papa

Daddy,

I'm sitting here at work trying to hold back the tears . . . Did anyone ever tell you that you have a real talent for writing?!? That was one of the most poignant, heartfelt, raw and touching pieces I've ever read (and the fact that it was about me is an added bonus!). Damn you for making me tear up at work!

I imagine you know already how much I love you. And how I thank my lucky stars each day that somehow someone decided that I would be the fortunate one to get you as a dad. (How I got lucky enough to have both you AND mom, I'll never know . . .) imagine that I must of learned some hard lessons in my previous lives and was set forth in this one to somehow use all my wisdom, luck, and blessings to make the world better for other people. It's the only explanation I have for why I've been given so much.

I can't think of anyone else that has the kind of parent/child relationship that we do. But I think the world would be such a better place if there were more families like us out there.

Thank you for everything daddy. You've taught me so many wonderful and valuable things in my 28 years . . . when writing, always hook the reader with your first sentence . . . in love, never settle . . . value yourself first and this will help you to value others . . . life is short, so enjoy it to the fullest. . . . everyone in the world is different, and that's ok . . .

Intentionally or not, you have molded me into the person that I am. I credit my strength to having wonderful parents who always stood beside me, cherished me, cheered me on, and shared their knowledge of the world.

I'll never be able to thank you enough.

Always,

terri lu

In August 2003, Terri Luanna married Brazilian Heron da Silva. The couple are living in Astoria, New York, where she is working on an M.A. in social work and he is studying engineering.

Love and War

⁂

*"I don't want to cause you any
anxiety or sorrow"*

A NIGHT OF DREAMS

The First World War – the Great War, the War to End All Wars – began in the summer of 1914 when Britain and her self-governing colonies, including Canada, confronted Germany over its designs on Russia, France, and Belgium. In October, **Chattan Stephens** *sailed overseas with the first Canadian contingent of troops as a lieutenant in the Royal Highlanders of Canada, the Black Watch regiment. From the Salisbury Plain training ground in the south of England, the twenty-six-year-old wrote Hazel, his wife of three years, at home in Toronto with their two young children.*

Nov 10th /14

Dearest Hazel

I have just come in from the usual days work and have read your letter of Oct 26th. It was one of the nicest letters you have ever writen me and when I get home I am going to show you that you have made no mistake in making me the trustee of such a wonderful love. You know very well that my gift of language is very small when trying to express myself in matters of this sort but if I could write down here how I feel towards you the paper would burn in my hands from the very expression of these thoughts. It is terribly hard for me to sit here at a table in the mess tent, and try to express

Chatten Stephens
(Courtesy Frances Ballantyne)

how I feel towards you when as soon as a thought of you enters my mind I look up from the paper and try to figure just what you are doing at the present moment and how you are looking. I take your picture out and looking at it I think what a wonderful mother you must be and what a wonderful wife I have got.

I hope both the kiddies will be as happy some day as I am with you. Tonight is not a time for me to write of my doings or of the happenings here. It is a night of dreams for me, for I will read your letter over and over again and don't want to think of anything else but you, so don't expect anything in this letter except the outpourings of a man's heart which is entirely in your keeping. Dearest I love you, have always loved you, and will always love you.

Your own but
very lonely to-night
Chat

Life's nightmares were to follow his night of dreams. An equally lonely Hazel Stephens soon joined her husband in England, bringing their two-year-old daughter, Frances, but leaving their infant son, John, behind with Chat's mother. The following spring the grandmother decided to bring the boy to his family and sailed on the British steamer RMS Lusitania, *which a German submarine torpedoed south of Ireland. She and the child were among the twelve hundred passengers who died. Chattan had fought on the*

*Hazel Stephens with daughter, Frances,
and doomed son, John* (Courtesy Frances Ballantyne)

front lines in Belgium for only a few weeks before catching trench fever. He was an invalid after returning to Canada in the summer of 1915 and died in the Great Flu epidemic three years later.

AN AFFAIR OF THE MIND

Talbot Papineau was destined by birth, education, inclination, and personal charm to be a leader in Canadian politics. He was the great-grandson of Louis-Joseph Papineau, who led the patriote struggle against Britain for control of Lower Canada's political institutions. Young Talbot studied political economy, was one of Canada's first Rhodes Scholars, and in 1911 campaigned for Laurier's Liberals. When war broke out he was a thirty-one-year-old lawyer in Montreal. He immediately joined the Princess Patricia's Canadian Light Infantry, a regiment founded by his friend Hamilton Gault. After fighting in Belgium at St. Eloi and Bellewaerde Ridge (and receiving a Military Cross for bravery), he was given a desk job at Canadian Headquarters, but asked to rejoin his regiment. His pencilled wooing of Beatrice Fox, a twenty-four-year-old sculptress from Philadelphia – conducted without a face-to-face meeting – began on the front line in Flanders.

Armentieres –
France, June 24th
1915.

My dear Miss Fox,
You will be surprised to receive this letter – you may even be indignant – though I doubt the latter as I am informed you are intelligent. Intelligence mingled with feminine curiosity will induce you to condone a certain social irregularity. You may have heard of me

but you have forgotten. You certainly
have not met me or to put it more for-
mally I have not been introduced. But
I am prepared to do that for myself
and I have your picture. American
publicity of personalities is to blame
– also the curious chain of coinci-
dences which I am about to relate – If
I am a little obscure or erratic you
must forgive as I am in a dugout
within a hundred yards of the Bosches
and they send an occasional rifle
grenade or a Whizz-Bang in my direction. I have just inspected rifles and
respirators and it seemed to me the
enemy had a personal interest in my
inquiry as explosives followed me

Talbot Papineau in April 1916
(Talbot Mercer Papineau col-
lection/Library and Archives
Canada C-013222)

down the trench. I have returned to amuse myself by writing you
instead of sensibly lying down to sleep before the watchful hours of
twilight and darkness. However to return to my chain. Your picture
came into my hands yesterday in the following manner.

While in England which is still principally London for me alas
– and before we came upon this mad adventure I made friends
with the mother-in-law of our Colonel – We are friends still and
grow better each day. She is intelligently eccentric and a critic
and a raconteur of force. She is also a friend of yours! Among
other things we discussed the United States and then Americans –
The dear lady is of strong prejudices and open expressions. We
developed an argument – (interrupted here by a sudden change in
wind – blowing from German trenches and I have ordered the
sentries to lay their smoke-helmets on the parapet in case we get a

gas attack) I am three-quarters American. I am a believer in the U.S. I am an admirer of their future and of some of the past – consequently we argued – Then it appeared that Lady Donoughomore had met some charming Americans – few but of good quality – To be explicit – yourself and your family – Thereupon, I was interested – I was interested because I was told you were many things I find it difficult to believe a woman can be – all at the same time – Intelligent – Lovely – Amiable – You were talented without freakishness. This of course was a matter of opinion – As a matter of fact you were of Philadelphia and I was again interested. I received my first education in Philadelphia or if I am a Spartan I was trained twenty years before I was born in Philadelphia – My mother was born there. My uncle lives there. I sometimes visit there. Therefore I wrote to my uncle and yesterday I had his reply – two months late – enclosing a newspaper picture of you – two of them in fact – The one in which you fondle a bust and wear a big apron I did not care for – the printing was bad. I sent it to Lady Donoughomore. The other – a full face – in evening dress with a glint of sunlight in your hair I liked and I have kept it – So may any other purchasers of the Public Ledger of North America – such is the price of fame – I am not sufficiently a Cubist or Futurist or whatever it may be not to regret the absence of an eye – One eye is clear and good and amiable – the other is principally printers ink – The same may be said of the left of the lips – the right discloses a very pleasing pleasantness and perhaps a sense of humour. The whole is decidedly attractive but may be due to the art of Mathilda as much as to Nature!

My uncle tells me you lived near him for years in Haverford and that you were invited to dinner to meet me – if you please – the last time I was there – You didn't come because you were out of town. I take it rather unkindly of you. I might then have known your address and your colouring. I am really quite exercised as to whether you are "brune, blond or rousse."

To have completed my chain – the links are a little concealed perhaps in the weeds of my discourse – but I am forgiven. For the moment I am inoccupied and I have only flies, rifles and roar of distant cannon to listen to. I should sleep but the fresh adventure of writing to an unknown rather appealed to me. Would you forbid me the appeal and deny the poor soldier – I can work that poor soldier gag rather well – a slight diversion – After all what does it or does it not matter – Like the Kaiser I should be a trifle unbalanced – since August I have been a licensed killer – since January I have tried to kill – I have succeeded in not being killed at any rate. Out of forty officers I am the only one neither killed, wounded nor sick. Rather a record of good fortune – but a record which may be broken this evening or in ten minutes for all I know. Living on such volcanoes and flipping a coin for consciousness or speculative Valhallas destroys my sense of decorum and something of my Philadelphian conventionality. The paper today has something of us in it and I may send you a clipping. If I do I outrage my modesty but fairness seems to demand you should know a little of your mysterious correspondent. By the way my uncle is James S. Rogers – my grandfather was Talbot of the same ilk – from whom I am named.

I could write indefinately but I must sleep. I really must – and what would old friends say if they knew of my occupation – when I write if I write at all – "too busy to write"! My earthly address is Captain Talbot M. Papineau.

> P.P.C.L.I.
>
> (Princess Patricia's Cand. Light Infantry)
>
> 80th Brigade
>
> 27th Division
>
> British Expeditive Force, Eng.

(p.t.o.) [please turn over]

This [the address] I give though against the Censors' regulations –
I should like to know if this reaches you – You may just say "yes"
– or you may abuse me – or you my write a folio – or [you] may
have your father write to threaten me – or you may have a fiancé
and say so – Only don't ignore me – !

The storm is over – the sun shines beautifully – I look up to
the fringe of a wheat field filled with blood red poppies – below
the earth is brown and muddy – We are moles and high explosives
are searching to destroy us. Thousands of flies buzz about these
rather unsavoury underground homes where men have lived and
died for seven months. Would you like to hear more? Then continued in my next perhaps –

Yours

Talbot M. Papineau

I shall confess to Lady D. what I have done in my next to her
– The shelling is getting a little too active for my liking.

*The long-distance romance, pursued in letters between the battle
and home fronts, deepened as the months passed.*

General Headquarters Staff

Canadian Army Corps.

March 7ᵗʰ 1916

My dear Bee.

May I call you a darling? Surely if I am your valentine I may be
permitted at least once this very natural out burst. Today especially for this morning I received your beautiful box of cigarettes
so prettily wrapped and so extensive as to assure me "smokes"
for a long time to come. Here I have room to do them credit and

together with the heart shaped box of candy they ornament a large chest in a corner of my "sitter" . . .

. . . I am very glad you said in your last letter that our correspondance was now upon a different footing and was no longer merely existent for the entertainment impersonally of a "lonely soldier" – That purpose it has indeed served beyond all expectation but beyond that again we have I am glad you agree become interested in each other as definate personalities. I am proud of your work and your success and I want to remain connected no matter what may change my own life – place or affaires de coeur – or anything. I think I expressed a fear in my last letter that you might think otherwise but I am reassured by what you have said. None the less I shall be glad to hear a repetition of your view.

My position now makes it perhaps more difficult for me to mention our operations as I may not distinguish between what is interesting rumour and what is important information that I may actually acquire.

Everybody is more cheerful than I have seen them for quite a while. I am under impression that at length Germany's astounding strength is beginning to wane. I think of great fat wrestlers, one grimly, desperately hour after hour holding up his shoulders against the inevitable fall . . . I love the little touches of feeling you sometimes manifest . . . I must now go to my dinner. So farewell my dear Bee.

Talbot.

April 21st 1916.

My dear B.

I have so much to acknowledge and so much to tell you that I am confronted with a task almost beyond my powers. First let me tell you how I received the memorial photo from Frederick Palmer.

On April 13th I suddenly received orders to return to England for investiture by the King of my Military Cross . . .

. . . I have enjoyed your letters enormously. They were substantial and interesting. None the less I am a trifle puzzled. How can I reconcile your stern admonition that our letters should be matter of fact and impersonal with the charming kiss – blown it is true and only sisterly – but nevertheless a wild flight of sentimental frivolity for the serious B. I am convinced we shall never be quite understood until our actual meeting – but why should we – Why not be a mystery to each other at least until the end of the war? . . .

Yours ever

Talbot

G. H. Q.

April 28th 1916

My dear B.

. . . Here we have a few days of glorious weather – The leaves and flowers are showing and the countryside is beautiful – At least until we reach the belt of utter desolation about Ypres. Even there I find an occasional touch of beauty. Yesterday by the ruins of a farmhouse just behind the firing lines I saw a fruit-tree whose black branches were covered with white blossoms as thick as clinging snow. An interesting expedition altogether. The night before the Germans exploded a mine, bombarded and attacked. The line was held and I went over to report – An unpleasant spectacle – many unburied bodies – One officer with his head off. In front of me a man was hit and his arm shattered – blood everywhere. Many places I had to crawl flat on my face and I was muddy and wet and sandy by turns. I went into the crater – Not a sign of all the men who had been in that line before. They simply disappeared. I wonder if they felt anything. What were their last thoughts! Are they as sentient-conscious beings anywhere now or are they gone – knowing nothing? . . .

I hope my photos have reached you safely and are not unpleasant surprises. When am I to have another of yours. I await your next with pleasurable anticipation.

Talbot.

May 8th 1916

My dearest B –

What an impulsive darling you are and with the kindest heart I have ever met – Moved to compassion by my loveless state you put yourself upon the sacrificial [altar] and taking courage you write me your charming letter of the 19th and send me gifts emblematic of your impulse. I have hastened to the Signal Office and I have directed a cable to your address with the one word "Congratulations" – not you must understand that that is the word I would have selected myself to send – rather to receive – but because it is the code word which you had suggested. You will notice I do not send "Congratters" but that is because I am sure the ignorant telegraphists would have mistaken it for a secret code and it would never have been transmitted. From that moment our contract has been completed for it is established in jurisprudence that the acceptance of an offer takes effect from the time of posting a letter or the deposit of a telegram and not at the time of its reception by the offeror. The P. O. or the Telegraph O. is considered the agent of the offeror and notification to the agent is legally equivalent to notification to the principal. Consequently my dear B we are engaged – We are lovers – tho I should judge very timid ones – You do indeed in the courage of your first impulse promise me "real love letters" but I mark the gradual oozing of your resolution and the sudden break lest our "courage" or was it your love should altogether go. You repent the cable suggestion and then you insert the saving sheet to say that all is "beautiful nonsense". Yet a few moments before you had actually written "When I say I really love you well there isn't any come back" – But when at some distant date you have scanned me through a mask and decided to really love me then there shall be no withdrawal? I imagine that is what you mean. But why should I direct your writing when as a matter of fact I thoroughly know your state of mind and could tell you about yourself more clearly than even you could . . .

So please do love me, love me dearly. I like it. I like it over much. I shall like your love letters. And though you may say you place no obligations upon me yet I shall be as faithful and as long as I can. Shall you not expect something in return really? Shall it be only play after all and shall the serious game be with someone else? We can not possibly tell – not until after the war and after the meet. In the meantime it is safe to play. I am a dangerous one to be serious with. There is no reason why this evening or tomorrow I should get in the way of a shell and so cause unnecessary regrets. I want you to love me and write me love letters for they will charm and amuse me but I don't want you to really care. I want in return to amuse and interest you. I don't want to cause you any anxiety or sorrow. It is bad enough to have Mother to think about in that way . . .

You are a darling and I am very fond of you.

Affectionately

Talbot

P. S. Horrors! I nearly forgot to tell you how much I am going to prize the little silver heart box and the ring and the elephant and the silver heart. They are beautiful things and I know they represent

beautiful thoughts and feelings. I shall treasure them and I shall
ever be grateful and better for the associations –

Your

Talbot

21st October 1917

My very dear Beatrice,
You are the really only clever girl I think I have ever known. I am
never quite sure how to deal with the situation! Your "Quest of the
Boots" arrived last night and also the boots. The former was so
diverting that it seemed a real shame that all the fun should be for
my own personal enjoyment only. It is a thing worthy of very
general circulation. How do you ever think of so many amusing
things? If sculpture and other things ever failed you you could still
be sumptuous as a writer! I shall preserve the edition which I hope
we may enjoy together sometime. As for the boots they are the
most wonderful things I have ever seen. But my dear B. how could
you think I would deliberately ask for anything so expensive. I only
meant a pair of the canvas running boot with a rubber sole. The
support to the ankle in running is what I wanted – the low shoes
which are all I can get here do not provide this. I am positively
ashamed that you should have sent such an elaborate gift. I am on
the eve of grave events and I have only a short minute in which to
write but I wished to make sure that you heard from me . . .

. . . Believe me always affectionately and gratefully.

Your

Talbot.

*On October 30, 1917, Talbot went "over the top" with the first
wave of Canadians at Passchendaele. He was killed instantly by a
shell. The* Montreal Herald *wrote, "It is no exaggeration to say*

that the death of Captain Talbot Papineau is a matter for national regret." He died without ever meeting Beatrice Fox. His lifelong friend, John Archibald, later wrote her to express his condolences: "Talbot knew, on his last leave, that he was going into a place from which he was likely enough not to return, but I never knew him happier or quieter in mind. He was glad to be back with the regiment and refused to consider an offer of a staff position in England. After all, the front line was his element and he felt it. His death is a calamity to his mother and almost as much to some others of us – but not to him . . . it was no tired, blunted life he gave up . . . If we meet some day in the future, as may happen, we shall talk about Talbot, for I think that you too appreciated what he was."

To a far country

Many Canadian soldiers wrote "last letters" to be mailed if they died in battle. Few were as passionately composed as this one by **Gregory Clark,** *a popular feature writer with the* Toronto Star. *He had joined the Canadian Army as a junior lieutenant and married Helen Scott Murray just before leaving for Europe. On the eve of his departure from England to the Continent, the twenty-three-year-old wrote a fateful letter to be held for possible delivery to his new wife.*

[Folkestone, Kent]
[August 1916]

My darling,

So it is, after all, farewell!

I am writing this, my last letter to you, at Napier Barracks. The date – does it matter?

For now I am bidding you farewell forever. Farewell, instead of that sweet au revoir we said so many, many days ago!

But, my only love, what good can we do cursing Fate or hurling reproach at the dumb and heedless heavens?

When you receive this, I shall be gone to a far country and there can be no return. No dear eyes will be to welcome me. No soft arms to guide me in the great darkness. No soft breasts to rest my weary heart.

Hush! No tears. No repining.

Remember only this, dear soul of my life, that in my childhood I loved the dream of you that was in my heart. In my youth, I lifted mine eyes unto the hills and watched afar for your coming. I was faithful to you, my beloved.

And then when I found you, the silent harps of my being sprang to life and filled my soul with music. The garden of my life, which I had prepared for your coming, sprang miraculously into blossom.

And, oh, my dearest, I have loved you!

When we parted, something came to me and whispered that I would not return. That moment, madness came upon me, and I have not since been free. And what was that madness, laddie boy? The madness of my love for you. Add together all the love of the past three years and you would not have the love of one day in these many days I have been alone. My beloved, I mean it when I say that I have been afraid, terribly afraid, of the intensity of that love. I have feared that God would grow angry at my worship of you, and that the angels in Heaven would strike me down for daring to love as I have loved.

My wife, I have reached the ultimate in love. Take comfort in this that before I went forever away, I had reached the pinnacle of love, and had given my soul forever into your beloved hands.

See, laddie, how helpless I am? What I want to say will not come. I have no more words.

What of you? There is no use me saying what I have said each day – that I should never have left you. We are in the hands of a grim and deaf Fate. And, anyway, it is too late. But, oh, I have prayed that I might be broken and torn and crippled so long as I could come back to you.

God, I can't speak! Helen, Helen, pray for me, that my soul may rest in peace and not range forever the endless skies, troubled and broken over your lonely heart.

Boy o'mine, I simply cannot write here about what you will do after I have gone.

Only this: be brave. Do not let that lovely heart be broken. You are young. Dad will arrange about the pension. Leave it all to either your Dad or mine.

And do not be afraid to live. Do not go lonely, thinking I would sooner have you lonely. Take this poor offering of a piteously given love – my love is all I have to offer. But do not imagine that your life is over. There is much in life. Oh, my darling, don't I know that!

Life!

If only we could have had one little son –

You cannot read the like of this forever. I know it will only make your anguish greater. But I also know you will expect this from me.

Good-bye, then, lover of my soul. And know this: that I am somewhere, somewhere, living in a dream, over and over again, a dream of all our happy days, of all the times I have held you in my arms, of our shoppings and our canoe trips and our nights of eternal joy.

And so laddie will you at last come to me and we can live eternally those blissful dreams – together.

I love you. I adore you. I worship you. May God keep you and bless you. I am your lover,

Gregory Clark

Greg fought with the 4th Canadian Mountain Rifles in northern France to capture Vimy Ridge in the most famous of all Canadian battles. He survived the war and came home to deliver the letter in person to Helen. They raised a family and he became one of Canada's most beloved storytellers. The columnist, who helped his friend Ernest Hemingway get a reporting job with the Toronto Star *in the 1920s, wrote for the* Star Weekly *and* Weekend Magazine *and won the Stephen Leacock Medal for Humour. During the Second World War, he was a war correspondent in Europe, where their eldest son, Murray, was killed in battle. Greg Clark died in 1977.*

BE A TRUE BOY

A less common form of a soldier's final letter to loved ones was addressed to children – like this one written by Nova Scotian **James Howard Tupper**. *At home on leave in March 1915, two months before he sailed to England and on to northern France, he composed letters to his two sons, which his wife, Letty, was to pass on them later. This one was delivered on June 2, 1916.*

TO: Master Borden Tupper – Your Daddy
(To be given when he is 12 years old)
My dear Son:
How dear you are to me you will never know or how hard it is for me to leave you, perhaps never to return, you can never understand

James Tupper
(Courtesy Anne Davison)

unless you go through the same ordeal yourself some day and I hope you may never have to but if you do, face it boy, face it bravely. Do not back down. I love you with all the power of love within me and now on the eve of my departure for war I am writing you and if I do not come back this will help you to understand why I went, why I took such a risk, why it was necessary. I count my life cheap in the scale compared with the empire. I am a man and being a man I could not stand by and see our country in danger and not do my best to save it. It does not appeal to all alike. As you grow older you will realize more fully what I mean. Perhaps when you read this the war will be over and peace in the world once more.

It may be my lot to fall and not return with the troops and if so I would like you to always remember that I loved you better than life itself. I have looked forward to the time when you would be a little older and I would be helping you shape your future and give you a father's council and you would have the benefit of the years of experience I have had. We would be good friends, you and I, the best of friends. You are my oldest son and I hope you will grow up to be as good a man as you promise to at present.

My boy, always be good to your mother. If my actions deprive you of a father, you will still have one of the best of mothers. You cannot afford to neglect her. Honour her and love her above all else and you can safely rely on her councils and judgement. Be kind and true to Grandma. She is Daddy's mother and has a great store of wisdom for boys and girls.

I must think of you as a boy of twelve, a big boy, a true boy, a boy who will make a man. True men are not plenty and all boys are not true boys. Be a true boy. There are things to be true too. First, be true to your "God". Second, be true to yourself. Third, be true to your country. You can be true to your God by obeying His commands, carrying out His will and being kind to all His creatures.

You can be true to yourself by treating yourself fair. God has given you a body to go through this life. Use your body in the way He would wish you to. Keep your body clean, that will keep it healthy. Keep your mind clean by reading good books, thinking good thoughts and doing kind acts. Choose clean friends and always be friendly. Never go back on a friend. One good friend is worth a great many poor ones. In your play and daily contact with your friends and school fellows be clean in your conduct to them, particularly with the girls. Remember you are a gentleman and treat them as ladies. No matter what they are like it will not excuse you. Avoid the bad ones. You cannot afford to spend time with them. That would not be treating yourself fairly.

To get an education God has given you a time of youth to prepare your mind, knowledge gained every day but only one day at a time. You will get tired of school and you will see boys who do not do very much and you will think they get along just as well but they will not and they will perhaps find it out in time. Study your lessons each day, one day at a time and you will find the better you know your lessons the better you will like to go to school. You will not be true to yourself unless you learn your lessons each day as they come along. You are storing up knowledge that will be most useful bye and bye. Get your storehouse "your mind" well stored with the useful knowledge you get at school and as you go through life you will always find use for it and no man can take it from you and you cannot lose it. You will always have it.

Be true to yourself in your play. Play fair or not at all. A boy who will not play fair is likely to make a man who will cheat in his business. They are both on the same road. The business comes a little further along.

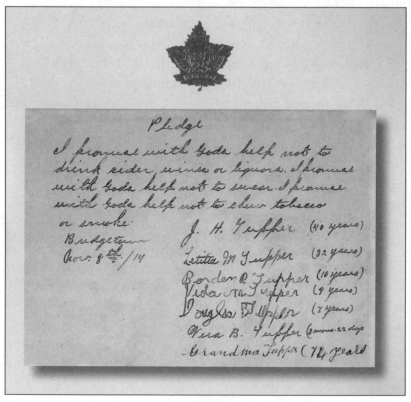

The pledge of abstinence signed by Tupper and his family,
including Borden (Courtesy Anne Davison)

You can be true to your country by being a good citizen, one ever ready to defend what is right and oppose what is wrong. As you grow to manhood you will have to decide on many questions, "public questions" and take one side or the other. It is your duty to do that. Decide honestly and then act accordingly. If filling any office of any society, or in any public capacity, do your best. This is all included in "citizenship" of the right kind. It is not always necessary to die for your country to serve her. You can live for her, only do your duty as you see it and you will be fulfilling your obligations.

I have many friends upon whom you can rely for council and help. I cannot name them all but only a few of my nearest and dearest ones . . . You will of course have your own friends and companions but you can remember these as some of my best and truest friends . . .

And now my own dear boy may God keep you, protect you and watch over you and make you worthy of the love bestowed upon you.

Be kind to your sisters. You have two sisters now and I hope you will have them for many years. You and Douglas love each other which is right. I know you both love your sisters and they love you. How happy you will all be.

My own dear boy I must close. I cannot express my love for you. May God keep you and watch over you.

Your loving Father,
J. H. Tupper

Three months after Borden read this letter, his father – now a major in the 25th Battalion, part of the Second Canadian Contingent – was killed in France during the horrific Battle of the Somme in September 1916. Borden and his brother grew up to be ministers

*and their two sisters became nurses. Borden's daughter, Anne
Davison of Parrsboro, Nova Scotia, recalls, "The letter to my father
had a profound influence, not only on my father as a twelve-year-
old boy, but on my generation, on my children and their children.
It still brings tears to our eyes and inspiration to our souls as we
read it and ponder it for our own lives."*

LASSIE IN BLACK

*Alice (Lassie) Bray of Ottawa was twenty-six when she shipped
out as a voluntary aid detachment nurse with the British Red Cross
Society in the autumn of 1916. On a steamer from Quebec City
to Liverpool, she recounted for her mother, Elizabeth, the life
aboard ship while bemoaning the severity of her ugly black
nursing uniform.*

Steamer Grampian
Sept 16th/16

My own dearest little Mother.
Well here we all are it seems so strange to think actually on our
way to Old England. Funny how things do come doesnt it who
would have <u>thunk</u> this time about three months ago where I would
be at this time.

Oh my love take care of your little self. I am doing what you
told me & just trying to enjoy everything as much as I can after
all there is nothing <u>should</u> happen to you is there & honestly lovey
I just feel fine so dont worry the least bit about me. You should
have seen the meals I tucked into my little 'innards' this day. No
more starving for me for I guess we will work off all we put on so
I dont care . . . My we all look like crows dont we. I nearly die

laughing when I look along the line of black heads at the table &
then think I am one of them myself. I do hope we can take them
off sometimes. They say we get six days furlough when we first
land in London & think there we can get out of them. Goodness
I hope we can.

. . . It is strange how little you see of people. I only have seen
that Mr. Todd for one little 'How do you do in the morning.' There
are so many little ins and outs you pass each other a dozen times
& dont know it I guess. But there doesn't seem anything worth
while trying to make a hit on & there would be no use trying in
these duds so I am just going to rest read & enjoy myself for I
guess it would be attempting the impossible to make a hit in this
outfit, & anyway we all look so much alike that someone else
would reap the benefit of your best endeavours . . . My goodness
though Mother when you do see some of them you feel quite a
beauty. Goodness aren't they the homely bunch.

The gulls were flying all round the boat this morning lovey &
honestly they just looked like white spirits in the lovely early
morning light. Wont you love gulls. They seem such gentle things
to me. Somehow almost like doves . . .

. . . Today is just unbelievably nice and my only fly in the oint-
ment is the awful blots on the landscape our uniforms are. Not that
I dont like them alright & on a rainy day they look fine but alas
& alack when the sun comes out they do look so out of place . . .

I guess I had better stop now. Give my best love to Father &
thank him a thousand times for all his goodness to me. Oh my
dearest I feel never in the world can I thank you enough. You have
both done so much for me . . .

Love and kisses & take care of your two dear selves.

Lassie

Alice worked at hospitals in Birmingham and Woolwich until early 1919 when she returned to Ottawa for further nursing studies. Shed of her crow-coloured uniform, she finally "hit on" George Samuel Abbott, marrying him in 1923.

THE KNOWLEDGE OF HER LOVE

*Emma Griffis of Calgary was a distant cousin of Ontario-born **Harold McGill**, a thirty-seven-year-old doctor to Native people on the Sarcee reserve near Calgary. They both went overseas in the Great War, she as a nursing sister at the Canadian military hospital in Bramshott, England, and he as a medical officer with the 31st Battalion on the Continent. At first they came to know one another better through their correspondence, which grew increasingly intense.*

March 27/1916.

Dear Miss Griffis; –

Your very interesting and newsy letter of Feb 29 came to hand a few days ago when we were out of the trenches and I did not get time to answer it before we came back in again . . .

A serious misfortune has befallen me. My mouse trap, which a Belgian girl gave me as a present, is out of order and I felt like an infantryman left unsupported by artillery. The mice invaded my dugout in strong force when I first took it over but I soon cleaned them out with the trap. The trap also caught the fingers of a brother officer whose language upon the occasion was not what one would expect from a soldier of the Onward Christian variety. Now however that my mouse trap is out of action, the mice have returned not as single spies but in battalions and are rapidly regaining the moral ascendancy . . .

Sincerely yours
Harold W McGill

France, Oct 1, 1916.

Dear Miss Griffis; –

It is so very long since I have heard from you that I am greatly afraid that you have been ill again. Of course I have not written often either lately but I have been waiting to hear from you, and besides for past two months we have been leading very strenuous lives indeed and time for letter writing has been at a premium . . .

. . . In the last show we were in my stretcher bearer sergeant, the finest little fellow in the battalion, had his leg torn off by a shell and died of wounds in the F [Field] Ambulance dressing station. I saw him after he was hit. He bid me good bye saying he had tried to do his work and was sorry he was not able to carry on to the end. It made me feel like a baby to hear him talk like that and I could very easily have made a fool of myself. He was the last one left of the stretcher bearers I brought from Calgary and was known and loved through-out the battalion. It is not so much the loss of him as a stretcher bearer that I feel as the personal loss of a friend. Teddy Barnes was his name

Harold McGill in 1914 (Glenbow Museum NA-4938-16)

and he had brought honours to the battalion by his athletic prowess. I must write to his mother . . .

Sincerely yours

Harold W McGill

By the following spring, after Miss Griffis came to France and the couple met in person, Dr. McGill began addressing her as "Dearest Emma" and signing himself "Yours with fondest love, Harold" – although in the following letter, after meeting her in London on leave, he reverted to closing with his full name.

France, July 12 '17

11²⁰ P.M.

My dear Emma; –
I have just arrived at the aid post of the battalion which is in the front line. The aid post is in the cellar of a chateau that has been wrecked by shell fire . . .

Emma Griffis McGill outside the old general hospital in Calgary in the early 1900s (Glenbow Museum NA-4938-10)

My leave seemed almost too good to be true especially when you told me you liked me and gave me the promise I so longed to receive. I was prepared to have that taxi drive around London until the petrol gave out or I knew my fate. But do not think dear girl that I do not realize what a terrible responsibility I took when I asked you for that promise and the trust in one that it involves. The knowledge that you love me is very sweet and before long I

hope we may be able to begin our lives afresh together. In the
meantime we must both "carry on" . . . Can you tell me what size
of a ring you will wear for me? I wish to send you one as soon
as possible.

When I next get leave I shall ask for a month and we can be
quietly married and spend it together . . .

Yours lovingly

Harold W McGill

*In a letter ten days later he gave her a brief biography of himself,
described his family, and blessed the lucky sprained ankle that had
allowed him to meet her in London.*

France, July 22, 1917.

My dearest Emma; –
You ask me why I did not give you a hint of what I was thinking
– <u>when I thought.</u> I do not exactly get your meaning but I have
thought of you every day since I first came to the war, and surely
my dear girl you know I cared for you before I told you so . . .

We don't know much about each others' family relationships,
do we? But I know that you are a good lovely girl with a keen sense
of humour. Did you ever think what a terrible thing it would be
for two people, neither with the sense of humour, to live together?
Small jolts would be detonated into mine explosions. As for myself,
a few unimportant particulars . . . So far as I know, apart from the
hazzards of my present occupation, I am a first class risk for a life
insurance company. I have never served a term in prison, and my
religious belief is very unorthodox. And lastly as I think I warned
you I do not belong to the class of predatory rich . . .

Yours lovingly

W McGill

By year's end, they were married in England and Harold was "looking forward longingly to the time when we can really begin living our lives together. In the meantime I must get on with my small part in the war. There is a long rough road ahead of us." Back home in 1919 they found the road smoother as they raised two daughters, she was on the executive of the Women's Canadian Club and the Women's Conservative Association, and he became a Conservative member of the Alberta legislature and later director of Indian affairs.

THE RELUCTANT SOLDIER

James Charles Aitchison, a Scottish carpenter in his mid-forties, moved to Saskatoon about 1910; his wife, Elizabeth, and seven children followed two years later. They soon had another son and daughter. In 1916, when major building projects were interrupted in the city, the forty-year-old father reluctantly enlisted and went overseas as a private. His first letter came from a training camp in England.

A Coy 53rd Battalion
C.E.F.
Stationed at Bramshott
May 24th 1916

My dear wife
I have just received your letter, telling me of our sad bereavement. How I wish I was beside you to comfort you, my dear wifie. Although I was partly prepared by your last letter, yet I was always hoping for the best, it is hard to lose one of our children even although we have so many, and although I have not seen a

great deal of him, still he is my own flesh and blood, and I feel his loss. Yet dear it is you I grieve most for, he is away from a life of trial and trouble, and is an angel now, but I know how you love your children, and what a want it must be for you, especially when I am not at home, to share your sorrow, and help to make it lighter for you. It is as you say the worst trial we have had in our married life as it is the first one we have lost, how my heart goes out to you in this trial. I think it will bind us closer together if that is possible, as we have always been an affectionate husband and wife. I hope dear that the others will soon get over it, and that you will be able to get some rest. Now dear you will have to compose yourself as well as you can, for the other children's sake and mine. I don't know that I can write any more. I am in the best of health and I have been wearying yet fearing for your letter. In sorrow, as in gladness

Your ever loving husband
Jim

His oldest daughter, Pringle, later wrote him that the second of his two infant children had died, largely from malnutrition.

Stationed at Somewhere in France
June 10th 1916

My dear wife

I got Pringle's letter, telling me of our little darling Nettie's death, just the day before leaving for France. I am so sorry about it as I did love that child. You are having a very bad time of it, losing two children in so short a time, and I wish I could see you to comfort you. I hope the other two are getting better of the whooping cough and that the rest of you are keeping well. Now dear don't worry about me, for I will take every care of myself, consistent with my duty, and if I fall, you have the satisfaction of knowing that I died a soldier's death. You must not worry if you don't get letters as often as you would like, as it may be difficult to write at times . . .

I hope you are bearing up well after our double bereavement, but I know you must suffer terribly as you were so fond of both of them . . .

Your ever loving husband
Jim

Jim was badly wounded in the Battle of the Somme in the autumn of 1916.

Roy Herbert Hospital
Woolwich
Oct 3rd 1916

My dear wife

I had to stop the last letter rather suddenly, so I am writing again. I was under the Xrays yesterday, and nurse tell me that I have a large piece of metal in my leg. I am inclined to think it may be a piece of high explosive shell, that got me, not that it matters, only if so it will be a more ragged wound. Fancy I walked miles over very rough ground with it. I did not become a stretcher case until I reached Boulogne, I was hobbling about with a stick, when one of the doctors there, said, "put that man on a stretcher." Well dear I have been lucky, I am not injured permanently, and if you saw some of the poor fellows you would thank God, that I have got off so lightly. Oh how pleasant it is to lie in a clean bed, after the beds I have lain on these last 4 months, I think I would soon have been knocked up, I could not sleep at night for lice, I am sure there were thousands on me, I used to lie and pick them off the whole

James and Elizabeth Aitchison before the deaths of the two youngest of their nine offspring (Courtesy Margaret Maclean)

night. They kept me off my sleep worse than the shells. Well I am alright now for some time to come, and it is possible owing to my deafness they may not send me to the front again. Well dear I think we have got the Germans beat now . . . I am pleased to see by Pringle's letter that the garden is such a success, and that you have so many potatoes . . . I will close now, with love

from your ever loving husband

Jim

Twelve days later, he died of his wounds. His wife, struggling to raise their seven children, did not receive a widow's pension for a full year after his death and was sent a bill to cover the cost of his burial in his hometown of Innerleithen, Scotland. Their only surviving son, James Aitchison, was a professor and then head of the

department of political science at Dalhousie University in Halifax
until his death in 1994.

A SON OF UNTOLD WORTH

A mother can feel and express pure yet fierce passion for a child
now grown and gone to war to face imminent death. **George**
Herbert (Bert) Berry *was one of three children of George and* **Ada**
Berry. *He grew up on a homestead near Yarrow Creek, Alberta,*
and in Victoria before attending Upper Canada College in Toronto
and universities in Detroit and Toronto. In 1915 the hazel-eyed,
twenty-one-year-old student joined up and became a lieutenant
while serving with the ambulance corps during the third major
battle of Ypres-Passchendaele between July and November 1917.
His mother wrote him often.

> P.O. Box 40
> Strathmore, Alberta
> Sept 28 1917
> Friday Morning

My own darling Boy

Just a short note this morning dear one. It is such a beautiful
morning, and I am wondering where you are and what you are
doing and if it is as nice a morning with you dear – and I am pic-
turing what you would be doing were you home this morning, for
it is one of those lovely fall mornings we get here. I am writing this
at the office and am going over to the house in a few minutes to
take some snaps, and shall try to get one showing the hedge and
sweet peas as they are now, for the frost must surely come soon
and then the beauty will be gone, but I want you to have an idea of

how lovely the hedge looks. It is so green, and Dad has kept it trimmed down so beautifully, it thickened into a solid mass . . .

As I walked over this morning to the office and felt the lovely morning, I prayed you might be having your Paris leave and be at Boursault enjoying a little quiet and peace and rest, for the ceaseless horror must be so very hard on you dearest.

You are a mystery really, dearest, for I could not have believed you could have gone through all you have, but we are terribly proud of you dear, for I know how brave you have been and the wonderful courage you have had, and I only pray you may have your just reward for it dearest.

With all manner of kisses and hugs and love from all

Always

Mother

Sept. 5th, 1917

Dear Mother –

I am doing forward observing officer today – now don't get anxious – as I'm in a very safe place – just as safe as if I was in London. I'm in a tunnel way down under the ground at least 20 or 25 feet. Have a peek hole at the top of some stairs. I have a periscope to look through so don't have to show myself at all. Things are very quiet so its like having a day's holiday being here . . .

With fondest love and kisses to you all,

Bert

Thursday Morning

[October 10, 1917]

My own most precious Boy

We have just had a cable from the War office, my darling, to say you were wounded on the sixth. It is so terrible sweetheart, for we have no particulars and I am heartbroken my darling for I want to be near you so terribly now you are suffering. To be able to care for you, oh darling, I think you know. Daily I have feared this would come and now all I can do is to pray you are not suffering too much my darling. Oh, if it only means you will be out of it for the future, dearest, and that we may have you home to care for you, dear one, and nurse you well again. Something grips my throat and I feel [I] shall choke. You know what it is dear one. I am praying for you dearest so hard. May God help you through it all, the suffering and pain. My dear dear boy, I want to be near you so to love you dear one and hold you in my arms, oh darling how I love you. You know, don't you dear one . . .

Oh, darling, I can only think of one thing, and that is you lying and suffering dearest, away from all who love you so very very dearly, for you are more than life itself. I do pray that by now you may be feeling a little better. Oh, Bert darling, I suppose I really should not be writing as I am, but I feel I must, my poor darling boy . . .

You have always been so good and brave, such a comfort to me dear one, for when the world has seemed quite dark, and sometimes I have been depressed, I would think of you my darling, and all you meant to me – a son of untold worth, and I would thank God for such a gift, and feel my unworthiness, dearest . . .

I shall mail this today but shall write you again tonight. All our prayers my darling boy. All our love and kisses and hugs. You know just how we are thinking of you dearest.

Always
Mother

The letter was returned to his mother in an envelope stamped "Killed in action/Return to Sender."

THE HUNGRY HEART

Jessie Brecken was a Winnipegger who attended Havergal Ladies'
College in Toronto. She married Halifax-born Paul Brecken, a
University of Toronto graduate who became general secretary of
the Young Men's Christian Association (YMCA) in Calgary. After
he left to serve with the YMCA overseas late in the Great War, his
long-ailing wife lived with her parents in Toronto. Jessie wrote him
stirringly supportive letters, including this one on his departure.

[August 1917]

My precious Boy –
This is just a farewell note that carries a great deal of love for my
most precious husband.

Now, I want to tell you something and that is, that you must
be perfectly at rest about your wifie. I am so much better and
stronger than I have been for a long time, dear, and I am going to
such a nice home. You know that I am quite willing for you to go
overseas, and in spite of the heart hunger and times of desperate
loneliness, I know that day by day, grace will be given me to keep
bright & happy. During the past days of preparation strength has
come to both of us & it flows from a never failing source.

I wish that words might express what you have been to me
during these seven years of married life, dear. You have been so
patient through all the sickness, & your bright and happy ways
are just what I needed. God gave you to me, now & forever, and
many times I have thanked Him.

I am glad that you are to have an opportunity for service overseas, and I know that you will be made a great blessing. I shall ask
for this every day & also that you may be kept from harm & in
health and strength. O, how I love you, my very own boy!

Paul Brecken, circa 1920s
(Glenbow Museum NA-3506-1)

When you are lonely dear just think of the lovely times we have had together & of the time when we shall again be together. But most of all think of how much we love each other.

This little book, "Abide in Christ," has been a blessing to me Jacko, it is all so true & practical. I know it represents the life that every Christian should enjoy here. Read it as soon as possible, dear, for it is too good to keep waiting . . .

"The Lord watch between me and thee while we are absent one from the other."

With a heart full of love from

<u>Your</u> <u>Wife</u>

Paul was slightly gassed in September 1918. Jessie sent him a small, preserved maple leaf and later a four-leafed clover from Ontario's Muskoka Lakes vacation area.

109 Evelyn Crescent
Toronto, Canada
Nov. 11th 1918

Jacko Dear,

O joy! O joy! They say the Great War is over! They said so a few days ago but it was not true. About 4 a.m. today the whistles started to blow & as time went on more & more whistles added their shrill voices & other voices joined the din. By 5:30 the news boys were crying out – "Extra special! Extra special!" Automobiles

Jessie Brecken's letter of November 4, 1917, with pressed pansy and maple leaf (Glenbow Museum M 8532/5)

were rushing past with horns screeching. A man yelling at the top of his voice went along crying "Hurrah. Wake up. The war's over!" Some excited boys were out and setting off fire-crackers. I feel as if I had been drawn through a knot hole & am going to lie down soon . . .

I know you are just longing to see your Beau as she is longing to see you . . .

This morning your Beau made oat cookies & they turned out fine. Before long I hope I shall be making them for my Lover. Won't it be fine to sit down again together at our own home table & eat beau cooking . . .

Much, much love & more love to the best husband ever was from the bestest beau ever lived!

Lovingly
Jessie

After war's end the Breckens returned to Calgary, where Paul became a teacher, a one-term Conservative Member of the Alberta legislature, and a long-time city alderman.

A BROKEN HEART

Five letters found in the rafters of a Canadian attic tell a familiar wartime story of a soldier overseas who romances a local woman without being fully honest with her. As the First World War waned, the trusting **Mollie** *– working in the kitchen at a Red Cross hospital in London – mailed her letters to a military barracks in Canada, where her middle-aged lover picked them up and hid them in his family home. In the first one she comments on a photograph he'd sent her and mentions her grown-up daughter, "Girlie."*

9th March 1918
c/o The Hon
Mrs Franklin
50 Dorchester Terrace
London W2

My own dearest –,

What a lovely surprise I had last night when I came in from cooking. There were two letters from you and although I thought I was tired before I saw them I certainly was not when I got them in my hands and ran up to my room to devour them. You dear they were so cheery just like the dear sender but I can see from them that you do really miss me just as much as I do you and that you will really be pleased to see your troublesome bundle again some day and like you I hope it wont be long never mind if we do have to work so long as we can see each other. Keep on rubbing the charm and the War will stop to please us. Yes dear I did recognize the stamp on your Amusement Committee paper. You told me you would keep it and I know my Bobbie will. You have always kept your word with me. This is Saturday afternoon dearie the day I always miss you most and often think as it gets towards 12.30 I can hear your merry whistle instead your dear ones at home get it . . .

What have they been doing to my Bobbie that he is not looking so well and getting colds etc. Please take better care of my property there's a dearie. They have sent over for me to help a bit so I must go back and write more tomorrow . . .

. . . We had a very bad raid last Thursday night and some houses quite near here were smashed up and a lot of people who had gone down to the basement were buried in it and all killed. I stayed in my bed although the maid did come for me to go down but the bed did really rock when they dropped the bomb and made me think a bit but not enough to make me get up . . .

. . . I had a letter from Girlie this morning I am sending it on to you as I know you like reading her letters. This is a glorious spring day with a beautiful blue sky and the birds singing so merrily. It makes me feel hopeful of seeing my Bobbie again. thank you dearest so much but for the present I will not trouble you to send me anything as I have all my food at the Hospital where we seem to have plenty but it was sweet of you dear one it will go down in my book of memory like many more of your kind actions. I always send one letter per week so you may be sure if you do not get it dearest it is not my fault.

. . . I never quite know what you do when you are curling you will have to tell me. Anyway I am sure you enjoyed it and that is enough for me. I am so glad you are amongst all the things you love so much and wish I could have a look in sometimes. The sea is a big thing to put between us no jumping . . . Well bye bye dearest boy consider yourself kissed & hugged until you have no breath left, so you will know what to expect when we do meet. xxxxxxx

Ever yours

Mollie xxx

On March 18, Mollie urged him to stay in Canada until the war was over – "I would much rather (much as I want and long to see your . . . face) know that you are safe at home . . . some day I hope we shall have all the dear old times over again and before long. You have been gone three months now dearest and they been long lonely ones but now the spring is here I hope time will move more quickly . . . You will be enjoying your weekly dances with the lassies don't flirt too much dearest only a little but leave the large corner in your heart to me." But as his flow of correspondence to her began to dry up, she became increasingly desperate, as these two letters show.

9th May 1918

My own dear –
So far I have not received your letters. It will be three weeks on
Monday since I had one from you dearest. I do hope they have
not gone to the bottom of the deep blue sea if so I shall feel like
diving in to get them. I shall still build my hopes on Monday post
then what a treat for me . . .

23rd May 1918

Still no letter dearest it will be five weeks on Monday since I heard
from you. I would not mind so much if I was sure you were well
dear one. Well I must wait with what patience I can until they do
arrive, but I hope it wont be long . . .

I shall soon be taking my first months money . . . I really shall
have to send you some of it when I get it to have a good smoke.
Bye Bye dearest with all my love and kisses

Ever yours
Mollie
XXXXXXXXX
XXXXXXXX
XXXXX
X

*That was the last of Mollie's poignant letters. Nearly eighty years
later they were found – stained and fading – in the attic of a house
in western Canada. According to his attestation papers, when
Mollie's lover enlisted in the Canadian Expeditionary Force he'd
lived at that address with his next of kin – his wife.*

A DOUBLE-DECKER NAMED DESIRE

Of course not all wartime romances end in tragedy. One that didn't had its start in the happenstance of a chance encounter atop a double-decker bus in Liverpool. George Florence, a Scottish emigré to Canada in 1910, joined the Royal Flying Corps during the war and transferred to the cavalry when he went to England in 1918. George never faced combat but fell victim to the great influenza pandemic that year and had just recuperated when he visited the port city. There he met Katharine Owen, an eighteen-year-old store cashier, riding the bus to visit her well-to-do fiancé. Although she was the only person on the upper deck, George asked if the seat next to her was taken. The following day he typed this letter to her.

Records Office,
Knotty Ash Camp.
Sunday, March 16th 1919

My dear Miss Owen,
you will observe, my little girl, that I have NOT forgotten, as you hinted. How could I possibly? Have you never had the misfortune to be away from home and your friends? If so then you would realise just what it means to meet with someone who you think is really nice, someone you have a feeling of respect for. That is the way I felt when I had the honour of meeting you last night, and I am writing to you in the hope that you will give me the opportunity of meeting you again, and that in the very near future.

As I said last evening there often is times, and such times usually are more apparent in the vicinity of pay-day, when I find myself with enough money to take someone "Really Nice" to a show, but so far I have had to content myself with going alone, I never enjoy a theatre then, or I spend what I have in some way equally to my dissatisfaction.

On my return to the "Parisien Cafe" last night I found that I was too late, it had closed for the day, so I had to be content with a bag of sweets, that was your fault, so you really owe me a visit to that Cafe, you will have to let me take you there for dinner, or for tea, some evening – Will you? PLEASE?

I am commiting a dreadful breach of etiquette in writing to you in such a manner, I refer to my using this mechanical means, in place of the pen. I hope you will overlook that shortcoming of mine, but I find that I can use this way much easier tha[n] the other, for when I am tapping the keys the Officer in charge thinks that I am doing work for him and consequently I may write as long as I wish, it is rather hard that we chaps here have to resort to subterfuge when we wish to communicate with anyone, for altho our boss is a very nice fellow, there is always some of the "Big Bugs" sticking around, thus the camouflage.

I sincerely hope you will soon find an evening on which I may call for you. I really want you to help me to enjoy a show or a movie very, very soon, this may sound like a foolish request, and you might very well say "Take some of your chums with you."

I could do that, but thats what I have been doing for the past six months and I want a change, and as I said before "I want to enjoy the evening."

Hoping that this epistle leads to our better acquaintance, I will close now anticipating an early reply from you,

Your Canadian friend
in all sincerity
Gnnr. George K.C. Florence

[Handwritten:] P.S. I simply cant help reminding you to write soon.

G.K.C.F.

Seven weeks later George and Katharine were married and on their way to Toronto, where they raised two children. He died in 1965; she kept this first letter in her purse until her death at ninety-one.

A ROMANTIC ABROAD

In July 1936 a civil war broke out in Spain between General Francisco Franco's Fascist regime and the grassroots Popular Front Party. More than fifteen hundred Canadian volunteers left to join International Brigades fighting the government, which was backed by Germany's Adolf Hitler and Italy's Benito Mussolini. Among them was **Thomas Beckett,** *the twenty-year-old chairman of a Toronto chapter of the youth wing of the Co-operative Commonwealth Federation (CCF) – Canada's socialist party. Tom was already a veteran of anti-capitalist marches against the Canadian government during the Depression. In early 1937 he and four other Torontonians were at the brigades' headquarters in southeast Spain, where Tom wrote home to a girl from his neighbourhood he was sweet on. His message is a romantic mix of personal manifesto and tentative love letter.*

Albacete, Spain

17/1 [1937]

Dear Audrey:

You may be surprised to hear from me and at this distance, when you didn't hear from me very much when I was only one block away. I don't know why I am writing you. Maybe it's because I can't forget you. Or maybe it is because the dark-eyed Spanish girls remind me of you. There are many of them who look enough like you to be your sister, and they are modest and shy, with fresh clear complexion, and soft friendly eyes, and womanly virtuous morals.

You no doubt know why I am here. It is because I am what you did not want me to be, a Communist. You also no doubt know what I am doing here. Considering what is going on in Spain at the present time, you will probably think me wrong, or foolish, or wicked, for doing such a thing. As will also Rita, Laurie, and many others. Would you please show them this letter, as a request, in case I do not come back to explain?

I have travelled through half of Spain, and have been able to see and learn about the conditions, the people, their customs, traditions, their nature, and it brings to mind a saying often heard in Canada "Oh! the Spanish are different, they're always fighting about something. Let them fight, they're all crazy anyway."

Things are being changed here now, but they have not had time to erase the effects of a brutal society of rule by . . . the church, and the capitalists. Much newspaper propaganda about Spain, the average Canadian's conception of Spain, is very much wide of the mark. But the stories of the poverty that exists here and still exists, cannot be worse than the actuality. It is true, the Spaniards are different to Canadians. The people in Canada would fight <u>more</u> there all the time if they had had to put up with half of what the people here had. I have seen many things that I can't tell you. But I can tell you enough.

Travelling down the coast of the Mediterranean Sea, for some few hundred miles, I marveled at the beauty of the countryside. Sunshine, huge wooded hills, snow-capped mountain peaks. Fertile well-tilled valleys, more lovely than any artist could paint. Huge

Thomas Beckett in Spain between 1936 and 1939 (Library and Archives Canada PA-194600)

rambling castles on the crest of hills. Little villages and hamlets on the mountain sides, orange and lemon groves, vineyards, and simple, kindly, and generous peasants, who competed with each other in showing their gratitude to the "Americans" who had come to smash the chains of slavery that bound them to a life of toil, misery and poverty, in a land of marvelous wealth and beauty . . .

. . . Even if I had no political beliefs and was not a Communist, my abhorrence of cruelty, of unnecessary suffering, brutality, greed and tyranny, would lead me to do the same thing. My desire to help bring peace, happiness and freedom to the people of any and every country would demand this. And my experience has taught me that only through Communism can this be accomplished . . .

I feel as though I was talking to you, and would like to go on. I could write pages, but it is necessary for me to close now, for reasons that I might tell you some day, if all goes well. As I said in the post-card – "Wish me luck?"

To yourself the best of good luck and wishes and I hope this letter finds you well and happy.

Sincerely,

Tom.

Tom trained with the Abraham Lincoln Battalion, joining the first ninety-six American volunteers near Albacete. In mid-February, writing to his mother after the Lincolns had just been called into action, he said: "Time's up now, will write a longer letter as soon as I get a chance." He never had the chance. On February 17, he was in a truck with twenty others that drove across enemy lines, where they were captured and executed. Tom Beckett was Canada's first victim of the Spanish Civil War, in which about half the Canadian volunteers died.

DROPPING A DAISY

When a renascent Germany invaded Poland on September 1, 1939, Britain and France launched the Second World War two days later. Within a week, Canada had joined the Allied forces, and in December the infantrymen of the 1st Canadian Division sailed to England to start training. Alex Shatford was a schoolteacher in White Rock, British Columbia, who told his students, "I might have a date with my friend Hitler." He meant that he was about to sign up with the Army, which he explained to the police who called on him after some suspicious parents took his ambiguous remark too literally. Alex was an unusual fellow, as he demonstrates in his letters to Doris Gunter of Victoria, before and after he went over-seas as a sergeant with the 3rd Light Anti-Aircraft Regiment.

[1941]

Dear Doris,

I promised you I'd drop a line before I left for good. Well, I'm off to see the Wizard, so its cheerio to you all. We, the Anti-Aircraft, got back to Windsor, and found it was the same old run around. – Just sit down and wait, maybe months we'd get away.

A bunch of us applied for transfers, and five of us got them. I'm now a sergeant gunner in one of Mr. King Georges airplanes, so I'll be seeing the country.

I'm having one of the boys post this a week after I leave, so by the time you get it you can figure I've reached my goal at last.

I'll take the mate to this daisy along for remembrance. – Don't ever forget to say "No" Doris. It may be hard, but I sure admire you for it.

Always
[Alex]

21/6/41

Dear Doris.
Remember me? I'm the "Daisy Planter." Lots of water has gone under the bridge since then, but I thought you'd like to know that I planted the mate to the daisy I sent you. It was glued to the south end of a beautiful bomb that dropped in Berlin somewhere. Now I think I'm going to follow it.

No regrets, Doris, and believe me our short time together has never left my memory.

Alex

In an irony of war, in 1942, while Alex was dropping bombs with daisies in Germany, an RCAF aircraft accidentally dropped an explosive on Doris's house in Victoria. It is believed to be the only residence to be bombed in Canada. After the war, the couple never did pursue their relationship. Alex married someone else, raised four adopted children, and became a Canada Customs inspector before managing an estate in British Columbia.

FORGET LITTLE DIFFERENCES

Alfred Childs had been a star football and badminton player at high school in Woodstock, Ontario, before becoming a bank teller and, in 1939, enlisting to serve overseas – without telling his father, George, and seven motherless siblings. Like many Canadians eager to be airmen during the war, he joined #12 Squadron of the Royal Air Force. In 1941 Sergeant Childs was a twenty-one-year-old tailgunner as the squadron, in Vickers Wellington bombers, made daring night attacks on enemy ships, German industrial targets, and even Berlin.

[September 11, 1941]

To my dearest Dad and Family:

By the time you receive this I shall have been reported "missing due to enemy action". At the moment of writing this I am in a quandary. I'm not sure just what I want to say to all of you. Please don't take it badly because I have been lost. You must remember that thousands of families are hurt many times more. I have no fear of death. If it comes, it will be mercifully quick – but it is very difficult for those I leave behind me. Once again I say, don't feel too badly about it all. It is far better to die, as far as I am concerned, than have to stay at home and let someone else take the rap for me . . . I guess I just wasn't built that way, and I'm happier that things are like this.

And Dad – about our little differences – they were just little things, and please don't remember any of them. I'm quite sure I've forgotten anything unpleasant that ever happened.

I am going on my first raid tonight. It is an easy target and everything should be okay. If it is, I shall reconstruct this letter and try to say everything I want to say. It wouldn't be me if I had

Alfred Childs
(Courtesy Anne Childs)

anything to leave behind, Dad – but of course the money entrusted to George is yours if you want it. If not, I'd like it to go to George – also my watch. Anything else can go to all the rest.

In closing I just want you to know, Dad, that you are the grandest father a boy could wish to have, – and to the family goes the same. Cheerio Dad, Marie, Margaret, George, Josephine, Agnes, Charlie, and Rosemarie. I love you all very deeply, and may God watch over you and protect you. I shall be waiting with Mother to greet you in heaven.

All my love,

Alf

Exactly one month later, Alf died when his plane was shot down during a night raid over Holland, where he was buried. His niece Anne Childs recalls a family story about this final letter from her uncle: "My father, who was a teenager at the time, received the mail and there in his hand was a letter from his brother. He knew the letter was from Alf because he knew Alf's handwriting on the envelope. He knew he had something big; he had proof that his brother was still alive. So he ran with the letter to the foundry (two blocks from the house) where his father was at work and he excitedly presented the envelope to his father. Of course, the letter was not the proof that my father believed he had, but it was a piece of mail that is treasured to this day."

A LETTER UNSENT

A letter never mailed during the war was written by **Marjorie McIntosh** *of Toronto the day after Japan's attack on the American fleet in Hawaii's Pearl Harbor. The reflective young woman was writing to her deeply philosophical fiancé, Thomas Jones, a math teacher from Renfrew, Ontario, who served as a flight commander with the RCAF in England.*

Box 474
Tillsonburg, Ontario
December 8, 1941

Hello dear,

Even though it is 4:30 a.m. in your land, I still would like to say 'hello'. I did just a moment ago, in fact, and you answered as though you weren't asleep at all – as you should be. How are you?

There doesn't seem to be a thing of consequence which I should relate to you, and so will you talk instead? You see it's so very long since I've heard from you that I have no question of yours to answer, and no story of your adventures to comment upon. It's much more than three weeks since you ended your Halifax letter with "I love you with my whole heart." I miss hearing from you Tom; I miss it more as each day goes by.

But that is to speak very foolishly. I suppose I should think of the much more important matters that concern our world. You have something greater to attend to first, I know. Just the same, that knowledge doesn't prevent me from crying out against all this horror – old and new; it doesn't prevent me from believing as I've always done, that there is no justification for all the bitterness and heart-ache which can turn ordinary people into strange unknowns. I don't care how they talk about 'honour' and 'aggression' and 'our sacred duty'. Not one of those words is an excuse for the catastrophe.

Probably it's because I don't believe that the love and peace which we are supposed to be fighting for can ever be achieved through war. How can good grow out of that monstrous evil? Just to have heard the American hysteria this week end was enough to have realized that the unity they have achieved at last is only the unity of beasts. That's a horrid thing to say, but it can't be right for one nation to say, "we'll lick the hell out of them"; that's horrid too.

I'm so sorry to have said all this, but somehow I had to. You won't laugh at my notions too much, will you, even though you don't share them? And I know that you don't. They are the feelings which have made me not bitter so much just sad.

And that's all for to-night, dear. I shall not mail what I have written; instead I think I'll put this away somewhere so that on a far, beautiful day I can take it out, read it, laugh and throw it all away.

With all my love, I say good-night, dear officer of mine.

Marjorie

She did put the letter away. Tom Jones died in battle August 10, 1943. For his bravery under fire, he was one of 247 Canadian officers and warrant officers who earned a Distinguished Flying Cross for acts of valour, courage, or devotion to duty performed while flying in active operations against the enemy. Marjorie didn't open the letter again until December 5, 1976, thirty-five years after writing it.

JOEY'S NEW WORLD

*When Charles (Chas or Chuck) Swayze was born in Niagara Falls, Ontario, in 1943, his paternal grandfather nicknamed him Joey after comedian Joe E. Brown, who also had prominent jug ears. Joey's twenty-seven-year-old father, Major **James F. Swayze**, missed his birth while in England in advance of the arrival of the 1st Battalion of the Lincoln & Welland Regiment that summer. He wrote to explain to his son that he did have a dad, after all.*

February 19 [1943]
Lincoln & Welland Regiment

My dear Chas:

Or should I call you "Joey"? I have left off writing to you for the last few weeks as I realize that since the 23rd of January, things have been a bit unsettled for you as it must have been a rather upsetting experience for you to suddenly be born in our enormous world. However, I hope that by this time you have readjusted yourself sufficiently to overlook some of the inconveniences that being a baby causes to be thrust upon one and that you are able to valuate your surroundings and general situation.

To begin with your first thought must have been, (that is after the inevitable "Where the heck am I?") "Where is my pa?" I guess I have to first straighten you out on that score. As your Mother has probably told you, you have a father and I am he. Under normal circumstances, I would have been among the first to greet you upon your arrival, but as I shall explain, that was totally impossible.

You see, Joey, (I hope you don't mind my calling you "Joey") long before you were ever born, or before your Mother and I were ever married, there was a certain man who lived in a far away

James Swayze
(Courtesy Kathryn Swayze)

land. Now the world had had trouble with the people who live in this land years and years ago, when your Mother & I were even as small as you. However no one thought we would ever be troubled again so we just ignored those people who live a long, long ways away.

Well, this certain man was the kind of fellow who feels that everyone else in the world is against him and that naturally he is against everyone else in the world. Now you may find that hard to understand because there were no people like that in the land from whence you come, were there? Unfortunately, there are a lot of people like that here and we just have to put up with it.

Well this ugly fellow managed to talk long enough and loud enough to the people in his country to make them decide that all the other countries in our world were against them and so they were against everyone else. He told them that the only way for them to be happy was for them to work very hard to make machines to kill all of the people who didn't live in their country.

I know you are going to think that that is very silly. Well, actually you are right but things like that happen in this world. You as a little child think far more clearly than to ever do such a stupid thing but you'll find that men, as they grow older, have their thinking warped terribly out of shape by just living in the world.

To make a long story short, most of the other countries didn't take the stupid man and his country very seriously. First because we didn't think it possible for a whole country to be like that and secondly because this man told us all a great number of lies and said that actually he had no intentions of doing anything bad at all. This man and his country then suddenly started to fight with everyone around them. They, like all bullies, jumped on the smaller ones first and gobbled them up. They thought that they could get going so quickly that they could also gobble up England and later us, but they were mistaken.

So in order, as they thought, to be happy, these people went around shooting everyone who wasn't a member of their country. They dropped bombs out of airplanes and destroyed buildings and killed everyone who was under them. Even to little fellows as small as you are. It is a pretty terrible business right now and so we have to go out to stop it. You see Joey, if these other people had their way you wouldn't be able to grow up into a young man with your Mother and me. They would take you away to teach you how to think like they do. You see you are pretty lucky to be born where you are Joey. By the time you get much older all this trouble will be over and you will be able to do exactly what you want as long as it is right, and to say or think anything you want whether it is right or wrong. These are very great privileges, Joey. You will realize that more and more as you grow older. They are things which are dearer than even living and if defending them means dying there are a lot of fellows who are not living in this ugly person's country who feel that it would still be worthwhile.

That explains Joey, why so many of your friends and you especially arrive to find no father to greet them. I hope you'll pardon me and I know you'll understand. I also hope that you will never have to do what has to be done right now as it is a pretty horrible business and when there are so many other nicer things to be doing.

I hope you find your Mother satisfactory. I am sure you will and will love her even as much as I do. She loves you Joey, very much. She tells me so every time she writes. Incidentally, Joey. Your Mum is a pretty swell person. I don't want to brag but I feel that she is one of the niftiest wives in all the world. You'll also find out that you have one of the most loving mothers of any of your companions of Jan. '43. So all in all you're a pretty lucky guy.

Now I know that for a long time you will have people kissing you, washing you and keeping you clean – in general making life miserable for you. So when they do, don't forget to tell them about it.

After a while you and I are going to have a lot of fun together. In fact, the three of us will. (Your Mum and I always have a swell time.) I am going to teach you how to play games like baseball, basketball, rugby, and a million other wonderful things. I'm looking forward to some really swell times.

But meanwhile, there is a job of putting this stupid man and his stupid people back where they belong. So until then, be a good boy, love and take care of your Mother just like I would do if I were there.

All my love, son

Your Dad

Jim Swayze fought in Europe, receiving the Distinguished Service Order after a shell knocked him senseless in 1944. As the war ended he became commanding officer of the 1st Battalion, later CO of the entire regiment until 1952, and then the Lincoln &

Welland's honorary colonel. After studying law, he set up a legal practice, which his grown-up son (now known as Chuck) joined to form Swayze & Swayze and which still operates in Welland, Ontario. The senior Swayze, nicknamed Gentleman Jim by his friends, died in 1988. "He was a gentle man and a fine soldier. His sense of honour and duty guided everything he did, including fatherhood," his daughter Kathy says of his war service. His son says, "I was into my teens before I knew the effect of that letter." Rereading it recently for the first time since then, Chuck was in tears: "It has all come back to me what a wonderful father I had."

THE LONELY CANADIAN

*Private **William Rempel** was with Canada's #1 Intelligence Company when he went to England in 1942. His game plan was to follow up on a contact he'd made through an English airman while riding a train through the Prairies.*

July 13/42

Dear Miss Tillingham,

You will no doubt be surprised to get a letter from a perfect stranger and a Canadian soldier at that. You might be wondering how I got your address. Well I'll tell you how I got your address and why I'm writing.

On May 21, 1942, I was going home on my embarkation leave. While I was traveling through Sasketchewan, a fellow from the R.A.F. came into the same coach I was in. We started to talk about different things and I mentioned that I would probably go to England in the near future. I asked him whether he could give me a few address of people or girls in England. He said yes, so he gave me some addresses including yours and your sister Elsa.

By the way, I nearly forgot to tell you who the fellow was. His name was Tillingham and you were his sister.

We had a very nice time talking about different things in general.

I don't know anybody in the whole of England and I decided I would write to you and get acquainted with somebody.

I have been here for one month and I like the country, only I get very lonesome, because I don't know anybody.

So if you would care to write and let me know whether you received this letter, I would be pleased. I would also like to meet you if it were possible.

I remain
Your sincerely
Bill Rempel

Joyce, living in Leicester to avoid the bombing of southern cities, did respond to the perfect stranger's letter. Bill visited her there and later at her home in London, and they continued to write one another through 1943, becoming engaged that Christmas. "My RAF brother was concerned. He said, after all, he really didn't know the fellow he had met on the train!" They were married in London's historic St. Mary Magdalene Church in 1944, honeymooned for a week in Sussex, before Bill took part in the Allies' Normandy landing in June. In 1946 she joined him in Canada, where they raised two sons and two daughters. "Sadly," Joyce says, "my husband died in 2000, after fifty-six years together – a love story that started long ago with a lonely Canadian soldier."

DEATH AND CHOCOLATE

*In August 1940 **Heimir Thorgrimson**, his brother Thor, and six other men from the mainly Icelandic-Canadian community of Lundar, Manitoba, signed up with the 8th Field Ambulance Corps. Although believing they would be sent to Iceland as interpreters, they served in England, Italy, Sicily, and Holland. Thorgrimson, who became a sergeant, wrote forty-seven letters to his mother, wife, and his two daughters, aged four and three – translated here from Icelandic.*

Field, England
July 28, 1942

Dear Mother,

. . . There are no truer words than that we are dying a spiritual death, but that is a painless death and is not disturbing to me. Everything is different now than before when all was new over here with death impending at any moment. We were awake and our senses were alert, but now we don't hear the bark of a dog, let alone anything else.

Your loving son,
Heimir

March 23, 1944

Dear Lara and Ada,

Thank you ever so much for your lovely Valentine Card and the lovely parcel. It must have taken a lot of savings to buy all the chocolate bars and things. It is nice having thoughtful little daughters like that. Will you also thank your mother for the coffee and sugar, that was very nice, too.

Heimir Thorgrimson
(Courtesy Pamela Klawitter)

Laufey Thorgrimson, with
daughters Ada (left) and Lara
(Courtesy Pamela Klawitter)

I have eaten a lot of the chocolate but some I have given to little girls and boys in town. Most of them get no chocolate and they keep asking us for everything under the sun. They do not speak English but they usually say, "Hello, chocolate?, Hello – matches?, Hello – shoes? Hello – socks?", all sorts of things like that. We can't give them any shoes or stockings but we do give them chocolate and a small box of matches occasionally. The poor people seem to think that the Canadian soldiers have everything.

The people here are very crowded and sometimes there may be a family of ten or twelve in one large room or two small ones. They have hardly any firewood except small twigs. They burn those in an open fireplace and when they get some hot coals they put them in big metal bowls called "braziers". This bowl is placed just under the table and then the whole family sits down around the table.

Pretty soon it will turn warm but today it snowed in our town. It is on the top of a big hill in the mountains. The houses are built of stones, mostly two or three stories. The basements are usually big and there they keep their wine which they drink, with their meals, instead of water. There they also keep their pig, if they have one, also maybe a donkey – a funny little animal not much bigger than a sheep, but built like a horse. It has great big ears as you can see from your picture books. Many people here have a few goats. Some of them are large and black with long hair and curved horns.

You will see that Italy is very different from Manitoba and nearly as good but it is beautiful. Maybe when you grow up you will be able to see it. When I come home I'll tell you all about it and also about England which is very different.

We have a little house all to ourselves. It is called the "Sergeants' Mess". It has four rooms; two for sleeping, one for a kitchen and a big dining room. There are four men sleeping in my room. I sleep on the floor but I found some straw which I stuffed into a blanket and it makes a good mattress, not very soft though. I use my kit-bag for a pillow. We are quite comfortable and have plenty to eat but sometimes it isn't very good – not like the meals your mother makes for you.

Your mother tells me that you are very good and that Lara is smart at school. I am very glad to hear that. I enjoyed the letter very much and hope you write again soon.

Give all my love to your mother and tell her I am writing her shortly. All my love to you and be good to your mother.

Your dad, Heimir

He came home to his wife and children, soon moving to Winnipeg, where he worked for the Department of Veterans Affairs for two

decades and then the Department of Justice. Shortly after retiring,
Heimir died in 1971. The family destroyed the many letters between
him and his wife after her death in 1985.

CHRISTMAS WITH ANDREA

Surrounded by death, a soldier always welcomes reports of new
life back home. George Blackburn's troop train pulled out for
Halifax June 12, 1942, three hours after he'd said goodbye to his
*new wife in Ottawa. **Grace Blackburn** was pregnant with their*
first child and on the following Christmas Day gave birth to
Andrea, whose newspaperman father was now an artilleryman
with the 4th Field Regiment in England. Grace sent George more
than three hundred letters – many of them emblazoned with a lip-
stick kiss – that detailed her daily life while he was overseas.

Letter 54 (reserving comment on your beautiful
Christmas necklace until next letter)
Christmas Day – Andrea's birthday 1942
Civic Hospital, Room 338

My Darling,
With "White Christmas" playing on our radio . . . after hours of
carols, etc., your Twinkle is in a world of Wonder! Yes, George,
our adorable baby daughter arrived this morning, Christmas Day
at 1.18 A.M. and is the Christmas novelty around the hospital,
being the first born on this festive day. She is to be put in a special
cradle "on display" in the private patients' nursery this afternoon
and evening. She's a honey, Darling . . . 7 pounds 10 oz . . . with
" 'mature' schoolgirl complexion" of white with pink cheeks and
nose. Her mouth is nicely shaped, wide, and promises to be full.

Her hair is definitely dark right now. As all babies are born with blue eyes, Andrea's dark blue ones may give promise of turning brown, eh? When they brought her to me for two minutes this morning, I found her feet and arms all tucked into a closed nightie, so could not peek. And is she smart! Some babies are difficult to teach, but when they brought her in a pink blanket for her first meal to-day at 2 o'clock, she squinted out of her darling eyes and caught right on to what she was to do. Her wide-open eyes are shut most of the time just yet, but they

Grace Blackburn with Andrea,
born Christmas Day 1942
(Courtesy George Blackburn)

really concentrated on the target at 2 o'clock. We miss the 6 P.M. feeding to-night, so I have to wait until 10 P.M. to see her. Gosh, she's a pet, Darling! All the nurses and [Dr.] Kelley think so too, so there . . . I'm glad you were not here, Darling. Knowing you were waiting around would have made me miserable. Your long distance hand holding was very powerful . . . Thanks for the most wonderful Christmas present ever!

All my love,
Twinkle

George Blackburn came home at war's end to work with the federal government in Ottawa and to write three compelling books about his military career: The Guns of Normandy, The Guns of Victory, *and* Where the Hell Are the Guns? *He and Grace had two more children and a happy marriage until Grace's death in 2002.*

SEX AND THE MARRIED AIRMAN

Saskatchewan-reared **Ed Brunanski** *had just married a school-teacher named Jean before leaving Canada to serve in Yorkshire, England, with the* RCAF's *night-flying 428 Ghost Squadron. The airframe and engine master mechanic and Jean wrote often as they sorted out their young marriage.*

April 21st [1943]

My Own Dearly Beloved Wife: –

Hello my sweet, and how is my darling to-night? Gee darling I'm terribly lonesome and I miss you so much. Really dearest I'm very homesick for you and all that is dear to me in Canada. I remember when I was young (not so very young) I used to get so homesick that I could hardly swallow and the tears would almost overcome my restraining will. Well, darling, I feel exactly like that to-night. It's not just a physical longing it's far more deeper than that . . .

To-night I'll answer letter 77, which is very interesting because of the frank outspoken way you tell me about your book "Sex & Love Life." According to your version of it, I can see that the book deals quite clearly and in detail on the subject. Twice a week ought to be the limit; yes I think after awhile we can adhere to that rule if necessary.

April 22nd

. . . I agree with you dearest the reading of a subject like that [in a book he had, titled *Ideal Marriage*] will rouse one's emotions to some extent, but if I follow your advice and read it during the day it will not have too much effect. Darling is that book the first of its kind you've read & studied?

As 1943 wore on, the couple were writing about Ed's homecoming.

Nov. 8th

. . . No, I'm sure dearest whatever time of the day we meet that it'll be heaven, that supreme element of all the love we're capable of will merge as one living soul to live like that forever.

That reminds me sweetheart – that book you got on Sex and Love Life – how would you like to send it along in one of your parcels. After all we both must learn and right now I haven't a bit of literature on the subject. Just mail anything you think important for a husband to know and I'll study it. OK Pet?

Jan. 20/44

. . . Now I'll complete answering letter No 421. I'm patiently awaiting the parcel in which you included the book "Sex & Love Life." You know dearest I haven't read anything on the subject

Jean and Ed Brunanski (Courtesy Ed Brunanski)

since I sent you "Ideal Marriage." Not that it really matters because it's apparently useless with me over here & you thousands of miles away to try and learn anything or try and remember. I'm sure that we can read it & study it when we're together and make as good use of it as if we study it now.

Aug. 12th

. . . And now darling here I sit doing the most interesting thing of the whole day. Gee, darling, if instead of writing you I could be holding you in my arms tightly and kissing those sweet lips of yours it would be so much more fun when we could go to bed perhaps to rise to the greatest heights of ecstacy or just relax happy and contented – Maybe soon eh darling?

always & always faithfully

Your very own Hubby Ed

Ed and Jean Brunanski were reunited in Ottawa in November 1944 and returned to Saskatchewan to raise a family and buy a weekly newspaper in Wakaw that they published for a quarter-century. Jean (whom he called by a Hungarian pet name of Jelenka) died in 2001.

TEARING THEIR PLEASURES

Elizabeth Harrison was an accomplished war artist in Ottawa chronicling the home front during the 1940s while working at the United Kingdom High Commissioner's Office. Eric Harrison ("Benge" to Elizabeth) was a Queen's University history profes-sor then serving as the historical officer with the 1st Canadian Corps in Italy and overseer of Canadian war artists assigned to

work there, among them Lawren Harris and Charles Comfort.
Both thirty-seven, the Harrisons had been married since 1931,
when they moved to Canada from England. They were exuberant
letter-writers, she expressing her lust for him and he describing
the bittersweet beauty around him while not mentioning his
narrow escapes in the war-torn country.

> 334 Cathcart Street
> Ottawa, Ontario
> 9th April '44
> Easter Day.

My Darling

There's no doubt but that Spring is hell. It's against nature to be
without one's Benge in spring. I look at all the happy women with
their handsome males and am filled with envy. They don't have to
sublimate all their natural lusts in poetry, painting & music &
then feel even more unsatisfied! They can go home to their own
nice house, full of their own things, chosen by themselves, & they
can be as lustful as they like! . . . The root of all evil is not money
but lack of a lawful man when one wants him. A maleless woman
thinks all sorts of evil & licentious things about innocent males
who are doing nothing to attract their attention but just being
beautifully masculine. Just moving about & being bony & tall &
clean & painfully reminiscent. Just having deep voices & laughing & going off with their lawful wives and young women &
<u>belonging</u> to somebody. Damn them! If mine were here now we
would have a wonderful time wouldn't we? Like that never-to-be-
forgotten hot afternoon at Frank St. How shocked [a friend] would
be[,] could he but know what went on in his bed! . . .

　　The quality of love must change in wartime. All the gentleness
& the takings-of-time must be jettisoned for Andrew Marvell's

kind of love: "tear our pleasures with strife through the iron gates of life." No wonder the soldiers get a reputation for brutality and licentiousness! However, I must go and try to forget or rather to overlay my licentious aching for you by doing the laundry. Nothing like washing pyjamas & towels in the bath to set up a counter-ache in one's back. Especially on Easter Sunday. If the Spring is afflicting you like this too we must hope for the worst of it to be over very soon. – once the poignant sap-running is over and the leaves are out I suppose it won't be too bad . . .

I love you my Benge.

Your

Elizabeth.

Eric responded in kind.

25 Apr. 44

My Dear Darling,

This evening I have your beautifully poignant letter of the spring (dated 9 April). Yes, indeed, the season is hard to bear, and for me with so much dramatic and storied loveliness in the places I have been visiting of late, April without you is being most exquisitely painful.

I have told you of my leave in the mountains, where the spring leapt up the slopes after the retreating snow, and where I wept listening to the voice of the peasant girl singing across the valley, and then grew hard, and walking through the crocuses, could listen to the cuckoo and the lark and the roar of the waterfall with only a slight tightening of the throat. I wanted you to be there, sharing those soaring perspectives and threading those white and winding roads with the slope on one hand and the steep on the

other, following the donkey path, climbing after the goat, achieving the summit and gazing dizzily after the falcon riding the air.

I wanted you to be there because you belong to April and
because, such is my good fortune, you belong to me. I saw it all
with only one eye and I can only recall it tongue-tied: whereas had
you been there to hear the sheep-bells and to see the fresh brown
earth where the peasants had turned it, I should have carried a
fuller vision along with me and the bells of our joint recalling would
have pe[a]led together when the mountains were far away.

Seeing it alone and under the strange, abnormal conditions of
war, in the midst of this vast business, this horrible, massive, scientific savagery, leaves me with small affection for the country.
Besides, it is either blasted or deprived, hungry, pitiful, alien,
cadging, poor, primitive, and teeming, not yet recovered from its
tyrannies, squalid, apathetic, helpless, simple, naive, obliging,
laborious, lazy, lovely, stinking. It sings in the valley and shits in
the lanes and in the streets and on the slopes. It shits everywhere.
The flies do not bother it; it is carpetted with ordure, though the
women are always washing in the fountains and their clothes-lines
are as laden as the blossoming trees.

But what you say of women bereft of men, I have seen working
the other way among hundreds and thousands of men without
women. They sublimate their lack in blasphemy, letters, liquor,
their own company, whoring, discomfort (wet men, cold men,
frightened men make poor bed-mates) and with work, resignation,
preoccupation, endurance. Abstinence becomes habitual, fornica-
tion contracts V.D. Every town, especially if it is a large one, is
plastered with warning signs, though for those who are determined
to stand it no longer prophylactics and French letters are provided.
The best deterrent is a preference for cleanliness and blondes . . .

And when it comes to plain physical desire, then in this spring season, my Elizabeth, I have known it like a pain and writhed between my blankets with the ache of it and looked lecherously at women by the way. But as you wisely observe, when the sap has stopped running and the leaves are out, the sharpness of the senses will be dulled a little, and the heat and the dust and the war and the harvest shall be our sublimations. Your letter would provide some good dialogue for the play we ought to write on this interesting topic. How universal a theme.

In another letter I'll answer your other piece of news – though it was scarcely news to hear that the spring was a bother, since I also love <u>you</u>.

Your Eric

After serving Canadian general Harry Crerar as historical officer in northwest Europe, and retiring with the rank of lieutenant colonel and an Order of the British Empire, Eric returned to Queen's University, where he later became head of the history department. Elizabeth taught art in public schools in Kingston, wrote poetry, an autobiography, and an art-instruction book, and continued to paint and draw (Charles Comfort praised one of her shows as "objective paintings of exceptional originality, a new and magnificent apprehension of nature"). The Harrisons had one daughter, who took her own life in 1968. Eric died in 2000, Elizabeth a year later.

A GEM OF A MARRIAGE

The four hundred letters that Norah and **Fred Egener** *exchanged between 1941 and 1945, when he was a Canadian army lieutenant* *in Italy, present an intimate portrait of a married couple in wartime. They had met on holiday in their mid-teens, and in 1936, as university students frightened about the unrest in Europe, they secretly married but didn't live together for two years. By the time Fred, a lawyer with the Ontario health department, left for overseas, they were living in Oakville, Ontario, had a two-year-old son, and Norah was pregnant. A year after he left, she confessed to being "starved for affection" and sharing embraces with another man in his absence. Two years later he was reassuring her again of his love.*

May 6 [1944]

Dearest Norah:

. . . Darling, a letter of yours to England arrived recently. I didn't reply directly to it. I felt sure it had been answered over and over again. You need never think I may have found another girl. No husband, I feel sure, ever loved his wife more completely than I you.

Perhaps at times I've been reserved, perhaps a word more would have settled you, I don't know, but I do know that I have never loved anyone but you and never felt the least inclination to review my feelings toward you. I always loved you from our first days together. That love has grown, is growing. It has added many new sides. Like the facets of a diamond the new have added to the brilliance, but never changed the stone.

Fred and Norah Egener, on his university graduation day, 1936
(Courtesy Norah Egener)

You have outdone yourself in loyalty to me during the last three years. I expected it of you, I know, but your splendid showing with the children, the home, the family, have been more than one could expect. I expected much, in all honesty I say I demanded of you more than I probably had any right to do. I left with complete confidence, without really understanding what it would mean in work and bearing on your part. I understand now, and admire the strength you have put into your job . . .

I should tell you so daily, but of course I'm not one for saying much on any occasion. I only know, Norah dear, that I expected much of you and that I received that and more from you, which is just what I did expect.

All my love, darling,
Fred

"This is my favourite love letter," Norah Egener says today. "The letters were how we found meaning in chaos; they kept us close for four years to the day." Fred led a platoon in the Perth Regiment that was the first to crack the Germans' notorious Gothic Line in Italy, but returned home safely to set up a law practice in Owen Sound, Ontario. He retired as a family court judge a year before his death in 1988. Now in her late eighties, Norah says, "I am very active in my University Club, supporting good causes, and playing serious bridge. Time is of the essence."

THE LETTER AS WEAPON

In 1944 Alexander Ross of Embro, Ontario, was in Italy with the 17th Field Regiment of the Royal Canadian Artillery as it battled at Monte Maggiore, a village in the Apennine Mountains.

Back home he had been dating an Ottawa teacher named **Elizabeth**, *whom he hoped to marry. They kept corresponding until December 4, when his regiment was back in action in a village near Ravenna. The mail that day brought him what American servicemen in this war had nicknamed "the Dear John letter." The dreaded missive from a sweetheart back home, says Canadian military historian Terry Copp, "could be a potent weapon of war" by causing great personal distress that could precipitate a breakdown.*

12 November 1944.

Dear Alex,

This letter may be a very bad mistake, but ever since I received your last letter I've known I had to write it. I just hope I can state the facts plainly without sounding like a melodramatic ass.

When I was seventeen, and before I met you, I fell in love. You made me forget him – almost. The times when I wanted to call us quits and stopped writing for weeks on end were the times when the ghost of this former love returned to haunt me. Two years ago I thought I had it licked, but the last few months have proved how wrong I was.

It's something, Sandy, over which I seem to have no control – believe me; if I had, I should soon cease to be miserable. I thought I could keep on to you as one sweetheart to another, but the words stuck in my pen and won't come out. This other person doesn't know how I feel – and won't – in fact, none, but you now know what a complete fool I am capable of being! I can't kid myself any longer that it is simply a passing fancy, and so I am writing now to ask you to leave me to my misery, Sandy, and try to find happiness with someone else. Does that sound heartless? Forgive me if it does . . .

This had better be good-bye, Alex. I don't have to tell you how swell it was knowing you. Good luck and God bless you.

Sincerely

Elizabeth

The letter decisively spelled the end of their relationship. Alex later fought in the Netherlands and left the army in 1946 as a captain with a Military Cross. He married Irene Joan Porteous in 1950 (later writing a book called A Year and a Day *about their forty-four-year relationship) and became chairman of the English language and literature department at the University of Guelph. His daughter, Celia Ross, became president of Algoma University College in Sault Ste. Marie, Ontario, where Alex now lives.*

THE CRUEL SEA

Ronald Nicholson, a dark-haired, brown-eyed, twenty-one-year-old from Winnipeg, went to England in mid-1944 as a ground-crew member of the Royal Canadian Air Force. In Manchester he met a young woman and wrote his aunt about his intentions.

20/4/45

Dear Aunt Olive: –

. . . How are you all? fine I hope. I am OK, things are not very exciting at the moment. There is a dance here tonight but I have to many letter to write to bother going, besides I have stopped going to the station dances.

I have some news for you that I think will be rather surprizing to you. On the 16th of June I am going to get married. My bride is Jean Bailey of Manchester.

I don't think that I have ever told you much about Jean. I met Jean about a month after I came over here, but have not gone steady with her till the last six months.

Jean is about 5 ft. 4 inches tall, a strawberry blond, hazel eyes and a sweet baby face; she is 18 years old. I spent part of my last leave with Jean and it was then that we desided to get married; I had thought of it for some time before but did not make up my mind till the end of my leave.

I wrote to Mom & Dad and told them and they seemed to be quite pleased about it . . .

Love,

Ronnie

Ronnie's mother, **Bea Nicholson**, *announced the news to her sister.*

May 3. 1945.

Dear Evelyn:

. . . Take a good deep breath, set yourself firmly in a chair, and prepare for a surprise when I tell you what Roland & I were doing this morning. Ronald has been telling us the last few months about Jean – in Manchester. In Mar. he wrote that they would like to get married. The counselling officer, interviewing him about post war plans, advised him to get a wife, and he asked what we would think about it. Before he went away we would have advised him to wait till he got on his feet financially, but since so many are marrying young and these boys away from home have grown up quickly, it has made a change, so we gave our approval, if they were both sure they knew what they were doing. Before our reply came, he wrote again, asking us to place ourselves in their places, with thousands of miles between them if he came back without her, and he was sure he would regret it the rest of his life. He

seemed very sure of our disapproval and pleaded his case elo-
quently. He always was a very independent youngster and I am
surprised that he cared so much how we felt . . . At the end of 8
pages he said he was sending a Bond home, and would we get a
nice ring set and send them as soon as possible . . .

Love to all – Bea.

*The Nicholsons did send their son a diamond engagement ring and
an engraved wedding ring. Then two days after the couple's marriage, Jean's sister, **Margaret Bailey**, wrote to Ronnie's parents.*

Fyling Hall,
Robin's Hood Bay,
Nr. Whitby, Yorks.,
18th June, 1945.

My Dear Mrs. Nicholson:
This is going to be a very difficult letter to write, and I hope that
you will realize just how much I want to express to you.

Jean is my sister whom I love dearly, so please will you accept
my very deepest sympathy on her behalf and my mother's, to you,
Ronnie's mother. She is too ill to write and I have undertaken this
task on her behalf.

I know that you will want to know how it happened and his
actions just before this, so I will try to tell you. His wedding day
was beautiful. He was completely happy but for one vital thing;
he wanted you to be there. He spoke about you and said that you
would be thinking of him. He asked me to send the top tier of the
wedding cake to you on that day if possible, and I did this. He
wrote a letter to enclose in it, and then asked me to destroy that
one and wrote another. This in the middle of laughter and joy

and jokes and excitement. Then they went on their honeymoon, the happiest pair in the whole world, both of them adoring each other – so much in love and so full of plans.

Robin Hood's Bay is a beautiful spot, and he loved the people of the house here just as much as we do. He told Jean that she could not have brought him to a more lovely place. On Sunday afternoon, the day after the wedding, they decided to go for a bathe, and told Mrs. Shaw and Annie (the people in this house) that they would be back at four-thirty, as they wanted to go to Chapel in the evening. Ronnie knew that you would have wanted him to go to Chapel

Ronald Nicholson and Jean Bailey Nicholson, briefly wed in June 1945 (Courtesy Marjorie Hadaller)

when they decided upon this. They went down to the sea and changed into bathing suits and began to walk out into the sea. When it began to get too deep for this they turned to swim back. Jean not having walked as quickly as Ronnie, was before him when they turned, and she thought he was following her. She turned round and saw that he was in difficulties and tried to help him, but his body was rigid and she could not move him. It must have been cramp because he could not tell her what was the matter. Big waves were buffeting them all the time, knocking them down and finally separating them, and Jean could not find him. She called for help over and over again, but people did not realize that they were in danger, and she had to go back to the beach where she found a man to swim back to the place with her where he had disappeared. Others helped but they could not find him and the search is still going on.

You who love Ronnie must know what Jean is feeling, and can forgive her for not writing this letter. You know what she wants to convey to you, and mere words are inadequate. It must have been dreadful for her to see it happen, and to know that it was she who brought him here. Need I say that she is heartbroken. She is either crying or gazing at the sea, knowing that he is in it somewhere. Everything that is possible is being done. My mother and I came here on Monday morning. We travelled all night and are staying here until they find Ronnie.

He was a wonderful boy. I know that all mothers feel proud of their sons, but you have more need to do so than any. Everybody he met loved him and knew him for a fine, good, well mannered and thoughtful boy.

If there are any of his personal belongings that [you] would like Jean will send them to you. She will write as soon as she is able.

Forgive me now. I cannot write more.

Yours with very great understanding,
Margaret Bailey

Ronnie's body was found within ten days and he was buried in Manchester. Jean was pregnant with their son, Ronald, and in 1946 she moved to Canada so the child could be near his father's family. Many years later, she remarried and had another son. She died in 2000 in Brandon, Manitoba.

WINNIE THE WAR BRIDE

*Philip Rose of North Vancouver was doing administrative work in England for Victoria's Canadian Scottish Regiment when he asked a twenty-one-year-old English girl for the last dance of the evening under the dome of the Royal Pavilion in Brighton. Winifred, who made munitions and assembled engines for the army, fell in love with the tall, dark, and handsome young Canadian. They were soon married and she followed him back to Canada by ship. Her heartbroken mother, **Lily Sheppard**, sent letters to her and Phil at his parents' home to be read on Winnie's arrival.*

Kemptown
Brighton
Sussex
9th August, 1946

My Dear Little Daughter Winnie

Here is wishing every success and every Happyness. I sincerely hope everything will turn out all just as you have wanted it all to. I also hope that you had a nice Voyage over, we all miss you more than words can tell, and to-day Chum [their dog] went hunting everywhere for you . . .

And please tell Phil to take care of my little Winnie and make her happy. I think Phil will? Well dear if ever you don't like Canada you know what to do, Both come back home (England), with all my Love

Mummy xxxxxxxxxx

My Dear Phil

Make my little Winnie as happy as you can comfort her. She is a long way from her Mother and home . . . try and get your little

House and home on your own it will be much better for Winnie because she was downhearted when she went away at leaving us but if you make her happy and comfortable I think she will settle and now I will be longing to hear of her safely to you so please Phil do let me know at your very earliest will you that she is safely in your care goodby dear

All my Love xxxxxxxxxxxxx

Mummy

Winnie never saw her mother again; "I can still see her and my sisters waving goodbye at the Brighton rail station." Winifred Rose was one of about forty-four thousand European war brides who came to Canada after the war. In 1988, shortly before he became ill and died, Phil wrote Winnie a poem about meeting her at the Royal Pavilion, which ended: "The Dome, once used by Royalty,/is the place where we did meet./My War Bride, as she is now known,/had swept me off my feet."

THROUGH HELL'S FLAMES

*After the Second World War, Canadian troops went overseas to fight in the Korean War, to support the North Atlantic Treaty Organization forces in Europe during the Cold War, and to be United Nations peacekeepers throughout the world. In autumn 1994, Private **Kurt Grant** of Spencerville, Ontario, was with the peacekeeping 1st Royal Canadian Regiment in the Krajina region of Croatia, where Serbians and Croatian and Bosnian Serbs were attempting an ethnic cleansing of the Muslim and Croatian major-ity. Kurt and his wife had been married for five years; six weeks*

before he left for the Balkans, Catherine had been diagnosed with
multiple sclerosis. In his letters, he quoted from W.H. Auden,
Elizabeth Barrett Browning, and other poets.

0033 AM, 01 Nov. [1994]

My dearest Sweet Catherine

Today your love letter of 22 Oct arrived. It was in with several
others at the time, but I knew that this one was special. At first I
did not know why, but then it came to me; as I raised the letter to
my nose and inhaled the delicate scent which emanated from its
folded pages, I was struck by an overwhelming image of you. Not
a picture you understand, but the essence of you. So powerful was
it that when I closed my eyes, I had an uncontrollable urge to
reach out and hold you close to me. Yet being alone, I was moved
almost to tears for being without you.

As I write this, I am holding your note close to me, so that I
might continue to be reminded of you in ways which the written
word cannot emulate.

Lying in bed prior to coming on shift, I needed once again to
feel the length of your back pressing against me, the curve of your
hip under my hand, the swell of your breast, the warmth of your
leg against mine, and the scent of your hair. You are my North,
my South, my East and West, my working day, and my Sunday
rest. It is you who are responsible for who I am, and without you
I am but a face in the crowd.

"How do I love thee?" I cannot even begin to count the ways.
But, heaven forbid, should anything ever happen to me over here,
know this, with all the certainty of the morrow's rising sun, that I
shall walk through the very flames of hell itself to be by your side.
When you are in the garden and a gentle breeze moves your dress,

that will be me holding you close; when the sun warms your face, it will be my hand caressing you; and when you lay yourself down to sleep at night, I too shall lie with you, and watch over you, as you rest.

04 Dec.

My dearest Catherine

Forgive me, my darling, for not having written to you sooner. It has been a week now since last we spoke, and I long for the opportunity to converse with you. Sadly our phone has been temporarily removed from Rodaljice, and I don't know when it will be replaced. Therefore I am using this written form to communicate with you . . .

I continue to write daily in my diary, and in doing so lay your pictures out on the table before me. I have been smiled at many times for doing it but no one ever says anything for, to a man, they are envious as hell of me for having a wife as beautiful as you. The other night, for example, I brought your pictures on patrol with me. In spite of my telling the Serb women we visit regularly how attractive you were, everyone who saw the pictures simply could not believe what they saw. The Serb women huddled for a while around the photos, and were genuinely envious. The men just drooled. One guy who sat beside me couldn't take his eyes off you for the hour we were there.

It made me very proud to be married to you, but I did try my best to be humble. NOT! . . .

0315 AM, 07 Dec.

My dearest Sweet Catherine

I take pen(cil) in hand this evening in an attempt to cheer you up. My hope is that when you read this, some of the burden of your sickness will be lifted from your lovely shoulders, and a smile may again grace the face I so dearly love.

Our conversation this afternoon distressed me greatly. When I heard your voice labouring so painfully to reach out to me, I knew instantly that you were tired beyond words. With every fiber of my being, I wanted to rush to your side to hold and protect you as you recover, but in looking at my clothes and my surroundings, I can only be with you in spirit. The disappointment angered me.

My love for you, my sweet, seems boundless, and with each passing day I feel your absence more keenly. In spite of your insistence, the longer I am over here, the more firmly I believe I have done you a disservice by leaving you. My place is by your side, more so now than ever before. I long to see you smile, and feel your arms around me. I miss our walks together, and our quiet chats at our favorite coffee house. But most of all, I miss touching you. The softness of your skin, the smell of your hair, the gentleness of your smile. This separation has been hard on both of us.

Upon my return, we shall together purchase a cappuccino machine. I can think of nothing more pleasurable, than to sit on our porch, cappuccino in hand, my favorite girl by my side, and our zoo in attendance. This truly is the definition of living well.

Take heart my dear, at this writing there are but a scant three weeks until we meet in England . . .

When we meet in the airport, you will run to me, and I shall envelope you in my arms and protect you from the world. Then, lovingly, tenderly, I shall give you a kiss that will reach into the very center of your being, and caress you. It matters not who is watching, for in our world, there is just you and I and no one else, which is as it should be.

I hope I have been at least partially successful in achieving my stated aim. When we meet in England we shall create many new memories together.

My love to you always

Kurt

Kurt's six-month tour ended the following spring and he came home to Ontario, where he now works as a military researcher and writer for the federal Department of History and Heritage. Catherine's MS was treated with a new form of medication that has left her completely ambulatory a decade later. "I'm grateful," her husband says, "to live in a country where we can get medication for her condition."

MARK OF ARABIA

*He was a caring twenty-eight-year-old Nova Scotian in an uncaring corner of the world: the demilitarized zone between Iraq and Kuwait. Corporal **Mark Isfeld** was there in 1991 with Canada's 1st Combat Engineer Regiment, clearing land mines the Iraqis had left behind in the wake of Operation Desert Storm launched by the United States. With no formal stationery at hand, he wrote his mother a heart-bordered card he fashioned from the back of a carton from a Salisbury steak microwave dinner.*

HAPPY
MOTHER'S
DAY

MOM

NO RAIN!
NO SNOW!
NO SLEET!
JUST DUST AND DESERT HEAT,
NO MATTER HOW MY BRAIN GETS BURNED
I WON'T FORGET THE MOST IMPORTANT
THING I'VE LEARNED
I LOVE YOU

With
"warm"
Thoughts
Mark of Arabia

Mark was heartbroken by the suffering of the children he saw in Kuwait and later in Croatia. His mother, Carol Isfeld, began using

Mark Isfeld and dromedary in Kuwait (Courtesy Carol and Brian Isfeld)

scrap wool to crochet boy dolls with blue berets and girls with bonnets and sent them to her son, who handed them out to the kids he encountered while clearing land mines. In June 1994 he was guiding an armoured personnel carrier in southern Croatia when it set off a mine. Mark was wounded and, on his way to hospital in a helicopter, died. His mother and other Canadian women kept making the "Izzy dolls" by the thousands. Carol and Mark Isfeld, living in Courtenay, British Columbia, later became prominent activists in the Canadian-led campaign that eventually resulted in 107 nations signing the Mine Ban Treaty.

King Marco

Another remarkable Canadian peacekeeper was Sergeant Marc Léger of Lancaster, Ontario. A member of the Princess Patricia's Canadian Light Infantry (PPCLI) in 2000, he held a town-hall meeting to organize a group of neglected Serbian refugees, who dubbed him King Marco as he enlisted the aid of his superiors and the Canadian ambassador to help them restore their homes. Two years later he was in Afghanistan, where he was again concerned about the plight of the people. In April 2002 the twenty-nine-year-old died when an American jet fighter mistakenly bombed Canadian soldiers during their night-training exercise, killing four of them and wounding eight others. Marc had a wife of seven years, Marley Léger, who had miscarried their first child just before he'd left for Afghanistan. After her husband's death Marley wrote him a letter, which she read at his funeral.

My Dearest Marc:

We were so young when we met but as young as we were our love was so very strong right from the beginning.

I want to thank you for everything you have given me. You have touched a place in my heart that has made me come alive.

You have claimed a part of my heart that will always belong to you. You have taught me to love so deeply and touched me in places I never knew I had.

More than you know and more than I could ever say, I feel thankfulness in my heart for you. "I love you" just doesn't seem enough for someone whose smile brightened my days and whose laugh could make me forget the rest of the world.

I love you for the happy warm feeling that was mine when we were together and the cheerful tone in your voice that made my day so bright. I can't wait until we meet again. And until then, I'll hold you close to my heart and I promise to live my life as fully and completely as you did and I promise to keep your memory alive.

Marc, I am so very proud of the man that you've become and I'm proud to be called Mrs. Marc Léger.

I love you and I will always love you. Until we meet again, goodbye my sweet love.

Marley Léger has kept Marc's memory alive. In May 2003 she opened a restored community centre in the Livno Valley of Bosnia-Herzegovina in memory of her husband. With sixty thousand dollars from the Marc Léger Memorial Fund she launched, and funding from the Canadian International Development Agency, the PPCLI's 1st and 2nd Battalions oversaw the centre's final restoration and rebuilt the church next door to continue the work their comrade had begun.

ACKNOWLEDGEMENTS

Once again, we are enormously grateful to all those people across Canada whose enthusiastic cooperation made possible this third and final volume in our series featuring private Canadian correspondence of the past two centuries. Without the generous contributions of letters from individuals and the skilled assistance of archivists, this collection would never have appeared.

We thank especially the numerous employees who served us so effectively at the National Archives of Canada (among them, Rob Fisher, Lorraine Gadoury, Anne Goddard, and Maureen Nevins) and the National Library of Canada (notably Jeannine Barriault); Carol Reid at the Canadian War Museum; Doug Cass and his helpful crew at the Glenbow Museum in Calgary; Apollonia Steele and Marlys Chevrefils at the University of Calgary's Special Collections; Ralph Stanton and his small but efficient group at the University of British Columbia's Rare Books and Special Collections Department; Jeremy Heil and his colleagues at Queen's University Archives in Kingston; Carol Haber and her associates at the City of Vancouver Archives; Robert Paul of the Diefenbaker Canada Centre Archives at the University of Saskatchewan; Carl Spadonia and his fellow archivists at the William Ready Division of Archives and Research Collections at McMaster University in Hamilton; Selina Coward and Elizabeth Seitz at the University of Regina Archives and Special Collections; Theresa Regnier at the University of Western Ontario Archives; and Margaret Houghton, Special Collections archivist at the Hamilton Public Library.

At the following archives, libraries, and museums, we consulted the named fonds and selected letters written by the fonds' creator(s) and/or by the person whose name appears in brackets: Canadian War Museum: Thomas Reid Jones collection (**Marjorie McIntosh**).

City of Vancouver Archives: Henry John Cambie fonds; Yip Sang fonds (**Dian brothers**).

Diefenbaker Canada Centre Archives, University of Saskatchewan (**Mary F. Diefenbaker and John Diefenbaker**).

Glenbow Museum: William Berry family fonds (**Ada Berry and George Berry**); Paul and Jessie Brecken fonds; A.E. Cross family fonds (**Helen MacLeod**); Edwards, Gardiner family fonds (**Oliver Edwards**); Harold Wigmore McGill and Emma Griffis McGill fonds; James F. Macleod family fonds; Richard Barrington Nevitt fonds; Marion and Jim Nicoll fonds; Ethel Pearson fonds (**Bob**); Scollen family fonds; and Willison family fonds (**Carrie Northover Kosling**).

Hamilton Public Library, Special Collections: (**William Bruce**).

McMaster University Library, William Ready Division of Archives and Research Collections: Pierre Berton fonds (**Thomas Phillips Thompson**); David Helwig fonds (**Jane Rule**).

National Archives of Canada: Ted Allan fonds (**Norman Bethune**);

Alice H. Bray fonds; Norman Alfred Caplin fonds (**Leon Edel**); Samuel Cass fonds (**Eliezer Cass**); Gregory Clark fonds; William Donnelly fonds (**Margaret Thompson**); William Lawson and Maude Grant fonds (**Maude Parkin Grant**); Irene Heywood fonds (**Lionel LeMoine FitzGerald**); William Lyon Mackenzie King collection (**Mathilde Grossert**); Sir Wilfrid Laurier fonds; Mackenzie Papineau Battalion collection (**Thomas Beckett**); George Boyd MacMillan fonds (**Lucy Maud Montgomery**); Sir Ernest MacMillan fonds (**Elsie Keith MacMillan**); David Brown Milne fonds; Mary Eleanor Westcott Papineau fonds (**John Try Davies**); Talbot Mercer Papineau fonds; Herman Witsius Ryland and family fonds; Anne Savage fonds (**A.Y. Jackson**); and Jonathan Sewell and family fonds.

Queen's University Archives: Elizabeth Harrison fonds (**Elizabeth** and **Eric Harrison**).

University of British Columbia Library, Rare Books and Special Collections: Jack Shadbolt fonds; Neil Patrick Lane fonds (**Patricia Lowther**).

University of Calgary, Special Collections: Max Braithwaite fonds (**Farley Mowat**); Hugh MacLennan fonds; W.O. Mitchell fonds; Malcolm Ross fonds (**Margaret Laurence**).

University of Regina, Archives and Special Collections: Papers of Journalists and Max Bell Professors (**Gladys Arnold**).

University of Western Ontario Archives: Frederick and Evelyn Albright fonds.

Victoria University Library, University of Toronto: Northrop Frye fonds (**Northrop Frye** and **Helen Kemp Frye**).

Whitehern Historic House & Garden, City of Hamilton; (www.whitehern.ca) (**Mary Baker McQuesten**).

We are grateful to the hundreds of individuals and families who offered us correspondence or searched through family albums and storage boxes for photographs, generously copying them or entrusting us with originals. We regret that we couldn't publish all the very good letters and photographs we received. The following sent us letters we did include or gave us permission to use letters written by those whose names are in boldface type: Mary J. Anderson (**Mary Baker McQuesten**); Joan Andrew (**Maude Parkin Grant**); Frances Ballantyne (**Chattan Stephens**); Janet Beale (**Jonathan Sewell, Jr., William Henry Temple, William Smith**); George Blackburn (**Grace Blackburn**); Lorna Brooke (http://members.rogers.com/echoinmyheart) (**Frederick Albright** and **Evelyn Kelly Albright**); Mike Brough (**Alex Shatford**); Florence Bevel (**Mollie**); Barry Callaghan (**Morley Callaghan**); Anne Childs (**Alfred Childs**); Gregory Clark Jr. (**Gregory Clark**); Anne Davison (**James Tupper**); Loral Dean (**Homer Dean**); Marjorie Edel (**Leon Edel**); Norah Egener (**Fred Egener**); Sandra Florence (**George Florence**); Earl and Patricia Green (**Lionel LeMoine FitzGerald**); Marjorie Hadaller (**Bea Nicholson, Ronald Nicholson** and **Margaret Bailey**); Ann Harris (**Ann Eliza Cairns**); Brian and Carol Isfeld (**Mark Isfeld**); Eugenie Johnston (**Walter Keller**); Pamela Klawitter (**HeimirThorgrimson**); Jocelyn Laurence (**Margaret Laurence**); Pauline Le Bel (**Eulalie Rochon**); Beth and Chris Lowther (**Patricia Lowther**); Patricia MacKillop (**Charles B. Hill**); Margaret Maclean (**James Aitchison**); Ross A. MacMillan (**Sir Ernest MacMillan and Elsie Keith**); Ormond Mitchell (**W.O. Mitchell**); Jean Moore (**Eileen McFadden Moore**); Joanne Neufeld (**Peter Menlove**); Michael and Sheila Pauls (**David Pauls** and **Helen Toews Pauls**); Caroline Raymonde Plante (**Jacques Plante**); Joyce Rempel (**William Rempel**), Winifred Rose (**Lily Sheppard**); Alexander M. Ross (**"Elizabeth"**); Catherine Seton (**Eric Harrison** and **Elizabeth Harrison**); Beatrice Smith (**Arsène Goyette**); Kathryn Swayze (**James F. Swayze**); Maria Tippett (**Peter Clarke**); and Gwynneth Wallace (**Frederick DeMille Knowlton**).

The following permitted us to use their own letters: **Randy Bachman, Ed Brunanski, Mavis P.J. Butlin, Peter Calamai, Nina Callaghan, Margaret Crawford, Kurt Grant, Jane Eaton Hamilton, Carolyn Harris, Sarah Haxby, Jean Hubbard, Reva Hutkin (and L.G.), Adrienne Leduc, Marley Léger, Joy Masuhara, Farley Mowat, Susan Musgrave, Eric Nicol, Stephen Reid, Spider Robinson, Terri Luanna Robinson, Doris Tennant, Veronica Tennant, John Thomas, Mercedes and Pierre Trudeau, David Witty, Constance Wrigley-Thomas, Lorraine Wynes, Callon Zukowski, and Carolyn Harris Zukowski.**

For their expertise in languages, we thank Dr. Jan Walls, director of the David Lam Centre for International Communication and the Asia-Canada Program at Simon Fraser University, who deciphered Chinese symbols, and Babette Deggan, Taras Grescoe, and Pauline LeBel, who checked our translations of letters originally written in French.

Finally, we thank Alex Schultz, our patient, long-distance editor, and Heather Sangster, our keen-eyed copy editor; Terri Nimmo, who designed a lovely book; and Carolyn Swayze, our agent, who three years ago found a publishing home for this project.

BIBLIOGRAPHY

Anderson, Mary J., ed., *The Life Writings of Mary Baker McQuesten-Victorian Matriarch* (Waterloo: Wilfrid Laurier University Press, 2004).

Blondin, Robert, and Gilles LaMontagne, eds., *Chers nous autres: un siècle de correspondance québécoise*, tome 1 (Montréal, VLB Éditeur, 1978).

Callaghan, Barry, *Barrelhouse Kings* (Toronto: McArthur & Company, 1998).

Dick, David, *Engagement Letters 1926-1929 of Helen Toews and David Pauls* (Calgary: self-published).

Egener, Norah and Fred, *A Time Apart: Letters of Love and War* (Owen Sound, ON: Ginger Press, 1995).

Radcliff, Thomas, ed., *Authentic Letters from Upper Canada* (Toronto: Macmillan of Canada,1953).

Sissons, C.B., ed., *My Dearest Sophie: Letters from Egerton Ryerson to his Daughter* (Toronto: The Ryerson Press, 1955).

INDEX OF LETTER-WRITERS